Collateralized Debt Obligations:
structures and analysis

THE FRANK J. FABOZZI SERIES

Collateralized Debt Obligations:
structures and analysis

LAURIE S. GOODMAN
FRANK J. FABOZZI

John Wiley & Sons, Inc.

LSG
To my husband Mark
and my children Louis, Arthur, Benjamin, and Pamela

FJF
To my wife Donna
and my children, Karly, Patricia, and Francesco

For general information on our other products and services, or technical support, please contact our Customer Care Department within the United States at 800-762-2974, outside the United States at 317-572-3993 or fax 317-572-4002.

Wiley also publishes its books in a variety of electronic formats. Some content that appears in print may not be available in electronic books.

ISBN: 0-471-23486-9

Printed in the United States of America

10 9 8 7 6 5 4 3 2 1

contents

The market for collateralized debt obligations (CDOs) is the fastest growing sector of the asset-backed securities market. In 2000 and 2001, CDOs constituted over 25% of total ABS issuance, up from under 1% of the market six years earlier. Looked at differently, in 1995, one major bond rating agency rated only six deals, representing a combined par value of $1 billion. By 2001, that same rating agency rated 277 deals totaling $101 billion par value.

There have been numerous and dramatic changes within the CDO market as it evolved. For instance, bank balance sheet deals are now less important, arbitrage deals more significant, while synthetic deals have grown more rapidly than alternative structures. Collateral mix has also shifted dramatically, with high-yield bond collateral now less prevalent and structured finance collateral more common.

Our purpose in writing this book was to provide financial market participants with a basic, but comprehensive, understanding of the CDO market as it currently stands. And since this is an evolving market with new variations constantly appearing, we also provide a framework for examining new structures.

We gratefully acknowledge the expertise and participation of the UBS Warburg Securitized Products Strategy Team; Jeff Ho, Tom Zimmerman, Douglas Lucas, and Vicki Ye all made terrific contributions to this book. Jeff coauthored Chapter 12. Tom had a major impact on Chapters 4 and 5. Douglas coauthored Chapter 14 plus made significant contributions to Chapters 5 and 13. Vicki was involved at every step, from background research and data gathering to reading/critiquing the final product. In addition, we are grateful to Glenn Boyd, Laurent Gauthier, and Wilfred Wong, also of UBS Warburg's Securitized Products Strategy Team, who reviewed many a draft and made helpful comments.

We particularly thank the bond rating agencies Moody's Investors Service, Standard & Poor's, and Fitch, for allowing us to draw on the wealth of data and expertise they have provided to investors over time. Most specifically, we incorporated material on their rating methodologies, and default and rating transition studies.

Laurie S. Goodman
Frank J. Fabozzi

Laurie S. Goodman is a Managing Director at UBS Warburg and head of the U.S. Securitized Products Strategy Group. The team is responsible for the *Mortgage Strategist* and *CDO Insight* publications and for relative value trade recommendations across the U.S. securitized marketplace—RMBS, ABS, CMBS, and CDOs. In 2001, Ms. Goodman was elected to the Institutional Investor All-American Fixed Income Research Team for the ninth year. For the past four years, she has held the #1 slots for MBS Strategy, Agency Structured Product, and Non-Agency Structured Product. She is also Institutional Investor ranked for CDO Research. Prior to joining UBS Warburg in 1993, Ms. Goodman held similar research positions at Merrill Lynch, Goldman Sachs, and Citibank. She also had buy-side experience and spent four years as a senior economist at the Federal Reserve Bank of New York. She has published more than 150 articles in academic and professional journals, most on portfolio management and the valuation of fixed income securities. Ms. Goodman holds a B.A. in Mathematics from the University of Pennsylvania, and M.A. and Ph.D. degrees in Economics from Stanford University.

Frank J. Fabozzi is editor of the *Journal of Portfolio Management* and an Adjunct Professor of Finance at Yale University's School of Management where he teaches the structured finance course. From 1986 to 1992, he was a full-time professor of finance at MIT's Sloan School of Management. He is on the board of directors of the BlackRock complex of funds, the board of directors of the Guardian Life family of funds, and an advisory analyst for Global Asset Management (GAM). Dr. Fabozzi has edited and authored many acclaimed books in finance, including three coauthored with Franco Modigliani, recipient of the 1985 Alfred Nobel Memorial Prize in Economic Sciences, and an edited book with Harry M. Markowitz, corecipient of the 1990 Nobel Memorial Prize in Economic Sciences. He earned a doctorate in economics from the City University of New York in 1972 and is a Fellow of the International Center for Finance at Yale University. Dr. Fabozzi is a Chartered Financial Analyst and Certified Public Accountant.

CHAPTER 1

Introduction

A *collateralized debt obligation* (CDO) is an asset-backed security backed by a diversified pool of one or more classes of debt (corporate and emerging market bonds, asset-backed and mortgage-backed securities, real estate investment trusts, and bank debt). The list of asset types included in a CDO portfolio is continually expanding. When the underlying pool of debt obligations consists of bond-type instruments, the CDO is referred to as a *collateralized bond obligation* (CBO). When the underlying pool of debt obligations consists of only bank loans, the CDO is referred to as a *collateralized loan obligation* (CLO).

STRUCTURE OF A CDO

In a CDO structure, there is an asset manager responsible for managing the portfolio of debt obligations. There are restrictions imposed (i.e., restrictive covenants) as to what the asset manager may do and certain tests that must be satisfied for the debt obligations in the CDO to maintain the credit rating assigned at the time of issuance. We'll discuss these requirements in later chapters.

The funds to purchase the underlying assets, referred to as the *collateral assets*, are obtained from the issuance of debt obligations. These debt obligations are also referred to as *tranches*. The tranches are:

- Senior tranches
- Mezzanine tranches
- Subordinate/equity tranche

There will be a rating sought for all but the subordinate/equity tranche. For the senior tranches, at least an A rating is typically sought. For the mezzanine tranches, a rating of BBB but no less than B is sought. Since the subordinate/equity tranche receives the residual cash flow, no rating is sought for this tranche.

The order of priority of the payments of interest and principal to the CDO tranches is specified in the prospectus. We will describe how the cash flow payments are distributed in later chapters. What is important to understand is that the payments are made in such a way as to provide the highest level of protection to the senior tranches in the structure. This is done by providing certain tests that must be satisfied before any distribution of interest and principal may be distributed to the other tranches in the structure. If certain tests are failed, the senior tranches are then retired until the tests are passed.

The ability of the asset manager to make the interest payments to the debt holders and repay principal to the debt holders depends on the performance of the collateral assets. The proceeds to meet the obligations to the CDO tranches (interest and principal repayment) can come from

- Coupon interest payments from the collateral assets
- Maturity of collateral assets
- Sale of collateral assets

There are three relevant periods in the life of a CDO. The first is the *ramp-up period*. This is the period that follows the closing date of the transaction when the asset manager begins investing the proceeds from the sale of the debt obligations issued. This period usually lasts less than one year. The *reinvestment period* or *revolving period* is when principal proceeds received from the collateral assets are reinvested; this period is usually five or more years. In the final period, the collateral assets are sold and the debt holders are paid off.

A deal can be terminated early if certain events of default occur. These events basically relate to conditions that would materially and adversely impact the performance of the collateral assets. Such events include (1) the failure to comply with certain covenants; (2) failure to meet payments (interest and/or principal) to the senior tranches; (3) bankruptcy of the issuing entity of the CDO; and (4) departure of the asset management team if an acceptable replacement is not found.

SPONSOR MOTIVATION

CDOs are categorized based on the motivation of the sponsor of the transaction. If the motivation of the sponsor is to earn the spread between the yield offered on the collateral assets and the payments made to the various tranches in the structure, then the transaction is referred to as an *arbitrage transaction*. If the motivation of the sponsor is to remove debt instruments (primarily loans) from its balance sheet, then the transaction is referred to as a *balance sheet transaction*. Sponsors of balance sheet transactions are typically financial institutions such as banks and insurance companies seeking to reduce their capital requirements by removing loans due to their higher risk-based requirements.

Economics of an Arbitrage Transaction

The key as to whether or not it is economic to create an arbitrage CDO is whether or not a structure can offer a competitive return for the subordinate/equity tranche.

To understand how the subordinate/equity tranche generates cash flows, consider the following basic $100 million CDO structure with the coupon rate to be offered at the time of issuance as shown:

Tranche	Par Value	Coupon Rate
Senior	$80,000,000	LIBOR + 70 basis points
Mezzanine	10,000,000	Treasury rate plus 200 basis points
Subordinated/equity	10,000,000	—

Suppose that the collateral assets consist of bonds that all mature in 10 years and the coupon rate for every bond is the 10-year Treasury rate plus 400 basis points. Notice that the collateral assets pay a fixed rate but 80% of the capital structure is based on a floating rate (LIBOR). Thus, there is a mismatch with respect to the coupon characteristics of the collateral assets and the liabilities. One way that the asset manager hedges this mismatch is by using an interest rate swap. A swap is simply an agreement to periodically exchange interest payments with the payments benchmarked off of a notional amount. The notional amount is not exchanged between the two swap parties. Rather it is used simply to determine the dollar interest payment of each party. This is all we need to know about an interest rate swap in order to understand the economics of an arbitrage transaction. Keep in mind, the goal is to show how the subordinate/equity tranche can be expected to generate a return.

The interest rate swap that the asset manager would use would have a notional amount of $80 million. Suppose that the terms of the interest rate swap are as follows:

- The asset manager must pay a fixed rate each year equal to the 10-year Treasury rate plus 100 basis points
- The asset manager receives LIBOR

Let's assume that the 10-year Treasury rate at the time the CDO is issued is 7%. Now we can walk through the cash flows for each year. Look first at the collateral assets. The collateral assets will pay interest each year (assuming no defaults) equal to the 10-year Treasury rate of 7% plus 400 basis points. So the interest will be:

Interest from collateral assets = 11% × $100,000,000 = $11,000,000

Now let's determine the interest that must be paid to the senior and mezzanine tranches. For the senior tranche, the interest payment will be:

Interest to senior tranche = $80,000,000 × (LIBOR + 70 bp)

The coupon rate for the mezzanine tranche is 7% plus 200 basis points. So, the coupon rate is 9% and the interest is:

Interest to mezzanine tranche = 9% × $10,000,000 = $900,000

Finally, let's look at the interest rate swap. The asset manager is agreeing to pay the swap counterparty each year 7% (the 10-year Treasury rate) plus 100 basis points, or 8% of the notional amount. In our illustration, the notional amount is $80 million. The reason the asset manager selected the $80 million is because this is the amount of principal for the senior tranche. So, the asset manager pays to the swap counterparty:

Interest to swap counterparty = 8% × $80,000,000 = $6,400,000

The interest payment received from the swap counterparty is LIBOR based on a notional amount of $80 million. That is,

Interest from swap counterparty = $80,000,000 × LIBOR

Now we can put this all together. Let's look at the interest coming into the CDO:

Interest from collateral assets	$11,000,000
Interest from swap counterparty	$80,000,000 × LIBOR
Total interest received	$11,000,000 + $80,000,000 × LIBOR

The interest to be paid out to the senior and mezzanine tranches and to the swap counterparty include:

Interest to senior tranche	$80,000,000 × (LIBOR + 70 bp)
Interest to mezzanine tranche	$900,000
Interest to swap counterparty	$6,400,000
Total interest paid	$7,300,000 + $80,000,000 × (LIBOR + 70 bp)

Netting the interest payments coming in and going out we have:

Total interest received	$11,000,000 + $80,000,000 × LIBOR
− Total interest paid	$7,300,000 + $80,000,000 × (LIBOR + 70 bp)
Net interest	$3,700,000 − $80,000,000 × (70 bp)

Since 70 basis points times $80 million is $560,000, the net interest remaining is $3,140,000 (= $3,700,000 − $560,000). From this amount any fees (including the asset management fee) must be paid. The balance is then the amount available to pay the subordinate/equity tranche. Suppose that these fees are $634,000. Then the cash flow available to the subordinate/equity tranche is $2.5 million. Since the tranche has a par value of $10 million and is assumed to be sold at par, this means that the return is 25%.

Obviously, some simplifying assumptions have been made. For example, it is assumed that there are no defaults for the collateral assets. It is assumed that all of the collateral assets purchased by the asset manager are noncallable and therefore the coupon rate would not decline because issues are called. Moreover, as explained earlier, at the end of the reinvestment period the asset manager must begin repaying principal to the senior and mezzanine tranches. Consequently, the interest swap must be structured to take this into account since the entire amount of the senior tranche is not outstanding for the life of the collateral assets. Despite the simplifying assumptions, the illustration does demonstrate the basic economics of the CDO, the need for the use derivative instruments—in the example, an interest rate swap—and how the subordinate/equity tranche will realize a return.

Types of Arbitrage Transactions: Cash Flow versus Market Value

Arbitrage transactions can be divided into two types depending on what the primary source of the proceeds from the collateral assets are to satisfy the CDO debt obligations. If the primary source is the interest and maturing principal from the collateral assets, then the transaction is referred to as a *cash flow transaction*. If instead the proceeds to meet the CDO debt obligations depends heavily on the total return generated from the active management of the collateral assets, then the transaction is referred to as a *market value transaction*.

SYNTHETIC CDO TRANSACTIONS

A *synthetic CDO* is so named because the CDO does not actually own the pool of assets on which it has the risk. Stated differently, a synthetic CDO absorbs the economic risks, but not the legal ownership, of its reference credit exposures. The nonsynthetic CDO is referred to as a "cash" structure. Synthetic CDO structures are now widely used in both arbitrage and balance sheet transactions.

The building block for synthetic CDOs is a credit derivative. More specifically, it a credit default swap, which allows the transfer of the economic risk of a pool of asset, but not the legal ownership, of underlying assets. The dominant synthetic CDOs has historically been synthetic balance sheet CDOs. As explained in Chapter 8, where we discuss synthetic CDOs, the motivation of the sponsor is to obtain relief from risk-based capital requirements.

The fastest growing type of synthetic CDO is the synthetic arbitrage CDO, the subject of Chapter 9. As explained in that chapter, we expect that synthetic arbitrage CDOs will continue to grow because of the advantages of a synthetic structure relative to its cash structure counterparty.

USE OF DERIVATIVES IN CDO TRANSACTIONS

From our discussion of the structure of CDOs and the types of CDOs, we can see why it is common to have embedded within a CDO transaction a derivative instrument. Obligations to the counterparty of a derivative instrument embedded in a CDO have priority over payments to any of the CDO debt obligations.

In general, derivative instruments can be classified as futures/forwards, options, swaps, and caps/floors. Derivatives can be further categorized based on the type of risk that they can protect against: interest rate risk or credit risk.

Interest Rate Derivatives

An *interest rate derivative* can be used to protect against adverse movements in the general level of interest rates. We illustrated earlier in this chapter in explaining the economics of an arbitrage transaction one type of interest rate derivative, an interest rate swap. Exhibit 1.1 shows a flow chart of an interest rate swap where the reference rate for the floating-rate side is LIBOR. The interest rate swap can be used to provide a matching of the cash flow characteristics of the assets and liabilities. In this example, an interest rate swap was used to convert fixed-rate coupon payments from the collateral assets into a floating-rate payments in order to match the floating interest payments to the senior tranche.

EXHIBIT 1.1 Bond-Backed CDO and Interest Rate Swap

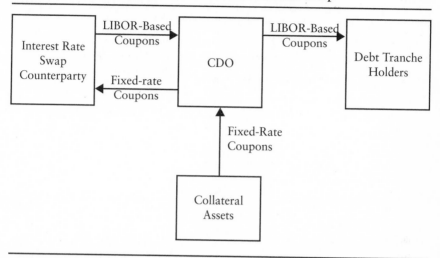

A more efficient way to hedge a bond-backed CDO transaction depending on market conditions may be to purchase an interest rate cap rather than entering into an interest rate swap. An interest cap is an agreement between two parties whereby one party, for an upfront premium, agrees to compensate the other if the reference rate is above a predetermined level (referred to as the "strike rate"). This protects the CDO transaction from an increase in its interest payments to the floating-rate tranches should interest rates rise. The party that benefits, if the reference rate exceeds the reference rate, is called the *cap buyer* and the party that must make the payment is called the *cap seller*. The terms of an interest rate cap include (1) the reference rate; (2) the strike rate that sets the cap; (3) the length of the agreement; (4) the frequency of reset; and, (5) the notional amount. The payoff for the cap buyer at a reset date, if the value of the reference rate exceeds the cap rate on that date, is the greater of zero and the difference between the cap rate and the strike rate multiplied by the notional amount (adjusted for the frequency of the payment). Exhibit 1.2 shows the flow chart for a bond-backed CDO deal with an interest rate cap.

EXHIBIT 1.2   Bond-Backed CDO and Interest Rate Cap

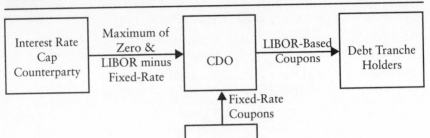

Credit Derivatives

Interest rate derivatives such as interest rate swaps and caps can be used to control the interest rate risk in a CDO transaction with respect to changes in the level of interest rates. Derivative instruments designed to provide protection against credit risk are called *credit derivatives*.

Credit risk can be divided into three types: default risk, credit spread risk, and downgrade risk. Default risk is defined as the risk that the issuer will fail to satisfy the terms of the obligation with respect to the timely payment of interest and repayment of the amount borrowed. Credit spread risk is the risk that an issuer's debt obligation will decline in value due to an increase in the credit spread. Downgrade risk is the risk that issue will be downgraded by a rating agency.

As explained earlier, credit derivatives are used in synthetic CDO transactions. While there are various types of credit derivatives—credit options, credit forwards, and credit default swaps—the one used in a synthetic CDO transaction is a credit default swap. This is used to protect against default risk. Since the term of a CDO is usually a minimum of five years, and the debt holder receives his or her money back at maturity, assuming defaults are limited, it is unnecessary to protect against credit spread risk and downgrade risk.

OVERVIEW OF BOOK

In Chapter 2 we discuss cash flow transactions—the distribution of the cash flows, restrictions imposed on the asset manager to protect the debt holders, and the key factors considered by rating agencies in rating tranches. Our focus in the chapter is on deals backed by high-yield corporate bonds.

In Chapter 3 we describe how the rating agencies view defaults and how they use them in developing the weighted average rating factors for CDOs. Because of the transparency of the rating methodology to investors, we then explain why relative value opportunities arise in the CDO market due to the way defaults and potential defaults are viewed by investors and how the opportunities can be identified by investors using credit analysis.

In Chapters 4 and 5 we discuss CDOs backed by structured finance products—residential mortgage-backed securities, commercial mortgage-backed securities, asset-backed securities, and real estate investment trusts. In Chapter 4 we review structured finance products. In Chapter 5 we then look at structured finance cash flow CDOs beginning with the similarities of and differences between structured finance cash flow CDO structures and high-yield corporate bond CDO structures. We then review the relative credit quality of structured finance debt versus corporate debt as CDO collateral, concluding that by using the same criteria to rate all types of CDOs, the rating agencies impose an extra burden on those backed by structured finance collateral. As a result, the ratings are conservative and thereby offer investors relative value opportunities.

In Chapter 6 we look at CDOs backed by sovereign emerging market bonds, focusing on the differences (that matter) between emerging markets and high-yield deals. We conclude that the rating agencies are far more conservative in their assumptions when rating emerging market deals than in rating high-yield deals. Again, this leads to relative value opportunities.

Market value CDOs are the subject of Chapter 7. While the number of market value deals is small relative to cash flow deals, they are the structure of choice for collateral where the cash flows are difficult to predict. We begin the chapter with an overview on the differences between cash flow and market value structures and then examine the mechanics of market value CDOs, focusing on advance rates. An advance rate is the percentage of a particular asset that may be issued as rated debt and is the key to protecting the debt holders. Our investigation of some volatility numbers suggests how conservative the advance rates used by the rating agencies really are and as such may result in relative value opportunities.

In Chapters 8 and 9 we cover synthetic CDO structures. In Chapter 8, we look at the basic structure and structural nuances of synthetic balance sheet CDOs, the unique challenges confronting the rating agencies in rating these CDOs, and the key differences between synthetic and non-synthetic (i.e., cash) transactions. Synthetic arbitrage CDOs are the subject of Chapter 9. This structure has a number of advantages over its cash counterpart and these advantages explain why synthetic arbitrage CDO issuance has grown dramatically and is expected to do so in the future. The advantages are that the super senior piece in a synthetic CDO is generally not funded, there is only a short ramp-up period, and credit default swaps often trade cheaper than the cash bond of the same maturity. In Chapter 9, we discuss these advantages and demonstrate how they impact the economics of a CDO transaction.

In Chapter 10, we explain the factors that structurers consider in creating CDOs. We show how to look at the CDO arbitrage and present a "quick and dirty" analysis for benchmarking CDO issuance. We then focus on how the arbitrage dictates deal structure. Spread configurations and the exact collateral used are important in determining optimal deal structure. As we explain, simply looking at percent subordination or percent overcollateralization as an arbiter of tranche quality is misleading. This is because since the arbitrage often dictates deal structure, these measures may communicate little about tranche quality per se.

One of the most interesting trends in the CDO market has been the increasing use of participating coupon structures—combinations of traditional debt securities plus an equity interest in the same deal. We discuss these participating coupon notes and identify the wide range of variations of the basic participating coupon structure in Chapter 11. These structures can be tailored to investor preferences, thereby offering investors the benefit of a rated instrument for regulatory and financial purposes, coupled with a higher base case yield than that on comparably rated CDO debt.

In Chapter 12 we provide a relative value methodology for mezzanine tranches of a CDO structure. We begin with a discussion of the risk-return profile of a mezzanine tranche and compare this profile to that of a corporate bond with the same credit rating. The methodology involves determining the better yielding investment alternative at the same level of risk by calculating breakeven default rates necessary to produce the same yield on the two bonds.

In Chapter 13 we explain how to analyze the equity tranche of a CDO. We begin with a review of where CDO equity cash flows come from. After explaining the framework for analyzing the equity tranche, we provide a brief review of the relative attractiveness of equity cash flows backed by different collateral and the impact of factors that drive CDO equity returns.

A payment-in-kind is a clearly disclosed, structural feature within some bonds whereby an issuer can—instead of paying a current coupon—increase the par value of the bond by paying the bond's then-due coupon with more of the same bonds, thus "paying-in-kind." A high default rate environment in the high-yield bond and loan market can cause some CDO tranches to stop paying current interest or to then "pay-in-kind." The tranches are referred to as PIK tranches. In Chapter 14 we take a close look at PIK tranches, discuss rating agency approaches to PIK tranches, and demonstrate the relationship between CDO PIK tranches and loss of internal rate of return among CDO tranches.

In the last chapter of this book, Chapter 15, we cover trading opportunities in the secondary market and a framework for managing a portfolio of CDOs.

CHAPTER 2

Cash Flow CDOs

As explained in Chapter 1, arbitrage CDOs are categorized as either cash flow transactions or market value transactions. The objective of the asset manager in a cash flow transaction is to generate cash flow for the senior and mezzanine tranches without the active trading of bonds. Because the cash flows from the structure are designed to accomplish the objective for each tranche, restrictions are imposed on the asset manager. The asset manager is very limited in his or her authority to buy and sell bonds. The conditions for disposing of issues held are specified and are usually driven by credit risk management. Also, in assembling the portfolio, the asset manager must meet certain requirements set forth by the rating agency or agencies that rate the deal.

In this chapter we will discuss cash flow transactions. Specifically, we will look at the distribution of the cash flows, restrictions imposed on the asset manager to protect the noteholders, and the key factors considered by rating agencies in rating tranches of a cash flow transaction. In our review of these key factors, we will provide insight into the differences in structuring deals based on collateral type (i.e., high-yield versus investment-grade corporate backed deals). In Chapter 5 we will look at structured finance cash flow transactions, and in Chapter 7 we will look at market value transactions.

DISTRIBUTION OF CASH FLOWS

In a cash flow transaction, the cash flows from income and principal are distributed according to rules set forth in the prospectus. The distribution of the cash flows is referred to as the "waterfall." We describe these rules below and will use an actual CDO deal to illustrate them.

The CDO deal we will use is *Duke Funding 1*. This deal, priced in November 2000, is a $300 million cash flow CDO and an excellent example of a "typical" cash flow structure. The deal consists of the following:

- $260 million (87% of the deal) Aaa/AAA (Moody's/S&P) floating-rate tranche
- $27 million ($17 million fixed + $10 million) Class B notes, rated A3 by Moody's
- $5 million (fixed rate) Class C notes, rated Ba2 by Moody's
- $8 million in equity (called "preference shares" in this deal)

The collateral for this deal consists primarily of investment-grade commercial mortgage-backed securities (CMBS), asset-backed securities (ABS), real estate investment trusts (REIT), and residential mortgage-backed securities (RMBS); 90% of which must be rated at least "Baa3" by Moody's or BBB– by S&P.[1] The asset manager is Ellington Management Group, LLC, a well respected money management firm.

Exhibit 2.1 illustrates the priority of interest distributions among different classes for our sample deal. Interest payments are allocated first to high priority deal expenses such as fees, taxes, and registration, as well as monies owed to the asset manager and hedge counterparties. After these are satisfied, investors are paid in a fairly straightforward manner, with the more senior bonds paid off first, followed by the subordinate bonds, and then the equity classes.

---

[1] At the time of purchase, the collateral corresponded, on average, to a Baa2 rating.

EXHIBIT 2.1   Interest Cash Flow "Waterfall"

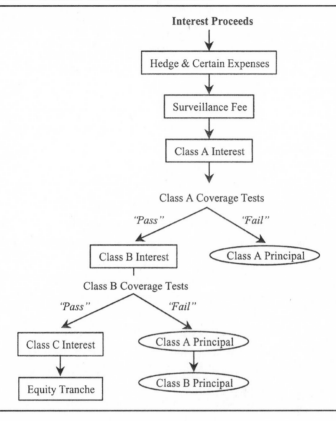

Note the important role in the waterfall played by what is referred to as the *coverage tests*. We'll explain these shortly. They are important because before any payments are made on Class B or Class C bonds, coverage tests are run to assure the deal is performing within guidelines. If that is not the case, consequences to the equity holders are severe. Note from Exhibit 2.1 if the Class A coverage tests are violated, then excess interest on the portfolio goes to pay down principal on the Class A notes, and cash flows will be diverted from all other classes to do so. If the portfolio violates the Class B coverage tests, then interest will be diverted from Class C plus the equity tranche to pay down first principal on Class A, and then Class B principal.

EXHIBIT 2.2   Principal Cash Flow "Waterfall"

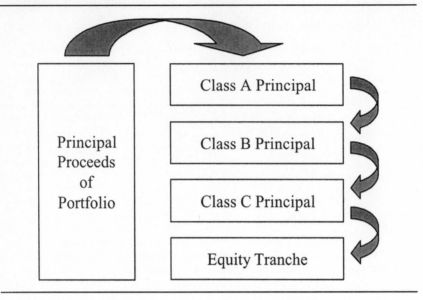

Exhibit 2.2 shows the simple principal cash flows for this deal. Principal is paid down purely in class order. Any remaining collateral principal from overcollateralization gets passed onto the equity piece.

In Chapter 13 we will take a closer look at this actual deal to see how the potential cash flow effects the equity tranche.

RESTRICTIONS ON MANAGEMENT: SAFETY NETS

Noteholders have two major protections provided in the form of tests. They are coverage tests and quality tests. We discuss each type below.

Coverage Tests

Coverage tests are designed to protect noteholders against a deterioration of the existing portfolio. There are actually two categories of tests—*overcollateralization tests* and *interest coverage tests*.

Overcollateralization Tests

The overcollateralization or O/C ratio for a tranche is found by computing the ratio of the *principal* balance of the collateral portfolio over the *principal* balance of that tranche and all tranches senior to it. That is,

O/C ratio for a tranche

$$= \frac{\text{Principal (par) value of collateral portfolio}}{\text{Principal for tranche} + \text{Principal for all tranches senior to it}}$$

The higher the ratio, the greater protection for the note holders. Note that the overcollateralization ratio is based on the principal or par value of the assets.[2] (Hence, an overcollateralization test is also referred to as a *par value test*.) An overcollateralization ratio is computed for specified tranches subject to the overcollateralization test. The overcollateralization test for a tranche involves comparing the tranche's overcollateralization ratio to the tranche's required minimum ratio as specified in the guidelines. The required minimum ratio is referred to as the *overcollateralization trigger*. The overcollateralization test for a tranche is passed if the overcollateralization ratio is greater than or equal to its respective overcollateralization trigger.

Consider Duke Funding 1. There are two rated tranches subject to the overcollateralization test—Classes A and B. Therefore two overcollateralization ratios are computed for this deal. For each tranche, the overcollateralization test involves first computing the overcollateralization ratio as follows:

$$\text{O/C ratio for Class A} = \frac{\text{Principal (par) value of collateral portfolio}}{\text{Principal for Class A}}$$

$$\text{O/C ratio for Class B} = \frac{\text{Principal (par) value of collateral portfolio}}{\text{Principal for Class A} + \text{Principal for Class B}}$$

---

[2] As explained in Chapter 7, for market value CDOs, overcollateralization tests are based on market values rather than principal or par values.

Once the overcollateralization ratio for a tranche is computed, it is then compared to the overcollateralization trigger for the tranche as specified in the guidelines. If the computed overcollateralization ratio is greater than or equal to the overcollateralization trigger for the tranche, then the test is passed with respect to that tranche.

For Duke Funding 1, the overcollateralization trigger is 113% for Class A and 101% for Class B. Note that the lower the seniority, the lower the overcollateralization trigger. The Class A overcollateralization test is failed if the ratio falls below 113% and the Class B overcollateralization test is failed if the ratio falls below 101%.

Interest Coverage Test

The interest coverage or I/C ratio for a tranche is the ratio of scheduled interest due on the underlying collateral portfolio to scheduled interest to be paid to that tranche and all tranches senior to it. That is,

$$\text{I/C ratio for a tranche} = \frac{\text{Scheduled interest due on underlying collateral portfolio}}{\text{Scheduled interest to that tranche} + \text{Schedule interest to all tranches senior}}$$

The higher the interest coverage ratio, the greater the protection. An interest coverage ratio is computed for specified tranches subject to the interest coverage test. The interest coverage test for a tranche involves comparing the tranche's interest coverage ratio to the tranche's *interest coverage trigger* (i.e., the required minimum ratio as specified in the guidelines). The interest coverage test for a tranche is passed if the computed interest coverage ratio is greater than or equal to its respective interest coverage trigger.

For Duke Funding 1, Classes A and B are subject to the interest coverage test. The following two interest coverage ratios are therefore computed

$$\text{I/C ratio for Class A} = \frac{\text{Scheduled interest due on underlying collateral portfolio}}{\text{Scheduled interest to Class A}}$$

$$\text{I/C ratio for Class B} = \frac{\text{Scheduled interest due on underlying collateral portfolio}}{\text{Scheduled interest to Class A} + \text{Scheduled interest to Class B}}$$

In the case of Duke Funding, the Class A interest coverage trigger is 121%, while the Class B interest coverage trigger is 106%.

Quality Tests

After the tranches of a CDO deal are rated, the rating agencies are concerned that the composition of the collateral portfolio may be adversely altered by the asset manager over time. Tests are imposed to prevent the asset manager from trading assets so as to result in a deterioration of the quality of the portfolio and are referred to as *quality tests*. These tests deal with maturity restrictions, the degree of diversification, and credit ratings of the assets in the collateral portfolio. As we will see, these tests have been quantified by rating agencies.

CREDIT RATINGS

There are three key inputs to cash flow CDO ratings. They are

- Collateral diversification
- Likelihood of default
- Recovery rates

While each rating agency uses a slightly different methodology, they reach similar conclusions. For this analysis we use a variation of Moody's methodology, as it is the most transparent plus allows us to change inputs to show the import and impact of each.

Moody's uses the same objective process for developing liability structures regardless of the type of collateral. Moody's determines losses on each tranche under different default scenarios, and probability-weight those results. The resulting "expected loss" is then compared to the maximum permitted for any given rating. While that whole iterative process makes for a tedious analysis, it does help highlight why, for example, a deal backed by investment-grade corporate bonds will have a very high proportion of triple A tranches and a low proportion of equity compared to a deal backed by high-yield corporate bonds.

Collateral Diversification

Moody's methodology reduces the asset pool to a set of homogenous, uncorrelated assets. For example, for CDOs backed by corporate bonds, a *diversity score* is calculated by dividing the bonds into different industry classifications. These industry classifications are shown in Exhibit 2.3. Each industry group is assumed to have a zero correlation with other industry groups. Two securities from different issuers within the same industry group are assumed to have some correlation to each other. At the extreme, two securities from the same issuer are treated as having 100% correlation, and hence providing zero diversification.

Reducing the portfolio to the number of independent securities allows the use of a binomial probability distribution. This is the distribution that allows one to figure out the probability of obtaining 9 "heads" in 10 flips of the coin. This distribution can also be applied to a weighted coin, where the probability of "heads" is substantially different than the probability of tails. Intuitively, each asset is a separate flip of the coin, and the outcomes ("heads" and "tails") corresponds to "no default" and "default." The use of this probability distribution makes it possible to define the likelihood of a given number of securities in the portfolio defaulting over the life of a deal.

EXHIBIT 2.3   Moody's Investors Service—Industry Classifications

Listing	Sector
1	Aerospace & Defense
2	Automobile
3	Banking
4	Beverage, Food & Tobacco
5	Buildings and Real Estate
6	Chemicals, Plastics & Rubber
7	Containers, Packaging and Glass
8	Personal and Nondurable Consumer Products
9	Diversified/Conglomerate Manufacturing
10	Diversified/Conglomerate Service
11	Metals & Minerals
12	Ecological
13	Electronics
14	Finance
15	Farming and Agriculture
16	Grocery
17	Healthcare, Education, and Childcare
18	Home and Office Furnishings, Housewares and Durable Consumer Products
19	Hotels, Inns and Gaming
20	Insurance
21	Leisure, Amusement, Motion Picture, Entertainment
22	Machinery
23	Mining, Steel, Iron and Nonprecious Metals
24	Oil and Gas
25	Personal, Food and Miscellaneous Services
26	Printing and Publishing
27	Cargo Transport
28	Retail Stores
29	Telecommunications
30	Textiles and Leather
31	Personal Transportation
32	Utilities
33	Broadcasting
34	Structured Products

Source: Table 6 (Industry Classifications) in Alan Brackman and Gerard O'Conner, "Rating Cash Flow Transactions Backed by Corporate Debt 1995 Update," Moody's Investors, Inc., (p. 13). *Note:* Updated by UBS Warburg CBO Desk.

One factor concerning investors in CDOs is the potential for the default on one bond to wipe out the equity. In fact, in addition to the general diversification methodology, there are entity concentration rules that protect against too large a concentration within securities issued by any single entity. It is customary for issuer exposure to be no more than 2%. To allow asset managers some flexibility, a few exceptions are permitted. In one actual deal, for example, four positions could be as large as 3%, as long as no more than two of these exposures were in the same industry. If two of the exposures greater than 2% were in the same industry, additional restrictions apply.

Historical Defaults

Likelihood of default is provided by the *weighted average rating factor* (WARF). This is a rough guide to the asset quality of a portfolio and is meant to incorporate probability of default for each of the bonds backing a CDO. To see where this comes from, we need to look at actual default experience on corporate bonds.

Exhibit 2.4 shows actual average cumulative default rates from 1 to 10 years based on Moody's data from 1983–2000. These data show that bonds with an initial rating of Baa3 experienced average default rates of 4.99% after 7 years, and 7.03% after 10 years. Compare that to the B1 default rate of 36.15% after 7 years and 48.01% after 10 years. Generally, as would be expected, bonds with lower ratings exhibit higher default patterns. Moreover, defaults rise exponentially, not linearly, as rating decline.

However, it is difficult to use these data to construct a stylized default pattern, as some anomalies appear. For example, Aaa bonds default more frequently than do Aa1 bonds. And Aa2 bonds default more frequently than either Aa3 or A1 bonds, while A2 bonds default more frequently than A3 bonds. Correspondingly, B2 bonds default less frequently than either Ba3 or B1 bonds.

EXHIBIT 2.4 Average Cumulative Default Rates from 1 to 10 Years—1983–2000 (%)

	1	2	3	4	5	6	7	8	9	10
Aaa	0.00	0.00	0.00	0.06	0.18	0.25	0.34	0.43	0.43	0.43
Aa1	0.00	0.00	0.00	0.21	0.21	0.35	0.35	0.35	0.35	0.35
Aa2	0.00	0.00	0.06	0.18	0.41	0.49	0.59	0.71	0.85	1.01
Aa3	0.00	0.09	0.17	0.26	0.37	0.49	0.49	0.49	0.49	0.49
A1	0.00	0.03	0.30	0.47	0.59	0.73	0.79	0.86	0.86	0.96
A2	0.00	0.02	0.16	0.41	0.62	0.84	0.99	1.35	1.63	1.71
A3	0.00	0.12	0.22	0.30	0.35	0.47	0.68	0.77	0.97	1.09
Baa1	0.07	0.30	0.53	0.86	1.19	1.43	1.82	2.05	2.20	2.20
Baa2	0.06	0.29	0.61	1.22	1.89	2.54	2.93	3.17	3.46	3.81
Baa3	0.39	1.05	1.62	2.47	3.15	4.09	4.99	5.95	6.54	7.03
Ba1	0.64	2.10	3.81	6.15	8.12	10.09	11.43	12.75	13.35	14.08
Ba2	0.54	2.44	4.95	7.32	9.27	10.88	12.59	13.60	14.27	14.71
Ba3	2.47	6.82	11.68	16.18	20.63	24.74	28.39	32.28	35.83	38.22
B1	3.48	9.71	15.59	20.56	25.62	30.78	36.15	40.30	44.16	48.01
B2	6.23	13.70	20.03	24.63	28.24	31.14	32.73	34.33	35.03	35.90
B3	11.88	20.18	26.71	31.95	36.68	39.89	42.81	46.80	51.42	53.53
Caa1-C	18.85	28.29	34.51	40.23	43.42	46.48	46.48	49.73	53.92	59.04
Investment-grade	0.05	0.17	0.35	0.60	0.84	1.08	1.28	1.47	1.62	1.73
Speculative-grade	3.69	8.39	12.87	16.80	20.39	23.61	26.44	29.04	31.22	32.89
All Corporates	1.21	2.72	4.12	5.34	6.39	7.30	8.05	8.71	9.23	9.61

Source: David T. Hamilton, Greg Gupton, and Alexandra Berthault, "Default and Recovery Rate of Corporate Bond Issuers: 2000," Moody's Investors Service (February 2001). Reprinted with permission from Moody's Investors Service.

EXHIBIT 2.5   Moody's Weighted Average Rating Factors

	WARF
Aaa	1
Aa1	10
Aa2	20
Aa3	40
A1	70
A2	120
A3	180
Baa1	260
Baa2	360
Baa3	610
Ba1	940
Ba2	1,350
Ba3	1,780
B1	2,220
B2	2,720
B3	3,490
Caa	6,500
Ca	10,000

Source: Moody's Investors Service. Reprinted with permission from Moody's Investors Service.

WARF Scores

Moody's smoothes these data and constructs a weighted average rating factor (WARF), shown in Exhibit 2.5. Thus, a bond with a Baa1 rating has a Moody's score of 260, while one rated Baa3 would have a WARF score of 610. Note that these scores exhibit the same pattern as did actual default numbers: Scores are nonlinear and increase exponentially as ratings decline. These scores are also dollar-weighted across the portfolio to deliver a weighted average rating factor for the portfolio.

The weighted average rating factor for the portfolio translates directly into a cumulative probability of default. The cumulative probability of default will be larger the longer the portfolio is outstanding. A WARF score of 610 means that there is a 6.1% probability of default for each of the independent, uncorrelated assets defaulting in a 10-year period. (In general, the WARF score translates directly into the 10-year "idealized" cumulative default rate.) The same 610 WARF would correspond to a 4.97% probability of default after 8 years, or a 5.57% probability of default after 9 years.

Note that the systematic bias in mapping actual defaults to WARF scores results in the rating methodology being more conservative for investment-grade corporate bonds deals than for high-yield corporate bond deals. This results in WARF scores for investment-grade bonds that are very close to the actual default probabilities, while the actual default rates for high-yield bonds are much higher than the WARF scores would indicate. Thus, for Baa3 rated securities, the WARF score is 610 (which corresponds to a 6.1% probability of default after 10 years), which is also very close to the average cumulative default rate of 7.03% after 10 years. For Baa2 bonds, the WARF is 360, corresponding to a 3.6% probability of default after 10 years. Actual cumulative default rates for Baa2 are a very similar level of 3.81%. By contrast, for bonds rated Ba2 and below (where most of the high-yield universe resides), WARF scores are considerably lower than the actual cumulative default rate. For a B1 bond, for instance, the WARF is 2,220 versus a cumulative default rate of 48.01%.

When the desired rating on the CDO tranche is the same as the rating on the underlying collateral, Moody's will use the probability of default derived from the WARF score. For CDO ratings higher than the ratings on their underlying collateral, Moody's will use a higher default rate. The multiple applied to the idealized cumulative default rate is referred to as a *stress factor*. Thus, for example, in an investment-grade deal (Baa-rated collateral), Moody's uses a factor of 1.0 to rate a Baa tranche. If the rating on the CDO tranche is Aaa,

Aa, or A, then Moody's uses a higher factor to stress the default rates.[3]

Recovery Rates

Moody's recovery rates are dependent on the desired rating of the CDO tranche. To obtain the highest ratings (Aaa and Aa), Moody's generally assumes recovery rates of 30% on unsecured corporate bonds. To obtain an A or Baa rating, recovery assumptions are slightly higher, at 33% and 36%, respectively. It should be understood that actual average recovery rates are higher than these assumptions. A Moody's study covering the period 1981 to 2000 showed that the median, or midpoint, recovery rate for senior unsecured debt was $44 ($47 average or mean). For subordinated unsecured debt, the median recovery rate was $29 ($32 average). The bottom line is this: Moody's is again conservative, as it uses a recovery value consistent with subordinated unsecured debt on debt that is in most cases senior—and that builds in "extra" protection for the investors.

Putting It All Together

Moody's has an expected loss permissible for each CDO rating. That expected loss is derived as follows:

Expected loss

$$= \sum_{i=1}^{n} (\text{Loss in default scenario } i) \times (\text{Probability of scenario } i \text{ ocurring})$$

---

[3] One factor concerning investors is the "credit barbelling" of the portfolio. In a portfolio with investment-grade corporate bonds, for example, that means buying a combination of an A rated security and a Ba rated security that has the same WARF score as the portfolio. Barbelling is used to increase portfolio yield. For example, most investment-grade deals average a Baa3 rating, but also tend to include 10–25% high-yield issuance. Given that default rates are nonlinear, this is a concern. However, rating agencies are well aware of the incentive to "barbell" a portfolio to increase portfolio yield. So they "correct" for that by treating the high-yield universe as a separate portfolio and examine that piece of the portfolio at a probability of default much higher than would be dictated by probability of default on the overall portfolio. More precisely, their adaptation for "barbelled" portfolios involves running a double binomial probability distribution. In addition, they place strict concentration limitations on the amount of less-than-investment-grade debt that can be held in a portfolio.

The following example, using an investment-grade corporate CDO, will help clarify this formula. Assume a typical CDO deal with 45 independent assets. Assume further that we are looking at a 10-year deal in which each asset has a probability of default of 5% corresponding to a WARF score of 500, which is well within the category of Baa rated assets. Moreover, we assume a capital structure with 85% of the bonds Aaa rated, 10% Baa rated, and 5% equity. The recovery rate is assumed to be 30%.

To create an example that can be replicated with a simple spreadsheet, we assume all interim cash flows are distributed, and all defaults occur at the end of the life of the deal. Moody's will actually run each scenario through its CDO cash flow model in order to determine the loss to each bond in the CDO structure. Moody's will assume a number of different loss schedules and select the most detrimental.

We have simplified that whole analytical process to make it more transparent. Our methodology overstates losses to the bondholders, since we ignored all overcollateralization and interest coverage tests. As the portfolio deteriorated, those two tests kick in and would cut off cash flow to the equity tranche, redirecting cash flows to pay down the higher rated tranches. We have also ignored the excess spread on these deals, which provides a very important cushion to the noteholders.

The probability of a scenario in which none of the 45 securities default is (probability of no default)^{45}, or $(0.95)^{45}$. This is equal to 9.94%. If there are zero defaults, there is obviously no loss. The probability of only one loss is found as follows:

$$[(\text{Probability of no default})^{44} \times (\text{Probability of 1 default}) \times 45]$$
$$= (0.95)^{44} \times 0.95 \times 45 = 23.55\%$$

This frequency distribution is shown in the column of Exhibit 2.6, labeled "Probability."

EXHIBIT 2.6 Expected Loss on BBB Class, Investment-Grade CDO Deal (Given 45 Assets)

No. of Securities: 45
Portfolio loss for single default: 1.56%
Expected BBB loss: 3.9205%

No. of Defaults	Portfolio Loss (%)	Probability (%)	BBB Loss (%)	BBB Loss × Probability (%)
0	0.00	9.94	0.00	0.0000
1	1.56	23.55	0.00	0.0000
2	3.11	27.27	0.00	0.0000
3	4.67	20.57	0.00	0.0000
4	6.22	11.37	12.22	1.3895
5	7.78	4.91	27.78	1.3629
6	9.33	1.72	43.33	0.7460
7	10.89	0.50	58.89	0.2973
8	12.44	0.13	74.44	0.0940
9	14.00	0.03	90.00	0.0246
10	15.56	0.01	100.00	0.0052
11	17.11	0.00	100.00	0.0009
12	18.67	0.00	100.00	0.0001
13	20.22	0.00	100.00	0.0000
14	21.78	0.00	100.00	0.0000
15	23.33	0.00	100.00	0.0000
16	24.89	0.00	100.00	0.0000
17	26.44	0.00	100.00	0.0000
18	28.00	0.00	100.00	0.0000
19	29.56	0.00	100.00	0.0000
20	31.11	0.00	100.00	0.0000
21	32.67	0.00	100.00	0.0000
22	34.22	0.00	100.00	0.0000
23	35.78	0.00	100.00	0.0000
24	37.33	0.00	100.00	0.0000
25	38.89	0.00	100.00	0.0000
26	40.44	0.00	100.00	0.0000
27	42.00	0.00	100.00	0.0000
28	43.56	0.00	100.00	0.0000
29	45.11	0.00	100.00	0.0000
30	46.67	0.00	100.00	0.0000

EXHIBIT 2.6 (Continued)

No. of Defaults	Portfolio Loss (%)	Probability (%)	BBB Loss (%)	BBB Loss × Probability (%)
31	48.22	0.00	100.00	0.0000
32	49.78	0.00	100.00	0.0000
33	51.33	0.00	100.00	0.0000
34	52.89	0.00	100.00	0.0000
35	54.44	0.00	100.00	0.0000
36	56.00	0.00	100.00	0.0000
37	57.56	0.00	100.00	0.0000
38	59.11	0.00	100.00	0.0000
39	60.67	0.00	100.00	0.0000
40	62.22	0.00	100.00	0.0000
41	63.78	0.00	100.00	0.0000
42	65.33	0.00	100.00	0.0000
43	66.89	0.00	100.00	0.0000
44	68.44	0.00	100.00	0.0000
45	70.00	0.00	100.00	0.0000

With one default, the defaulted bond comprises $\frac{1}{45}$ of the portfolio, or 2.22%. However, since a 30% recovery rate is assumed, that loss is lowered to 1.56% (2.22 × 0.7). Thus, the "Portfolio Loss" column of Exhibit 2.6 shows that the loss with one default would be 1.56%. But the 5% equity in the deal acts as a buffer, and there would be no loss to the BBB bond. In order to impact the BBB bond, losses must total more than 5%.

Assume four defaults among the 45 assets. This means that 8.89% of the assets ($\frac{4}{45}$) are defaulting, and portfolio loss becomes 6.22% (8.89% × 0.7). The probability of this occurring is 11.37%. If that case does occur, the Baa bond would lose 12.22% of its value. That is, the equity would be eliminated, and the $10 Baa tranche ($10 per $100 par value) would be reduced by ($6.22 − $5.00), or $1.22, for a 12.22% reduction. Thus

$$[(\text{Baa loss}) \times (\text{Probability of loss})] = 1.38\%$$

or

[(11.37% probability of scenario) × (12.22% loss if scenario materializes)]

Similarly, if there were five defaults (a 4.92% probability), the portfolio loss would be 7.78%. This corresponds to a loss of 27.78% on the Baa bond. The expected loss to the Baa bond in this scenario is (4.91 × 27.78), or 1.3629%. Note that if portfolio losses total more than 15%, the Baa bond is eliminated, and only then does the Aaa bond start incurring losses.

Adding expected losses in each of the scenarios across the binomial probability distribution, we find that the expected loss on this Baa CDO tranche is 3.92%. Realize again that this example is for illustrative purposes and will overstate losses to the bondholders. It ignores overcollateralization and interest coverage ratios and the excess spread in the deal.

Importance of Diversification

We can now readily show the importance of diversification. No matter how many assets we have, if the probability of default on each is 5% and recovery is 30%, then the expected loss on the portfolio is 3.5%. However, this does not address any distribution of losses, which is certainly important to the bondholders.

In fact, the Baa bondholders are concerned about the likelihood of losses exceeding the amount of equity in the deal, while the Aaa bondholders are concerned about the likelihood of losses exceeding the amount of equity and Baa bonds. The greater the number of assets, the greater the likelihood that losses on those assets will cluster around 3.5% and the lower the likelihood that losses will exceed the 5% equity cushion and impact the Baa piece. On the flip side, the smaller the number of assets, the greater the likelihood that losses will exceed the 5% equity cushion and will hit the Baa bonds.

EXHIBIT 2.7   Benefits of Diversification

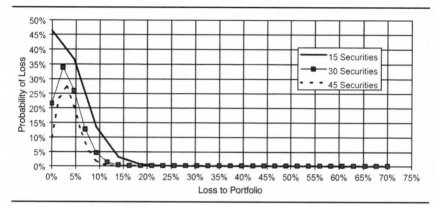

EXHIBIT 2.8   Diversity and Expected Losses (%)

No. of Securities	15	20	25	30	45	60
Aaa losses	0.0273	0.0091	0.0032	0.0012	0.0001	0.0000
Baa losses	9.1520	8.5074	6.8720	5.6216	3.9205	2.9262

Exhibit 2.7 shows probability distributions for losses on pools of 15, 30, and 45 securities. Note that the fewer the number of assets, the greater likelihood that losses will exceed a 5% equity cushion.

Exhibit 2.8 supports the point that with fewer assets, expected losses to the Baa rated tranche are much higher. Thus, for 15 assets, the loss to the Baa tranche is 9.15%; for 30 assets it is 5.62%. For 45 assets, the loss to the Baa tranche is 3.92%; and for 60 assets, it is 2.92%. Note also that the benefits of diversification diminish as more assets are added. The loss to the Baa tranche is 5.5% lower in moving from 15 to 30 assets. It only drops 1.7% in moving from 30 to 45 assets and only 1% from 45 to 60 assets.

What's "Too Much" Diversification?

The above analysis suggests that greater diversification is always better, since it means less variation of collateral returns. However, a higher diversity score also means that it may be likely the asset manager pushed for, and achieved, less equity in the deal. In fact, with a diversity score of 60, the same losses on the Aaa and Baa bonds could have been achieved with less equity (on the order of 4.5% rather than the 5% required on a deal with a diversity score of 45).

Is there any such thing as too much of a diversification "good thing"? That depends on the asset manager. A large, broad-based asset manager may have considerable strength across all sectors and should be able to handle the analysis—and risks—of a highly diverse portfolio. Even here, a very high diversity score can limit flexibility by requiring an asset manager with broad expertise to invest in an industry he does not like. Whether or not flexibility is being limited too much by a very high diversity score is dependent on the range of assets employed and the strengths of a particular asset manager.

Too much diversification is even more a major problem for a smaller asset manager, where the portfolio may have selective strengths in fewer industries. This asset manager may be stretching to take on additional diversity to achieve a lower required equity. Investors should certainly be wary of deals in which very high diversity scores are achieved by managers straying from their fields of expertise.

Loss Distribution Tests

As can be seen from the discussion above, Moody's approach to rating CDOs involves (1) developing a diversity score; (2) calculating a weighted-average rating factor; (3) using the binomial distribution to determine the probability of a specific number of defaults; and (4) calculating the impact of those defaults on bonds within the CDO structure. One element needed to calculate that impact is a distribution of defaults and losses across time. Let's look at this distribution of defaults and losses.

Moody's stresses bonds via six different loss distributions, and a bond must pass each test. The six loss distributions are shown in Exhibit 2.9. Moody's basic approach assumes 50% of the losses will occur at a single point in time, and that remaining losses are evenly distributed over a 5-year period. This single 50% loss is assumed to occur at a different point in each of the six tests. For example, Test 1 assumes that the single 50% loss occurs at the beginning of the deal.

Liability Structure

The structure of the liabilities will be primarily determined by the credit quality of the assets, the amount of diversification, and excess spread. That is, the combination of credit quality, diversification of assets, and excess spread dictate expected losses on each tranche. That is then compared to losses allowed to achieve a given rating. Realize that the structures have been optimized. If a structurer sees one of the tranches passing expected loss tests by a large margin, that means there is room to improve the arbitrage. That can be accomplished by leveraging the structure more (i.e., reducing equity, reducing the amount of mezzanine bonds, or both).

The results above clearly indicate that with less diversification, more equity is needed. Indeed, it's ludicrous to think a CDO can achieve a Baa rating with 15 securities, equity of 5%, and an expected loss of 9.15%. As diversification declines, equity must rise. However, the rating agency methodology indicates, for example, that in an investment-grade, corporate-backed CDO deal, in comparison to a high-yield corporate bond-backed deal, a very diversified portfolio of highly rated collateral can be structured with a high percentage of Aaa bonds and a low percent of equity.

EXHIBIT 2.9 Moody's Loss Distribution Tests

Year	Percent of Total Losses Occurring at Start of Each Year					
	Test 1	Test 2	Test 3	Test 4	Test 5	Test 6
1	50	10	10	10	10	10
2	10	50	10	10	10	10
3	10	10	50	10	10	10
4	10	10	10	50	10	10
5	10	10	10	10	50	10
6	10	10	10	10	10	50

EXHIBIT 2.10 Liability Structure of Cash Flow Deals (% of Deal)

	Investment-Grade Corporate Bond Deal	High-Yield Bond Deal	ABS/MBS Deal
Aaa	82–85	75–78	78–83
Baa	10–15	12–15	15–17
Equity	3.5–5	8–10	4–6

Capital Structures versus Collateral

Exhibit 2.10 compares typical capital structures for deals backed by investment-grade corporate bonds and high-yield bonds. The comparisons are generic, and assume the CDO transaction contains only bonds rated Aaa and Baa, plus equity. In Chapter 5 we will look at the capital structure for cash flow deals backed by structured products (commercial mortgage-backed securities, asset-backed securities, and residential mortgage-backed securities collateral)—structured finance CDOs.

While most deals of a given genre have Aaa and mezzanine percentages within the bands shown in Exhibit 2.10, there will be exceptions. These outliers generally stem from the fact that collateral baskets differ slightly from generic ones (e.g., collateral is better or worse or collateral is more barbelled) or there may have been further optimization of the deal structure (introduction of an A rated class, for example, lowers the percentages of both Aaas and Baas).

Focus on Exhibit 2.10 more closely. High-yield deals require a much higher percentage of equity and, correspondingly, carry a much lower percentage of triple A tranches at any given rating level than investment-grade corporate bonds. But the methodology we used above does not allow an easy comparison to the high-yield market. That's because excess spread, which has been intentionally ignored in the analysis, actually provides quite a cushion for bondholders. This cushion is even more important in CDO deals backed by high-yield bonds than in deals backed by higher-rated collateral. The protection provided by that excess spread is actually heightened further by the overcollateralization and interest coverage tests. These two tests can be tripped at higher thresholds on high-yield deals than on investment-grade corporate CDOs (and even structured finance CDO deals discussed in Chapter 5). This can be seen in Exhibit 2.11.

As can be seen in Exhibit 2.11, at the Baa level, typical overcollateralization tests are 105–112 on a high-yield CDO deal versus 102–105 on an investment-grade corporate CDO deal. Typical interest coverage tests are 110–120 at the Baa level, rather than 100–105 on investment-grade corporate deals. So as collateral deteriorates, the overcollateralization and interest coverage tests are breached. When the Baa overcollateralization or interest coverage tests are breached, then the cash flow spigot is turned away from the equity tranche, and onto paying down the Aaa bonds. When Aaa overcollateralization or interest coverage tests are breached, then interest payments to the Baa tranche are suspended and those flows go toward paying off the Aaa class. These triggers are important on all deals, but particularly so on high-yield deals due to the higher thresholds and greater excess spread.

While the simple, intuitive framework presented in this chapter misses intricacies of an actual deal, it is clear that a higher probability of default on each security must be accompanied by a capital structure with more equity and less Aaa debt. So to achieve the same loss on each tranche, the tranche in the CDO backed by high-yield bonds needs to have greater subordination. In the simple framework presented, the typical high-yield capital structure (75% Aaas, 15% Baa, and 10% equity) with a diversity score of 45 produces the same losses as does the investment-grade deal (assuming a default rate of 11.5% on that investment-grade CDO).

EXHIBIT 2.11   Overcollateralization and Interest Coverage Test (%)

	Aaa		Baa	
	O/C	I/C	O/C	I/C
High-Yield CDO	115–130	120–130	105–112	110–120
Investment-Grade Corp. CDO	108–115	115–125	103–105	100–105
ABS/MBS CDO	110–125	115–125	103–105	100–105

CALL PROVISIONS IN CDO TRANSACTIONS

We conclude this chapter with a discussion of commonly used optional redemption features in CDO transactions.

Call Protection for Bond Investors

There are many different variations of the basic CDO structure in which the deal is callable at par after a preset lockout period. Two of the most common variations protecting bondholders are prepayment penalties and coupon step-ups.

Prepayment penalties can take two forms: Either the investor is compensated with a premium call, or there is a "make-whole" provision. The most typical premium call is an amount equal to one-half the annual coupon, which steps down over time. Essentially, the effect of the prepayment penalties is to make the call less attractive to the asset manager.

Coupon step-ups are somewhat rare in deals. If the tranche is not called on a certain date, the coupon "steps-up" to a higher level. A coupon step-up is only used if the asset manager wants to signal to investors that it is unlikely that the deal will extend beyond a certain point. For example, deals with long reinvestment periods are more apt to have a coupon step-up to quell investor concerns about extension risk.

Variations of Call Provisions that Benefit Equity Holders

Not all call provisions will be exercised because the deal is going well. Sometimes if the deal is going very poorly, the equity holders may choose to liquidate because the deal is worth more "dead" than alive. This is partially true towards the end of the deal because the expenses of running a small deal with low leverage are too high. That is, it may act as a "clean-up call."

There are also customized call provisions to protect the equity holders from the whims of an asset manager. Some CDO deals have "partial calls," which allows each group of equity holders to exercise authority over their own piece of the deal. This is different from typical structures, in which the deal is only callable in whole by a majority of the equity interests. It is clear that the value of the deal on an ongoing basis will be different for the asset manager (who earns management fees) and an equity holder (who does not). In certain rare cases, a majority of equity holders may replace the asset manager. This is most common in those deals in which the asset manager does not own a piece of the equity. Both of these call provisions are meant to protect the equity holder (who is not the asset manager) at the expense of the asset manager. However, there are also consequences for the debt holders.

Refinancing Options

A minority of CDO deals have a *refinancing option*, that is, the ability to refinance the liabilities while leaving the collateral assets in place. However, this is subject to certain conditions. In particular, the terms of the debt obligations issued in a refinancing must be similar in form (floating over the same reference rate or fixed), in remaining tenor, and to the terms of previously issued debt obligations. Refinancing options allow the asset manager to change the issuance price, coupon, timing, and make-whole premium, if any. Moreover, at the time of any refinancing issuance, the issuer is required to obtain confirmation from each rating agency that the current rating will not be reduced or withdrawn on the refinanced securities. Note that all liabilities must be refinanced; that is, the equity holders cannot choose to refinance only one tranche.

This refinancing option will be exercised when the value of the liabilities has risen (rates have fallen or spreads have tightened) and there are reasons not to liquidate the collateral assets. That is, if the collateral assets are illiquid, and worth far more on an ongoing basis than on a liquidation basis, the collateral assets would remain constant and the liabilities could be replaced. This option is clearly meant to benefit the equity holders, but it is exercisable only under very limited circumstances.

CHAPTER 3

High-Yield Default Rates and Their Application to CDO Analysis

Critical to the analysis of CDOs backed by high-yield bonds is the expected default rate. There is a good deal of research published on default rates by both rating agencies and academicians. This chapter begins with a review of this research, explaining not only default rates but the various measures in computing them.

In Chapter 2, we described how the rating agencies view defaults and use them in developing the weighted-average rating factors (WARFs). This information is transparent to investors. What we then demonstrate in this chapter is that there are opportunities that arise because of the way defaults and potential defaults are viewed by investors. Much as investors use credit analysis seeking to find relative value in bonds that have lower credit risk than perceived by rating agencies and other investors that rely on those ratings, we will give a recent case where investors should have undertaken independent analysis in formulating opinions about the credit risk of CDOs backed by high-yield corporate bonds.

DEFAULT RATES

First, let's look at what research has found for the default rate experience of high-yield corporate bonds. We begin with the early studies of default rates.

Early Research on Default Rates

In their 1987 study, Edward Altman and Scott Nammacher found that the annual default rate for low-rated corporate debt was 2.15%, a figure that Altman has updated many times in his ongoing research on the subject (which will be discussed later).[1] The firm of Drexel Burnham Lambert (DBL), the major issuer of high-yield bonds at one time, estimated default rates of about 2.40% per year.[2] Paul Asquith, David Mullins, and Eric Wolff, however, found that nearly one out of every three high-yield corporate bonds defaults.[3] The financial press had a field day with the Asquith-Mullins-Wolff study suggesting that the high-yield bond market was an unattractive sector of the bond market.

However, the large discrepancy arises because the studies use three different definitions of "default rate"; even if applied to the same universe of bonds (which they are not), all three results could be valid simultaneously.

Altman and Nammacher define the default rate as the par value of all high-yield bonds that defaulted in a given calendar year, divided by the total par value outstanding during the year. Their estimates are simple averages of the annual default rates over a number of years. DBL took the cumulative dollar value of all defaulted high-yield corporate bonds, divided by the cumulative dollar value of all high-yield issuance, and further divided by the weighted average number of

---

[1] Edward I. Altman and Scott A. Nammacher, *Investing in Junk Bonds* (New York: John Wiley & Sons, 1987).

[2] 1984-1989 issues of *High Yield Market Report: Financing America's Futures* (New York and Beverly Hills: Drexel Burnham Lambert, Inc.).

[3] Paul Asquith, David W. Mullins, Jr., and Eric D. Wolff, "Original Issue High Yield Bonds: Aging Analysis of Defaults, Exchanges, and Calls," *Journal of Finance* (September 1989), pp. 923–952.

years outstanding to obtain an average annual default rate. Asquith, Mullins, and Wolff use a cumulative default statistic. For all bonds issued in a given year, the default rate is the total par value of defaulted issues as of the date of their study, divided by the total par amount originally issued to obtain a cumulative default rate. Their result (that about one in three high-yield bonds default) is not normalized by the number of years outstanding.

Although all three measures are useful indicators of bond default propensity, they are not directly comparable. Even when restated on an annualized basis, they do not all measure the same quantity. The default statistics from all studies, however, are surprisingly similar once cumulative rates have been annualized.

Recent Default Studies

Now let's fast forward to more recent studies of default rates. There are two major sources of information on speculative-grade default rates—Moody's Investors Service and Edward Altman and his associates. Moody's actually provides two data sets: defaults rates on all—and on U.S.—speculative-grade issuers.[4] (The financial press normally quotes information on "all" speculative-grade issuers.) This same "all" number is also used by Moody's in forecasting. Their second set using U.S. numbers is more comparable to data compiled by Altman.[5] In Exhibit 3.1 all three sets of default data are graphed. All numbers are annual, going back to 1970 for Moody's and to 1971 for Altman.

---

[4] Moody's data are contained in the report published by Moody's Investors Service entitled "Historical Default Rates of Corporate Bond Issuers, 1920–1999" (January 2000). The data are also on the company's website: www.moodyssqra.com/research/defrate.asp.

[5] Altman data are contained in Edward I. Altman with Naeem Hukkawala and Vellore Kishore, "Defaults and Returns on High-yield Bonds: Analysis Through 1999 and Default Outlook for 2000–2002" (January 2000), and Edward I. Altman with Brenda Karlin, "High-yield Corporate Bonds: Defaults Accelerate in Second Quarter 2000" (July 2000), New York University, Salomon Center.

EXHIBIT 3.1   Comparison of Speculative Grade Default Rates

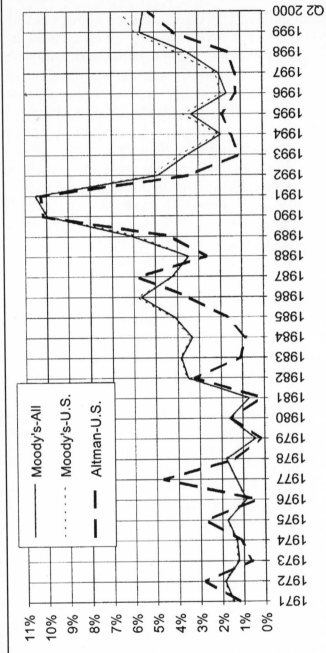

Source: Moody's Investors Service and Altman Report.

44

Note that historically there has been very little difference in Moody's data for "all" versus "U.S." speculative defaults. That's because U.S. issuers dominate the market, constituting most of the "all" category, and the default rates between the United States and the rest of the world have not been that different. However presently, Moody's-tabulated defaults for the U.S.-only series are considerably higher than for the total series. Twelve-month trailing default rate for all Moody's rated speculative bonds as of the end of June 2000 was 5.50%, versus 6.56% for the U.S.-only data. The two series diverge because U.S. defaults have been much higher than those elsewhere for 1999.

In any event, there has more customarily been a large difference between Moody's and Altman's data, with the former consistently higher (since 1992). For example, at the end of 1999, Moody's U.S.-only data showed yearly defaults of 5.87%, while Altman's default data read 4.15%. The end-June 2000 numbers exhibit the same pattern (6.56% for Moody's and 5.22% for Altman).[6]

The major difference between Moody's data for U.S. issuers and the Altman data is that Moody's weights all issuers equally, while as explained earlier Altman uses par value of issues outstanding.[7] Thus, Moody's default rate for a particular time period builds from numbers of issuers—those that actually defaulted on Moody's rated debt in a particular time period divided by the total number of issuers that could have defaulted. The Altman numbers use par value of speculative-grade bonds—those that actually defaulted during that year versus the sum of all such securities outstanding. Even with these differences, both series exhibit the same pattern, and the correlation between them is quite high.

---

[6] Realize that Moody's measures trailing 12-month defaults, while Altman measures defaults during the period. Thus, for the partial year, Altman measures defaults in the first half of 2000 and annualizes the 6-month number.

[7] There are minor differences, as well. Altman excludes cured defaults or convertible issues, while Moody's includes these issues. Moody's uses only its rated issuers, whereas Altman includes all issuers.

ANALYSIS OF FORECASTED HIGH DEFAULT RATES IN 2000

By the summer of 2000, the financial press focused on rising high-yield default rates. For example, the following appeared in August 13, 2000 issue of the *New York Times*:

> ... many large businesses and even entire industries are suffocating from their debts. A major portion of the health care industry is in shambles. In retailing, competition from category killers has contributed to huge consolidation. And some auto parts suppliers, already beleaguered, despite record car sales by Detroit last year, have no place to go but south. That's not all. Household names like Pathmark Stores and United Artists Theatre Company defaulted on bonds this spring, and are contributors to a total of $15 billion in defaulted debt across corporate America in the first half of 2000—a rate that could smash last year's record of $23.5 billion.... There is no doubt that a rising number of companies, running out of financing options, are having to default.

And, the following appeared in the July 10, 2000 issue of the *Wall Street Journal*:

> The U.S. is in a credit crunch, which means companies unable to raise funds from increasingly cautious lenders are being forced into default... . Only $8 billion in junk bonds were issued in the second quarter, down from $31.4 billion in the same period of 1999. Put another way, more junk bonds defaulted in the second quarter than were issued. About $9.4 billion in bonds defaulted in the quarter, issued by companies ranging from cinema operator United

Artists Theatre Co. to waste management company Safety Kleen Corp.... We can probably anticipate at least several quarters more of continued high defaults.

With this type of exposure, there were many traditional CBO buyers stepping back from their allocation to CBOs. They naturally questioned whether or not it was appropriate to buy new CBOs backed by high-yield debt. An analysis of the implications of higher default rates would have suggested that they are reflected in pricing and, as a result, at spread levels at that time, high-yield CBOs were indeed an attractive asset class.

The analysis of high-yield CBOs would have led investors to the following important conclusions:

- While the default rates at the time were high, they reflected relatively weak issuance during the looser credit standards of 1997 and early 1998. The deals by the summer of 2000 were made based on higher credit quality standards, which should be reflected in future performance.
- As demonstrated later, historically, defaults generally peak three years after issuance. This would have suggested the peak in defaults should occur the following year, 2001. However, the weaker credits from 1997 and early 1998, were defaulting much earlier than historical patterns would suggest. While it would have been reasonable to believe defaults at the time would continue to climb somewhat more, one could argue that they were closer to the peak than historical evidence would indicate.

The evidence that would support these conclusions is presented next.

The Relevant Default Rates

We previously reviewed the historical evidence on default rates. Which were the relevant default numbers for an investor looking to buy a high-yield backed CBO? One could argue that both the Moody's and Altman default series are overstated. They reflect defaults on weak 1997-1998 issuance and not the stronger issuance in 2000. Moreover, weighting by either measure (number of issuers or par amounts) over-states the impact of any particular default.

This is because the credit quality on bonds that will eventually default usually begins to trend downward several years before default. Thus, bonds that will default will typi-cally sell at a lower market values a year or two before default. Default rates should measure the actual cost to the portfolio. The cost to the portfolio depends on the initial purchase price of the security and will certainly be higher for a high-yield bond purchased at par than one purchased at a discount. A CBO manager, who entered the market in 2000 and 2001 with a new deal, would have been able to take advantage of the fact that weaker credits were at that time selling at large discounts, which reflected their higher probability of defaulting. Thus, if a default occurs down the road, the portfolio impact would be much lower than if the bond was purchased at par.

To show that measuring defaults either by the number of issuers or by par values overstates the portfolio impact, a simple portfolio consisting of seven securities was con-structed. The portfolio is shown in Exhibit 3.2 and has invested proceeds (at market value) of $500 million. Specifi-cally, the portfolio consists of:

{$100 million par of each of four securities selling at $100 [=$400 million]}

plus

{$50 million par of each of three securities; two sell at $50 ($25 mil-lion market value apiece) and one at par ($50 million market value) [= $100 million]}

=$500 million

Assume that one of the securities priced at $50 (i.e., not at "par") defaults at the end of the year. What is the default rate on this portfolio for the year? Moody's calculates it as

14.3%, based on one out of seven issuers defaulting (1/7 = 14.3%). Altman calculates it as 9.1% ($50 million par defaulted/$550 million par outstanding). However, for the portfolio in Exhibit 3.2, the default rate is 5%. That comes from dividing $500 million in market value securities into the $25 million ($50 million par × $50 price) defaulting. Thus, both Moody's and Altman overstate default rates as neither considers the current market value of the bonds.

Thus, the default rate that an "average" real life portfolio (of loss from actual default against market value going into the new position) is likely to experience is lower than either Moody's or Altman's numbers suggest.

Reasons Why Higher Defaults Were Expected

As can be seen in Exhibit 3.1, high-yield default rates were by historical measures very high by the summer of 2000. All three measures were around the relative highest that they had been, outside of 1991's peak rates. Moreover, Moody's at the time had widely forecasted that trailing 12-month default rates for all speculative issuance should increase from 5.50% at the end of June 2000 to 8.41% at the end of June 2001.

EXHIBIT 3.2   Default Calculations (Sample Portfolio)

Amount ($MM)	Price (MV/$100 par)	Total MV in Portfolio ($MM)	Defaults
100	100	100	N
100	100	100	N
100	100	100	N
100	100	100	N
50	100	50	N
50	50	25	Y
50	50	25	N

Moody's calculation: No. of issuers defaulting/No. of issuers = 1/7 = 14.3%.
Altman calculation: Par value of defaults/total par in portfolio = 50/550 = 9.1%.
MV calculation: Initial MV of defaulted securities/total MV in Portfolio = 25/500 = 5%.

Moody's based this gloom and doom on its default forecasting model. This model uses three major sets of explanatory variables to estimate default rates. The variables are changes in credit quality, an "aging effect," and macroeconomic indicators.

Two credit quality variables were used. The first captures relative size of the speculative grade subuniverse, measured as the percentage of total rated issuers holding a senior unsecured rating of Ba1 or lower. The second captures the percentage of speculative-grade issuers whose senior unsecured rating is Ba (Ba1-Ba3). This measures how much of the speculative-grade universe is in the upper (less risky) portion of the speculative grade range.

The "aging factor" comes into play because default likelihood for issuers historically peaks about three years after issuance and then starts to decline. At the time of and soon after issuance, borrowers are flush with cash, so default is easy to avoid. But as time passes, default likelihood increases as cash raised via the debt issue is exhausted—and as the feasibility of original business plans may prove weak or be threatened by unforeseen events. Studies have shown that likelihood of default peaks after three years.[8] In any event, once that critical period has passed, the probability of default declines as issuers typically generate sufficient revenues to service and pay down their debt. Thus, Moody's default forecasting model uses the number of newly rated issuers lagged approximately three years.[9]

Finally, the regression also inputs three macroeconomic variables, all on a lagged basis. The first is real industrial production—that is, industrial production adjusted by the producer price index (PPI). The more robust real IP, the lower the monthly default rates. The regression also uses the 10-year Treasury bond yield and the shape of the curve as mea-

---

[8] See "Predicting Default Rates: A Forecasting Model for Moody's Issuer-Based Default Rates," published by Moody's Investors Service.
[9] This includes only first-time rated issuers, whose initial rating was speculative grade (Ba1 or lower) at the senior secured level.

sured by the spread between the 10-year Treasury note and the 1-year Treasury bill. They are included because periods of decreasing liquidity and slowing economic activity, which auger poorly for defaults and tend to be associated with rising interest rates and a steepening yield curve.

Reasons Defaults Had Risen

Most of the anticipated increase in defaults at the time came from the fact that a large number of weak issuers entered the market during 1997 and early 1998. This led to higher default rates, higher downgrade rates, and an overall increase in the number of issuers rated B2 or lower. Reduced investor risk tolerance during 1999 slowed the flow of new, low-rate issuers, which would bode well for subsequent default rates once that critical "first three-year" period was over.

Exhibits 3.3 and 3.4 show this very dramatically, using variables similar or identical to those Moody's uses in forecasting. Exhibit 3.3 shows that the number of new speculative grade issuers accelerated dramatically in 1996 and 1997, and peaked in the spring of 1998. Subsequently, it tapered off quite significantly. The market appeared to have grown increasingly less tolerant of these borrowers.

EXHIBIT 3.3   First-time Speculative-Grade Issuer Counts

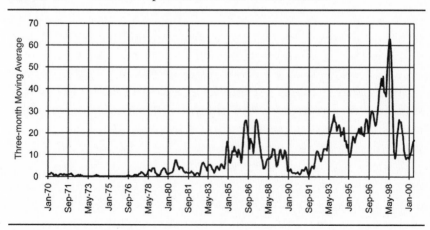

Source: Moody's Investors Service.

EXHIBIT 3.4   Corporate Bond Issuance—High-Yield as Percent of Total

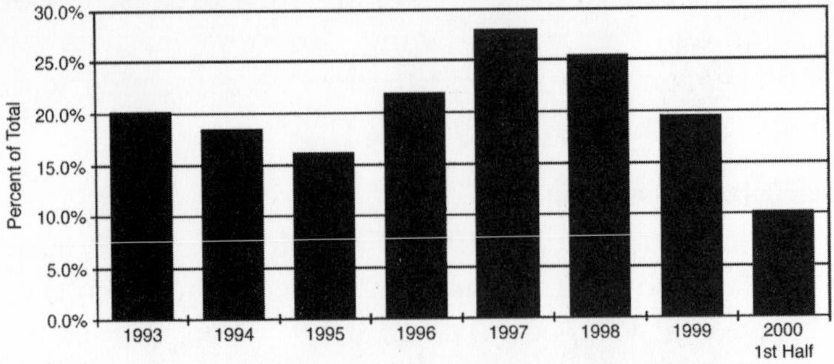

Source: The Bond Market Association, *Research Quarterly* (June 2002).

Exhibit 3.4 shows that new issue high-yield had fallen dramatically as a percent of total corporate issuance. This would indicate that the market was less receptive to speculative-grade paper than was previously the case, suggesting that the fewer issues that did come to market received closer scrutiny. Speculative-grade issuance was 21.8% of total corporate issuance in 1996; 28.0% in 1997; 25.4% in 1998; 19.6% in 1999; and 10.1% in the first half of 2000. Note that issuance in the first half of 2000 represented the lowest high-yield component since 1993.

On The Horizon

The analysis of default rates and their temporal pattern would have suggested an environment that bodes well for investors purchasing CBOs backed by high-yield bonds. Buying a new CBO backed by high-yield collateral would have delivered bonds of either recent issuance, originated in an environment of much greater market scrutiny, or bonds which had been outstanding for awhile, in which the market price reflects any likelihood of distress. In fact, market sensitivity at the time to this was reflected by the fact that over 17% of nondefaulted high-yield debt was selling at spreads more than 1,000 basis points over Treasury securities. (That spread of 1,000 over Treasuries at the time was the market's hurdle for defining what constitutes "distressed" debt.) And as shown in Exhibit 3.5, this percentage was by far higher than was the case since 1992.

EXHIBIT 3.5   Distressed Debt, as Percent of Total High-Yield Debt Market

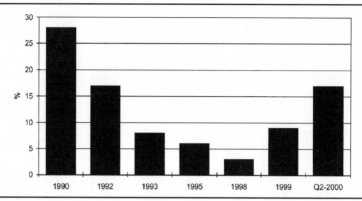

Source: NYU Salomon Center: Altman Report.

EXHIBIT 3.6   Spreads versus Default Rates

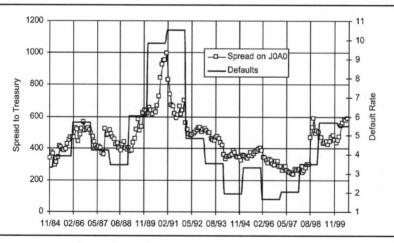

Source: Merrill Lynch Indices & Moody's Investors Service.

Wide Spreads Reflect High Current Defaults

Not only was the market differentiating weaker credits from stronger ones, but overall spread levels were quite high. In fact, high-yield spread levels, as measured by yield-to-worst on the cash pay Merrill Lynch High-Yield Index (J0A0) versus the Merrill U.S. Treasury Master Index (G0Q0), were at the time close to their October 1998 wides. This was the widest that they had been since 1991 (see Exhibit 3.6)

EXHIBIT 3.7   Three-Year Returns Are High After Periods of High Defaults

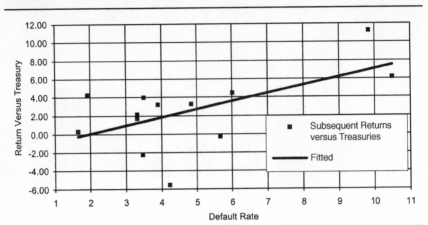

Moreover, narrow spreads on speculative-grade bonds tend to be correlated with periods of low defaults, and high spreads tend to be correlated with periods of high defaults. We believe that this correlation is not spurious. Environments in which spreads on high-yield bonds are narrow to Treasuries (as they were during 1987–1988 and 1997-early 1998) happen when risk tolerance is quite high. When all spreads are tight because of high risk tolerance, investors are more willing to reach for yield by underwriting marginal issuers. It is not surprising that this tends to bring out the weakest issuance. By contrast, in an environment of wide spreads and relatively high defaults (such as 1989–1991 and 2000), issuance was limited, as scrutiny was quite high on both new and existing bonds.

Expected Performance

In fact, periods in which defaults were low and spreads were tight were the worst times to buy high-yield debt. The best times are actually when defaults were high and spreads wide. This can be seen in Exhibit 3.7, in which the default rate in any given year (measured by Moody's default data for "all" speculative grade issuers) are graphed against total excess return of the Merrill High-Yield Index over the subsequent three years. "Excess return" on that high-yield index was measured as the return on the high-yield index (J0A0) versus the return on the Merrill U.S. Treasury Master Index (G0Q0).

The relationship between defaults and subsequent three-year performance is very strong. Buying bonds at the end of each of the two years with the highest default rates (1990 and 1991) provided the highest excess return over the next three years. As a specific example, buying the high-yield index at the end of 1990 (when defaults ran at 9.96%) delivered an excess return of 11.18% per annum. Similarly, buying the high-yield index at the end of 1991 (the year defaults hit a high of 10.50%) generated 6.13% annual excess return over the next three years.

By contrast, purchasing bonds during periods of low default rates showed only marginal excess returns the next three years. For example, if one had invested in the high-yield index at the end of 1988 (defaults were a relatively low 3.47%), then excess return for the next three years plummeted to −2.26% per annum. If buying the high-yield index at the end of 1994 (defaults hit their lows for the 1990s, at 1.93%), the subsequent annual excess return over the next three years would have been −0.02%.

This relationship was so strong that we fitted a regression line (also shown in Exhibit 3.7). Regression results show that buying the high-yield index at the end of a year in which default rates increased by 1% suggests an excess return 88 basis points higher over the next three years. Using this regression to forecast buying high-yield bonds in the environment at the time, with a 12-month trailing default rate in the 5.5% range, suggested a 3.12% excess return per annum over the next three years. But a quick look at Exhibit 3.7 indicates that the regression model was subject to a large standard error—hence this specific number should not be regarded as gospel. It does suggest an overwhelming likelihood that high-yield bonds will outperform Treasuries over the next few years.

Conclusion of the Analysis

Publicity that was given to the rise in default rates at the time made a number of market participants concerned about purchasing CBOs backed by high-yield collateral. We believe that analysis of the methodology for the calculation of default rates, coupled with an understanding of the temporal pattern of default rates, would have certainly demonstrated that higher returns were already priced in, and that the new high-yield bonds were far less likely to experience underperformance than weaker siblings issued during 1997–1998. Secondary securities already reflected a substantial amount of market tiering, since many of the weaker securities were selling at deep discounts at the time.

The wide spreads in the high-yield market at the time more than adequately compensated investors for the risks. In fact, buying high-yield bonds following a period of high default rates has historically been a good strategy as measured by total returns over the subsequent three years.

CBOs issued in the environment at the time were purchasing new issues and selective secondary issues, both at attractive spreads. Meanwhile, CBO liabilities were being issued at tighter levels than was the case in the prior year. Thus, the CBO manager was facing a very favorable arbitrage at the time. This was good news for investors in both rated notes as well as equity, as it suggested the CBO had much better potential for outperformance over deals issued several years prior.

SELECTING THE RIGHT DEFAULT RATES

Here is another case demonstrating where independent analysis of default rates would benefit investors. Investors most commonly assume that default rates on high-yield bonds used in CDO deals will be very similar to those of the high-yield market as a whole. But in fact, there are strong reasons to believe this is not the case. First, the portfolios of high-yield bonds used as collateral for CDO deals should incur lower default rates than the high-yield market as a whole. We then attempt to answer the question most often asked by market participants: What collateral default and recovery rates should I use as a "base case" in looking at deals backed by high-yield bonds?

The Fall 2001 Environment

In Fall 2001, investors were familiar with headline-grabbing numbers in the high-yield arena. Moody's trailing 12-month speculative grade default rate was 8.3%, measured by the number of issuers and 9.9% in dollar terms. Fitch's data were very consistent; its tally through June 30, 2001 indicated a 12-month dollar-weighted default rate of 10%.

Forecasting difficulty for the industry, Moody's expected even higher defaults ahead. That is, Moody's predicted that by year-end 2001, the 12-month default rate (as measured by the number of issuers) would rise to 10.1%, peak at 10.3% February 2002, and then decline to "only" 9.6% by June 2002. Exhibit 3.8 places these forecasts in a historical perspective, showing that default rates at the time were quite high (rivaling 1990–1991 peaks). Yet longer term, the average default rate on speculative grade (high-yield) corporate bonds over the 1980–2000 period was 4.18%, while the average over the 1995–2000 period was 3.27%.

The high level of defaults at the time reflected a weakened U.S. economy. But at some point the economy would be expected to recover and defaults drop. Some investors were aware of this, and so they used default vectors to evaluate CDO cash flows. Thus, they applied higher default rates for the first few years, followed by lower default rates thereafter. This is a practice that is strongly encouraged.

A Closer Look

At the time, many potential CDO investors noticed the then-current level of high-yield default rates, and immediately decided that CDO tranches backed by high-yield collateral were not even worth a further look. These potential investors were thus making the assumptions that default rates on bonds contained in CDOs would mirror the high-yield market as a whole, and that default rates would stay at these elevated levels forever.

An analysis of the data, however, would have supported the position that investor should not look at current default and recovery numbers for the high-yield market as a whole as an indication of default rates on CDOs. In fact, the case can be made that high-yield bonds contained in CDOs would have a lower default rate than the high-yield market overall. The reasons for this are twofold:

1. *High default rates are particularly concentrated in a few industries.* But for CDOs, diversification scores and concentration limits insure that a CBO will *not* mirror the high-yield universe.

EXHIBIT 3.8   Default Rate—Speculative Corporate Bonds

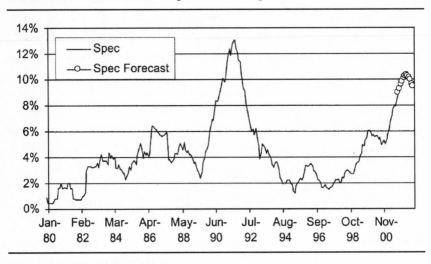

Source: Moody's Investors Service.

2. *The average CBO deal has quite a different rating composition than does the high-yield market as a whole.* That's because securities rated lower than B can initially constitute only a small percentage of a CBO, even though securities below B now represent 20% of the high-yield universe. Thus on average, CBOs have lower WARFs and fewer defaults than the high-yield market as a whole.

Each of these points was explained in turn. The conclusion—a 4% long-term default rate assumption—seemed both reasonable and fairly conservative at the time. Near term, defaults should be expected to be higher. Consequently, higher near-term default rates should have been used and scaled back to 4% as a long-term number.

Industry Concentrations

The overwhelming number of defaults by Fall 2001 had occurred within a very few industries. Fitch keeps tabs on this by sorting firms into one of 25 different high-yield industry groups (sectors) and calculating defaults by each industry group. For the first half of 2001, 71% of all the defaults Fitch recorded fell within just three sectors: 33% in telecommunications; another 24% in utilities; and 14% in bank and finance paper. Meanwhile, six sectors experienced zero defaults, including cable, real estate, insurance, computers and electronics, automotive, and supermarkets and drug stores.

Exhibit 3.9 shows default rates by industry. Notice that the default rate for the market as a whole over this six-month period was 7.8%. By contrast, the default rate for the utility sector was 27.8%; for the banking and finance sector it was 14.4%; and it was 13.4% for telecommunications.

EXHIBIT 3.9 Default Rates—2001 High-Yield Industry

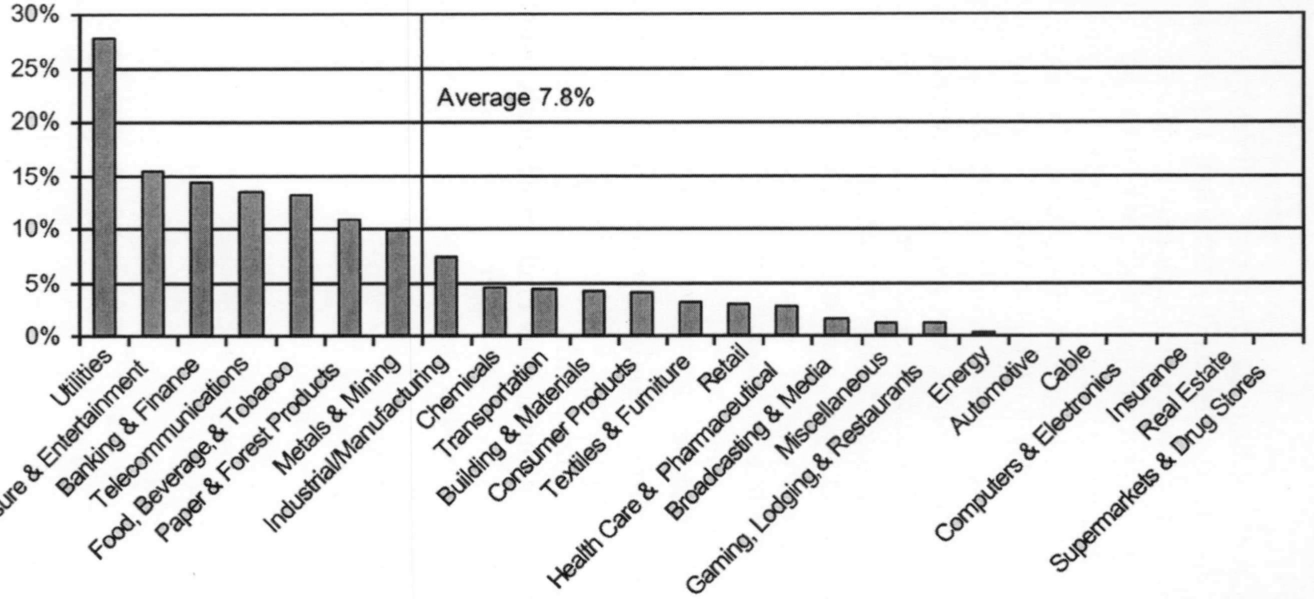

Source: Fitch.

Thus three industry groups jointly comprise 34% of the high-yield universe, yet they represent a default rate more than twice the 7.8% default rate generated by the total high-yield arena. Specifically, these three industry groups with a 34% "market share" defaulted at a 15% rate during the first half of 2001, while the remaining 66% of the high-yield universe defaulted at only 4.1%.

A Fitch press release in mid-October 2001 confirmed that this trend was continuing.[10] In the third quarter of 2001, there were $14.5 billion of defaults. Telecommunications contributed $6.1 billion, and banking and finance $3.2 billion. Thus, those two sectors jointly constituted 66% of actual defaults.

CDO Concentrations

In order for a CDO to merit good diversity scores (which allows for larger higher-rated tranches and smaller lower-rated tranches), most industry groups must be represented in the CDO portfolio. A CDO will usually include at least 25 industries (as defined and measured by Moody's). Fitch has fewer industry groups, thus Fitch-rated deals usually include at least 20 industry categories.

Putting those categories into play, most CDOs contain a general guideline that no industry group can represent more than 8% of outstandings. However, there is often an exemption for the highest concentration industry or two, as high as a 10–12% maximum in such cases. As a practical matter, given these diversity requirements, it is unlikely that any top three groups (by percentage representation) jointly comprise more than 22% of the high-yield universe.

Now, let's do a bit of math. If an investor-owned high-yield collateral issued by the three worst groups, which all defaulted at a 15.0% rate, while the remaining 78% of the portfolio's holdings defaulted at 4.0%, then the default rate for the investor's entire portfolio would be 6.4%.

---

[10] See Mariarosa Verde, "High Yield Defaults Rates 10.2% in September, 4.3% Excluding Telecom and Fallen Angels," Fitch Ratings (October 15, 2001).

In all likelihood, no CDO would be so concentrated in all three of the most poorly performing industry sectors. So let's make our exercise a little less punitive. If an investor held only 16% of his or her portfolio in two of the most poorly performing groups, then the blended default rate for the entire portfolio would be lower at 5.7%.

Finally, realize that different industries experience high default rates at different times. So, for example, 1990 was a big default year, and the three industries that had experienced the highest default rates were supermarkets and drug stores, retail, and textiles and furniture. Yet those were all low default industries in 2001. Consequently, long historical default series computed by industry tend to exhibit much less variation than do series that employ data for shorter time periods.

Exhibit 3.10 shows Fitch's data for high-yield default rates by industry for the period 1980–2000. Note that these data display much less default variation by industry than does the much shorter time frame (first half of 2001) represented by Exhibit 3.9. The average default rates for the longer 1980–2000 period, across all industry groups, was 3.4%. And no industry had a default rate much over 8%, even though all industry groups experienced some defaults.

The bottom line is that the high default rates by Fall 2001 were highly concentrated. Diversification structured into CDO securities helped prevent a CDO from having defaults as high as the universe as a whole. In other words, there's safety in numbers!

Market Composition Issues

Realize also that the rating composition of the average CDO was much different from that of the high-yield universe as a whole. That's because any given CDO is generally restrained from initially having more than 5% of its assets in any credits rated Caa or lower. Exhibit 3.11 depicts composition of the Lehman High-Yield index by rating. As can be seen from that exhibit, 38.6% of the index was rated Ba, 41.3% was rated B, and 20% was rated Caa or lower. So at the outset, CDOs start out their life by eliminating a hearty chunk of the lowest rated, most-likely-to-default credits.

EXHIBIT 3.10 Default Rates—1980–2000 High Yield Industry

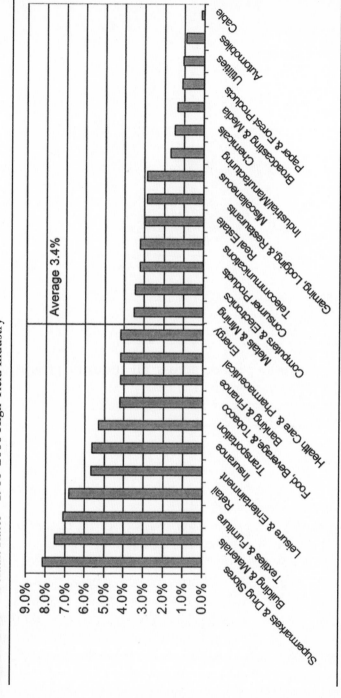

Source: Fitch.

EXHIBIT 3.11   Lehman High-Yield Index—Composition by Rating

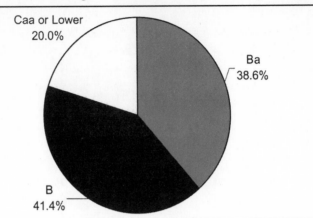

EXHIBIT 3.12   WARF Scores for the High-Yield Market

Rating	WARF	Share	WARF × Share
Ba	1350	38.6	521
B	2720	41.4	1,126
Caa & Lower	6500	20.0	1,300
All		100.0	2,947

And since the probability of default rises exponentially for lower ratings categories, that composition of the index also makes a big difference in the *ex-ante* WARF scores, plus the *ex-post* incidence of default.

Most high-yield CDOs have WARF scores in the range of 2,300–2,700, averaging out to about 2,500. To calculate the WARF score for the high-yield universe, the index composition given in Exhibit 3.11 and paired market share to the WARF for an "average bond" in the group are used. This exercise is shown in Exhibit 3.12. For example, the Ba market share of 38.6% is paired with the WARF for Ba2-rated bonds, and then the B market share with the WARF for B2-rated bonds. For the Caa and below universe, the WARF for a Caa bond is actually used because (1) Moody's does not publish WARFs for bonds with ratings below Caa; and (2) 80% of the bonds in this group have ratings of Caa, the "upper" end of the range. Using this methodology, the average WARF score for the high-yield market was 2,947, which is considerably above that on most high-yield CDOs. Moreover, this analysis slightly understated the average WARF score for the high-yield market, since the average WARF of a Caa rated security was assigned to all securities rated Caa or lower.

Using Moody's default numbers for 2000, the default rate on speculative-grade bonds was 5.7%, the average default rate on Ba rated bonds was 0.2%, while the default rate for B rated securities was 4.1%. An average WARF score of 2,500 can be obtained from a portfolio that consists of 20% Ba rated bonds and 80% B rated securities. The default rate on this particular portfolio would have been 3.32%. That is obviously much lower than the 5.7% default rate for the speculative-grade universe as a whole.

These two points suggested that the default rate on high-yield CDO assets (as measured by par values) would be lower than that for the high-yield market as a whole. An August 2001 study by Fitch[11] (and the only study we know of on this topic) supported this point. Fitch calculated a 1999 high-yield default rate of 4.30% and a 2000 default rate of 5.14%. Yet high-yield CDO assets only had a 1999 default rate of 1.83% and a 2000 figure of 3.87%. Thus, empirically, high-yield assets held by CDOs defaulted considerably less than did the high-yield market as a whole. One limitation of these data was that they ignore distressed sales; extensive use of distressed sales by CDO managers may artificially lower default rates on collateral backing high-yield deals.

Clearly then, investors using a high-yield index to gauge default rates would have been very misleading. We suggest instead that a long-term default rate of 4% would have been conservative, as it reflects the default rate of the high-yield

---

[11] See Brian D. Gordon, "An Empirical Study of CDO Asset Defaults and Recoveries," Fitch (August 9, 2001).

universe as a whole over 1980–2000. Also, CDOs should experience lower default rates than the high-yield universe as a whole. But refining that further, investors should be using a vector to look at high-yield default rates in order to account for the expected pattern of default rates in the near term.

Recovery Rates

In addition to uncertainty about default rates, investors are also unsure as to which recovery rates they should use. For example, recovery rates observed in 2000 indicated a decided slip from historical levels. Moody's data showed that historical recovery rates (1981–1999 as a percent of par) were in the 36–55% range for bonds (see Exhibit 3.13). However, for calendar year 2000, recovery rates were consistently lower across virtually all categories. For example, senior secured bonds (historical recoveries at 55.3%) showed recovery rates of 38.8% in 2000. Senior unsecured bonds (historical recoveries at 51.1%) had 29.8% recovery rates in 2000. Similarly, senior subordinated bonds (historical recoveries at 36%) slipped to 20.5% in 2000.[12]

EXHIBIT 3.13   Average Defaulted Values, by Security and Ratings (2000 versus Historical): Default and Recovery Rates for High Yield

	Historical 1981–1999	2000	Grand Total
Bank loan/Sr. unsecured	69.0	60.3	64.3
Bond/Sr. secured	55.3	38.8	53.9
Bond/Sr. unsecured	51.1	29.8	47.4
Bond/Sr. subordinated	36.0	20.5	33.3
Bond/Subordinated	32.5		32.3
Preferred stock	18.9		18.4
Average	40.0	33.2	39.1

[12] This information is within a study by David Hamilton, Greg Gupton, and Alexandra Berthault, "Default and Recovery Rates of Corporate Bond Issuers: 2000," Moody's Investors Service (February 2001). Recovery rates are calculated based on the secondary price of the defaulted instrument one month after default.

Researchers at Fitch found similar results. They observed that "Class of 2000 Defaults" produced an average recovery rate of 27%, down from 40% for the 20-year period from 1980–1999. Senior secured bonds defaulting in calendar year 2000 experienced average recovery rates of 56%, while senior unsecured and subordinated bonds generated average recoveries of 23%.[13] A Fitch study covering the first half of 2001 showed even lower recovery rates.[14] Fitch observed that excluding "fallen angels," senior secured bonds experienced a recovery rate of 22 cents, while senior unsecured and subordinated bonds experienced recovery rates of 10 cents. Much of this reflects low recovery rates among telecommunication companies, which only came in at 11 cents in the first quarter of 2000 and 5 cents in the second quarter of 2000.

In fact historically, periods of high default rates had been associated with lower recovery rates. Altman has shown that annual recovery rates as a function of annual default rates explain 61% of the variation in recoveries.[15] Thus, in years such as 1990, 1991, 2000 or 2001, investors could expect below-average recovery rates. It's simply a matter of supply and demand. During high default periods, there is a large increase in the supply of defaulted securities (both loans and bonds). By contrast, demand for such securities is less variable, so as the wise lay-lawyer Portia said, "the quality of mercy gets strained." Thus prices get knocked down to market-clearing levels.

This suggested that the low recovery rates observed in Fall 2001, for example, were a function of high default rates, and that the recovery rates that should be used to evaluate new

---

[13] See Mariarosa Verde, Robert Grossman, and Paul Mancuso, "High Yield Defaults Soar in 2000," Fitch (February 12, 2001).

[14] See Mariarosa Verde, Paul Mancuso, and Robert Grossman, "High Yield Defaults: First Half 2001 Review" Fitch (August 8, 2001).

[15] The Altman results are based on conversations with Edward Altman. His conclusions are obtained as part of an ongoing research project, funded by the International Swap and Derivatives Association (ISDA).

CDOs should more closely reflect historical numbers. Consequently, for purposes of the analysis below, recovery rates of 30% (a conservative number) and 40% (corresponding more closely to historical experience) will be applied.[16]

Loss Profiles: BBB and BB Bonds

Exhibit 3.14 shows the profiles on representative BBB and BB CBO tranches backed entirely by high-yield collateral. For the record, this generic deal is comprised 80% of senior securities (AAA, AA, and A), a 9% Baa2 tranche, a 2% Ba2 tranche, and 9% equity. The collateral is assumed to be well diversified, and has an average portfolio rating (WARF score) in the B2 range. We assumed a spread of LIBOR + 250 on the Baa2 bond and LIBOR + 675 on the Ba2 bond.

Note in Exhibit 3.14 that the Baa2 bond maintains its spread with a 30% recovery rate until defaults are above 9% for life. The Ba2 rated bond maintains its spread until defaults are above 8%. At a 40% recovery rate, the Baa2 bond maintains its spread as long as default rates are 11% or lower, while the Ba2 bond maintains its spread as long as rates are 10% or lower.

A more reasonable scenario for a mezzanine buyer is to assume high default rates for a few years and then lower rates thereafter. We assumed a default rate of 10% for 3 years in Vector 1, and 4% thereafter. Vectors 2 and 3 are less severe: 8% and 6% for 3 years and then 4%. Note that even when stressed (Vector 1), the Baa2 and Ba2 securities receive all promised monies.

Investment Implications of the Analysis

The investment implications of the above analysis for the Fall 2001 environment would have been as follows:

---

[16] Another conceptual alternative, which was not adopted here, was to assume a vector of recoveries over time, with lower recoveries up front, as would be expected from a high default period, and higher recoveries later, as we revert to historical norms. The simpler analysis was chosen because it is more in line with the way investors usually look at these bonds.

EXHIBIT 3.14 Mezzanine Spreads Under Various Default Assumption (BBB and BB Performance)

	Case 1 Assumptions		Case 2 Assumptions	
	Recovery Rate: 30% Annual Call Rate: 5%		Recovery Rate: 40% Annual Call Rate: 5%	
	DM		DM	
	BBB	BB	BBB	BB
Static Annual Default Rate				
0%	250	675	250	675
1%	250	675	250	675
2%	250	675	250	675
3%	250	675	250	675
4%	250	675	250	675
5%	250	675	250	675
6%	250	675	250	675
7%	250	675	250	675
8%	250	675	250	675
9%	250	30	250	675
10%	141	NA	250	669
11%	−185	NA	250	−672
12%	−580	NA	99	NA
With Default Rate Vectors				
Vector 1	250	675	250	675
Vector 2	250	675	250	675
Vector 3	250	675	250	675

Vector 1: 10% for 3 years and 4% thereafter.
Vector 2: 8% for 3 years and 4% thereafter.
Vector 3: 6% for 3 years and 4% thereafter.
In all scenarios, defaults start immediately with immediate recoveries.

■ Defaults in the high-yield market would be atypically high for the next year or two, reflecting the U.S. weak economy at the time. But those default rates should not be expected to persist indefinitely.

■ There were good reasons why CDO default rates should be lower than the high-yield market as a whole. In particular, CDOs have greater industry diversification than does the overall market, plus fewer bonds rated Caa or below.

- While recovery rates were at the time very low, a function of high default rates, investors should use recovery rates lower than historical rates, as defaults are apt to be high the next few years. However, we would estimate recoveries higher than levels by investors at the time, suggesting default rates that at some point will decline and recoveries will rise.
- Mezzanine tranches of CDOs were the unwanted stepchildren of the deal. Yet as has been argued above, under most likely scenarios new mezzanine tranches of CDOs will be "money good."

A corollary investment suggestion, resulting from a thoughtful investigation of where high-yield default rates were likely to be, would have been that mezzanine tranches of CDOs were likely to perform reasonably well.

CHAPTER 4

Review of Structured Finance Collateral

Structured finance (SF) collateralized debt obligations are CDOs backed by asset-backed securities (ABS), mortgage-backed securities (MBS), and real estate investment trusts. To be able to evaluate SF CDOs, the first step is to understand the investment characteristics and features of structured finance products. A review of structured finance products is provided in this chapter. Specifically, we review residential MBS, residential real estate-backed ABS, commercial MBS, credit card receivable-backed securities, auto-loan backed securities, student loan-backed securities, SBA loan-backed securities, aircraft lease-backed securities, franchise loan-backed securities, rate reduction bonds, and real estate investment trusts. In the next chapter SF cash flow CDOs will be discussed.

RESIDENTIAL MORTGAGE-BACKED SECURITIES

Mortgage-backed securities (MBS) are securities backed by a pool (collection) of mortgage loans. While any type of mortgage loans, residential or commercial, can be used as collateral for a mortgage-backed security, most are backed by residential mortgages. Mortgage-backed securities include: (1) mortgage passthrough securities, (2) collateralized mortgage obligations, and (3) stripped mortgage-backed securities.

We begin our discussion with the raw material for a residential mortgage-backed security (RMBS)—the mortgage loan. A mortgage loan, or simply mortgage, is a loan secured by the collateral of some specified real estate property, which obliges the borrower to make a predetermined series of payments. The mortgage gives the lender the right if the borrower defaults to "foreclose" on the loan and seize the property in order to ensure that the debt is paid off. The interest rate on the mortgage loan is called the *mortgage rate*.

There are many types of mortgage designs available in the United States. A mortgage design is a specification of the interest rate, term of the mortgage, and manner in which the borrowed funds are repaid. The two most popular fixed-rate mortgage designs are the fixed-rate, level-payment, fully amortized mortgage and the balloon mortgage.

The basic idea behind the design of the *fixed-rate, level-payment, fully amortized mortgage* is that the borrower pays interest and repays principal in equal monthly installments during the term of the mortgage. Each monthly mortgage payment for this mortgage design is due on the first of each month and consists of:

1. interest of $\frac{1}{12}$ of the annual interest rate times the amount of the outstanding mortgage balance at the beginning of the previous month; and
2. a repayment of a portion of the outstanding mortgage balance (principal).

The difference between the monthly mortgage payment and the portion of the payment that represents interest equals the amount that is applied to reduce the outstanding mortgage balance. The monthly mortgage payment is designed so that after the last scheduled monthly payment of the loan is made, the amount of the outstanding mortgage balance is zero (i.e., the mortgage is fully repaid or amortized).

The portion of the monthly mortgage payment applied to interest declines each month, and the portion applied to reducing the mortgage balance increases. The reason for this is that as the mortgage balance is reduced with each monthly mortgage payment, the interest on the mortgage balance declines. Since the monthly mortgage payment is fixed, an increasingly larger portion of the monthly payment is applied to reduce the principal in each subsequent month.

In a *balloon mortgage* the borrower is given long-term financing by the lender, but at specified future dates the mortgage rate is renegotiated. Thus, the lender is providing long-term funds for what is effectively a short-term borrowing. How short depends on the frequency of the renegotiation period. Effectively, it is a short-term balloon loan in which the lender agrees to provide financing for the remainder of the term of the mortgage. The balloon payment is the original amount borrowed less the amount amortized.

Every mortgage loan must be serviced. The servicing fee is a portion of the mortgage rate. The interest rate that the investor receives is said to be the net interest or net coupon.

Prepayments

Homeowners have the right to pay off all or part of their mortgage balance prior to the maturity date. Payments made in excess of the scheduled principal repayments are called *prepayments*. The effect of prepayments is that the amount and timing of the cash flows from a mortgage are not known with certainty. This risk is referred to as *prepayment risk*.

The majority of mortgages outstanding do not penalize the borrower from prepaying any part or all of the outstanding mortgage balance. In recent years, mortgage originators have begun originating *prepayment penalty mortgages* (PPMs). The basic structure of a PPM is as follows. There is a specified time period, the lockout period, where prepayments carry a stiff penalty. Depending on the structure, a certain amount of prepayments may be made during the lockout period without the imposition of a prepayment penalty. The motivation for the PPM is that it reduces prepayment risk for the lender during the lockout period.

Mortgage Passthrough Securities

Investing in mortgages exposes an investor to default risk and prepayment risk. Buying mortgages one by one is extremely cumbersome. A more efficient way is to invest in a *mortgage passthrough security*. This is a security created when one or more holders of mortgages form a pool (collection) of mortgages and sell shares or participation certificates in the pool. A pool may consist of several thousand or only a few mortgages. When a mortgage is included in a pool of mortgages that is used as collateral for a mortgage passthrough security, the mortgage is said to be securitized.

The cash flows of a mortgage passthrough security depend on the cash flows of the underlying pool of mortgages. As explained in the previous section, the cash flows consist of monthly mortgage payments representing interest, the scheduled repayment of principal, and any prepayments.

Payments are made to securityholders each month. Neither the amount nor the timing, however, of the cash flows from the pool of mortgages is identical to that of the cash flows passed through to investors. The monthly cash flows for a passthrough are less than the monthly cash flows of the underlying mortgages by an amount equal to servicing and other fees. The other fees are those charged by the issuer or guarantor of the passthrough for guaranteeing the issue. The coupon rate on a passthrough, called the *passthrough coupon rate*, is less than the mortgage rate on the underlying pool of mortgage loans by an amount equal to the servicing fee and guarantee fee. The latter is a fee charged by an agency (discussed later) for providing one of the guarantees discussed later.

Not all of the mortgages that are included in a pool of mortgages that are securitized have the same mortgage rate and the same maturity. Consequently, when describing a passthrough security, a *weighted average coupon rate* and a *weighted average maturity* are determined. A weighted average coupon rate, or WAC, is found by weighting the mortgage rate of each mortgage loan in the pool by the amount of the mortgage balance outstanding. A weighted average maturity, or WAM, is found by weighting the remaining number of months to maturity for each mortgage loan in the pool by the amount of the mortgage balance outstanding.

Issuers of Passthrough Securities

Issuers of passthrough securities include (1) the Government National Mortgage Association (Ginnie Mae); (2) the Federal National Mortgage Association (Fannie Mae); (3) the Federal Home Loan Mortgage Corporation (Freddie Mac); and (4) private issuers. While the first three are only a small part of the collateral in an SF cash flow CDO deal, they are discussed here for completeness. Private issuers will be discussed in the parts of this chapter that cover nonagency MBS and ABS backed by real estate.

Government National Mortgage Association passthroughs are guaranteed by the full faith and credit of the U.S. government. Therefore, Ginnie Mae passthroughs are viewed as risk-free in terms of default risk just like Treasury securities. The passthroughs issued by Ginnie Mae are referred to as *agency passthroughs*.

Fannie Mae and Freddie Mac are government-sponsored enterprises that issue mortgage passthrough securities. Although a guarantee of Fannie Mae or Freddie Mac is not a guarantee by the U.S. government, most market participants view the passthroughs that they issue as similar, although not identical, in credit worthiness to Ginnie Mae passthroughs. Fannie Mae and Freddie Mac passthroughs are referred to as *conventional passthroughs*. However, some market participants lump them together with Ginnie Mae passthroughs and refer to them as "agency" passthroughs.

Prepayment Conventions and Cash Flows

The difficulty in estimating the cash flows of a mortgage passthrough is due to prepayments. The only way to project cash flows is to make some assumptions about the prepayment rate over the life of the underlying mortgage pool. The prepayment rate is sometimes referred to as the "prepayment speed." Two conventions have been used as a benchmark for prepayment rates: conditional prepayment rate and Public Securities Association prepayment benchmark.

Conditional Prepayment Rate   One convention for projecting prepayments and the cash flows of a passthrough assumes that some fraction of the remaining principal in the pool is prepaid each month for the remaining term of the mortgage. The prepayment rate assumed for a pool, called the *conditional prepayment rate* (CPR), is based on the characteristics of the pool (including its historical prepayment experience) and the current and expected future economic environment. The CPR is an annual rate. To estimate monthly prepayments, the CPR must be converted into a monthly prepayment rate, commonly referred to as the *single-monthly mortality rate* (SMM).

PSA Prepayment Benchmark   The Public Securities Association (PSA) prepayment benchmark is expressed as a monthly series of CPRs. The PSA benchmark assumes that prepayment rates are low for newly originated mortgages and then will speed up as the mortgages become seasoned. Specifically, the PSA benchmark assumes the following prepayment rates for 30-year mortgages:

■ a CPR of 0.2% for the first month, increased by 0.2% per year per month for the next 30 months when it reaches 6% per year; and
■ a 6% CPR for the remaining years.

This benchmark is referred to as "100% PSA" or simply "100 PSA." Slower or faster speeds are then referred to as some percentage of PSA. For example, 50 PSA means one-half the CPR of the PSA benchmark prepayment rate; 150 PSA means 1.5 times the CPR of the PSA benchmark prepayment rate; 300 PSA means three times the CPR of the benchmark prepayment rate. A prepayment rate of 0 PSA means that no prepayments are assumed.

Average Life

The stated maturity of a mortgage passthrough security is an inappropriate measure of its final maturity because of principal repayments over time. Instead, market participants calculate an *average life* for a mortgage-backed security. The average life of a mortgage-backed security is the average time to receipt of principal payments (scheduled principal payments and projected prepayments), weighted by the amount of principal expected. That is,

$$\text{Average life} = \sum_{t=1}^{T} \frac{t \times \text{Projected principal received at time } t}{12 \times \text{Total principal}}$$

where T is the last month that principal is expected to be received.

Contraction Risk and Extension Risk

An investor who owns passthrough securities does not know what the cash flows will be because that depends on prepayments. As noted earlier, this risk is called prepayment risk.

To understand the significance of prepayment risk, suppose an investor buys a 10% coupon at a time when mortgage rates are 10%. Let's consider what will happen to prepayments if mortgage rates decline to, say, 6%. There will be two adverse consequences.

First, a basic property of fixed income securities is that the price of an option-free bond will rise when interest rates decline. But in the case of a passthrough security, the rise in price will not be as large as that of an option-free bond because a fall in interest rates will give the borrower an incentive to prepay the loan and refinance the debt at a lower rate. Thus, the upside price potential of a passthrough security is truncated because of prepayments. The second adverse consequence is that the cash flows must be reinvested at a lower rate. These two adverse consequences when mortgage rates decline are referred to as *contraction risk*. This characteristic of a security is referred to *negative convexity*. Negative convexity means that when interest rates decline, the percentage price gain is not as great as the percentage price decline for a large change in interest rates.

Now let's look at what happens if mortgage rates rise to say 13%. The price of the passthrough, like the price of any bond, will decline. But again it will decline more because the higher rates will tend to slow down the rate of prepayment, in effect increasing the amount invested at the coupon rate, which is lower than the market rate. Prepayments will slow down because homeowners will not refinance nor partially prepay their mortgages when mortgage rates are higher than the contract rate of 10%. Of course this is just the time when investors want prepayments to speed up so that they can reinvest the prepayments at the higher market interest rate. This adverse consequence of rising mortgage rates is called *extension risk*.

Therefore, prepayment risk encompasses contraction risk and extension risk. Prepayment risk makes passthrough securities unattractive for certain individuals and financial institutions to hold for purposes of accomplishing their investment objectives. Some individuals and institutional investors are concerned with extension risk and others with contraction risk when they purchase a passthrough security. Is it possible to alter the cash flows of a passthrough to reduce the contraction risk and extension risk for institutional investors? This can be done, as explained when we cover collateralized mortgage obligations.

Stripped Mortgage-Backed Securities

A mortgage passthrough security distributes the cash flow from the underlying pool of mortgages on a pro rata basis to the securityholders. A stripped mortgage-backed security is created by altering that distribution of principal and interest from a pro rata distribution to an unequal distribution. The result is that the securities created will have a price/yield relationship that is different from the price/yield relationship of the underlying passthrough security.

In the most common type of stripped mortgage-backed securities, all the interest is allocated to one class (called the *interest-only* or *IO class*) and all the principal to the other class (called the *principal-only* or *PO class*). The IO class receives no principal payments.

The PO security, also called a *principal-only mortgage strip*, is purchased at a substantial discount from par value. The return an investor realizes depends on the speed at which prepayments are made. The faster the prepayments, the higher the investor's return. An IO, also called an *interest-only mortgage strip*, has no par value. In contrast to the PO investor, the IO investor wants prepayments to be slow because the IO investor receives interest only on the amount of the principal outstanding. When prepayments are made, less dollar interest will be received as the outstanding principal declines. In fact, if prepayments are too fast, the IO investor may not recover the amount paid for the IO even if the security is held to maturity. An interesting characteristic of an IO is that its price tends to move in the same direction as the change in mortgage rates.

Both POs and IOs exhibit substantial price volatility when mortgage rates change.

Collateralized Mortgage Obligations

As just explained, an investor in a mortgage passthrough security is exposed to extension risk and contraction risk. Some investors are concerned with extension risk and others with contraction risk when they invest in a passthrough. An investor may be willing to accept one form of prepayment risk but seek to avoid the other. By redirecting how the cash flows of passthrough securities are paid to different bond classes that are created, securities can be created that have different exposure to prepayment risk. When the cash flows of mortgage-related products are redistributed to different bond classes, the resulting securities are called *collateralized mortgage obligations*. The creation of a CMO cannot eliminate prepayment risk; it can only redistribute the two forms of prepayment risk among different classes of bondholders.

The basic principle is that redirecting cash flows (interest and principal) to different bond classes—*tranches*—mitigates different forms of prepayment risk. It is never possible to eliminate prepayment risk. If one tranche in a CMO structure has less prepayment risk than the mortgage passthrough securities that are collateral for the structure, then another tranche in the same structure has greater prepayment risk than the collateral.

Issuers of CMOs are the same three entities that issue agency passthrough securities: Freddie Mac, Fannie Mae, and Ginnie Mae. CMOs issued by any of these entities are referred to as *agency CMOs*.

When an agency CMO is created, it is structured so that even under the worst circumstances regarding prepayments, the interest and principal payments from the collateral will be sufficient to meet the interest obligation of each tranche and pay off the par value of each tranche. Defaults are ignored because the agency that has issued the passthroughs used as collateral is expected to make up any deficiency. Thus, the credit risk of agency CMOs is minimal.

Types of CMO Structures

In all CMO structures there are rules for the priority of distribution of the interest and principal cash flows from the collateral. There is a wide range of CMO structures. In a *sequential-pay CMO structure*, the deal is structured so that each class of bond is retired sequentially. That is, no bond class receives a principal payment until a bond class with high principal payment priority is fully paid off. There are some bond classes that receive only interest. These are referred to as *notional IOs* or *structured IOs*.

A *planned amortization class* (PAC) CMO structure bond is one in which a schedule of principal payments is set forth in the prospectus. The PAC bondholders have priority over all other bond classes in the structure with respect to the receipt of the scheduled principal payments. While there is no assurance that the principal payments will be actually realized so as to satisfy the schedule, a PAC bond is structured so that if prepayment speeds are within a certain range, the collateral will throw off sufficient principal to meet the schedule of principal payments.

The greater certainty of the cash flow for the PAC bonds comes at the expense of the non-PAC classes, called the *support* or *companion bonds*. These tranches absorb the prepayment risk. Consequently, support bonds in a CMO structure expose investors to the greatest level of prepayment risk. Because of this, investors must be particularly careful in assessing the cash flow characteristics of support bonds to reduce the likelihood of adverse portfolio consequences due to prepayments.

The support bond typically is divided into different bond classes, including sequential-pay support bond classes. The support bond can even be partitioned to create support bond classes with a schedule of principal payments. That is, support bond classes that are PAC bonds can be created. In a structure with a PAC bond and a support bond with a PAC schedule of principal payments, the former is called a PAC I bond or Level I PAC bond and the latter a PAC II bond or Level II PAC bond. While PAC II bonds have greater prepayment protection than the support bond classes without a schedule of principal repayments, the prepayment protection is less than that provided PAC I bonds.

Nonagency Mortgage-Backed Securities

Mortgage loans used as collateral for an agency and conventional residential mortgage-backed securities are conforming loans. These are loans that meet the underwriting standards of

Ginnie Mae, Fannie Mae, or Freddie Mac. The collateral for residential nonagency mortgage-backed securities (referred to as nonagency securities hereafter) consists of nonconforming loans (i.e., loans that do not conform to the underwriting standards of the agency).

Nonagency securities can be either passthroughs or CMOs. In the agency/conventional market, CMOs are created from pools of passthrough securities. In the nonagency market, a CMO can be created from either a pool of passthroughs or unsecuritized mortgage loans. It is uncommon for nonconforming mortgage loans to be securitized as passthroughs and then the passthroughs carved up to create a CMO. Instead, in the nonagency market a CMO is typically carved out of mortgage loans that have not been securitized as passthroughs. Since a mortgage loan is referred to as a "whole loan," nonagency CMOs are also referred to as *whole-loan CMOs.*

Types of Nonconforming Loans

A loan may be nonconforming for one or more of the following reasons:

1. The mortgage balance exceeds the amount permitted by the agency.
2. The borrower characteristics fail to meet the underwriting standards established by the agency.
3. The loan characteristics fail to meet the underwriting standards established by the agency.
4. The applicant fails to provide full documentation as required by the agency.

There are alternative lending programs for borrowers seeking nonconforming loans for any of the aforementioned reasons.

Jumbo Loans   A mortgage loan that is nonconforming merely because the mortgage balance exceeds the maximum permitted by the agency guideline is called a *jumbo loan.*

Alternative-A Loans With respect to the characteristics of the borrower, a loan may fail to qualify because the borrower's credit history does not meet the underwriting standards or the payment-to-income (PTI) ratio exceeds the maximum permitted. Borrowers who do satisfy the underwriting standards with respect to borrower characteristics are referred to as *A credit borrowers* or *prime borrowers*.

Alternative-A loans (Alt-A loans) are made to borrowers whose qualifying mortgage characteristics do not conform to the underwriting criteria established by the agencies but whose borrower characteristics do. For instance, the borrower may be self-employed and may not be able to provide all the necessary documentation for income verification. In such respects, Alt-A loans allow reduced or alternate forms of documentation to qualify for the loan. An Alt-A loan borrower, however, should not be confused with borrowers with blemished credits, which is discussed in the next section below.

The typical Alt-A borrower will have an excellent credit rating—referred to as an "A" rating, and hence the loan is referred to as an Alt-A loan—which is especially important to the originator since the credit quality of the borrower must compensate for the lack of other necessary documentation.

What is appealing to borrowers about the Alt-A program is the flexibility that the program offers in terms of documentation, and borrowers are willing to pay a premium for the privilege. Typically, rates on Alt-A loans range between 75 to 125 basis points above the rate on otherwise comparable standard mortgage rates.

Subprime Loans *B and C borrowers* or *subprime borrowers* are borrowers who fail to satisfy the underwriting standards of the agencies because of borrower characteristics. These characteristics include a compromised credit history and a payment-to-income ratio that is too high. Borrowers who apply for subprime loans include both those who have or had credit problems due to difficulties in repayment of debt brought on by an adverse event, such as job loss or medical emergencies, to those that continue to mismanage their debt and finances.

The distinguishing feature of a subprime mortgage is that the potential universe of subprime mortgagors can be divided into various risk grades, ranging from B through D. The risk gradation is a function of past credit history and the magnitude of credit blemishes existing in the history.[1] Additionally, some of the higher grades in this loan category have also been labeled as "fallen angels" to indicate the fact that the creditworthiness of such borrowers was hampered by a life event, such as job loss or illness. Since such borrowers tend to pose greater credit risk, subprime mortgages command a pricing premium over standard mortgages. Subprime mortgages are virtually considered to be home equity loans and are considered to be part of the ABS market.

High LTV Loans   A characteristic that may result in a loan failing to meet the underwriting standards is that the loan-to-value (LTV) ratio exceeds the maximum established by the agency or the loan is not a first-mortgage lien. There are lenders who specialize in loans that exceed the maximum LTV. These lending programs are sometimes referred to as *high LTV* or *125 LTV* programs because the lender may be willing to lend up to 125% of the appraised or market value of the property.

Basically, the lender is making a consumer loan based on the credit of the borrower to the extent that the loan amount exceeds the appraised or market value. For this reason, lenders with high LTV programs have limited these loans to A credit borrowers. Mortgage-related products in which the underlying loans are 125 LTV loans are considered part of the ABS market and are discussed later in this chapter.

---

[1] The loans are actually scaled by originators from B to D. Every originator establishes its own profiles for classifying a loan into a risk category.

Deals with Mixed Collateral

There are deals in which the underlying collateral is mixed with various types of mortgage-related loans. That is, the collateral backing a deal may include collateral that is a combination of mortgages and products that are classified as asset-backed securities—home equity loans and manufactured housing loans—and are discussed later. The Securities Data Corporation (SDC) has established criteria for classifying a mortgage product with mixed collateral as either a "nonagency MBS" or an "asset-backed security" (ABS), which we discuss next. The purpose of the classification is not to aid in the analysis of these securities, but rather to construct the so-called league tables for ranking investment banking firms by deal type.

PSA Standard Default Assumption Benchmark

A standardized benchmark for default rates was introduced by the then Public Securities Association (now called the *Bond Market Association*). The PSA standard default assumption (SDA) benchmark gives the annual default rate for a mortgage pool as a function of the seasoning of the mortgages.

The PSA SDA benchmark, or 100 SDA, specifies the following:

1. The default rate in month 1 is 0.02% and increases by 0.02% up to month 30 so that in month 30 the default rate is 0.60%.
2. From month 30 to month 60, the default rate remains at 0.60%.
3. From month 61 to month 120, the default rate declines from 0.60% to 0.03%.
4. From month 120 on, the default rate remains constant at 0.03%.

As with the PSA prepayment benchmark, multiples of the benchmark are found by multiplying the default rate by the assumed multiple. A "0 SDA" means that no defaults are assumed.

Credit Enhancements

The major difference between agency and nonagency securities has to do with guarantees. With a nonagency security there is no explicit or implicit government guarantee of payment of interest and principal as there is with an agency security. The absence of any such guarantee means that the investor in a nonagency security is exposed to credit risk. The nationally recognized statistical rating organizations rate nonagency securities.

To obtain a credit rating, all nonagency securities are credit enhanced. That means that credit support is provided for one or more bondholders in the structure. Typically a double A or triple A rating is sought for the most senior tranche in a deal. The amount of credit enhancement necessary depends on rating agency requirements. There are two general types of credit enhancement structures: external and internal.

External Credit Enhancements   External credit enhancements come in the form of third-party guarantees that provide for first loss protection against losses up to a specified level, for example, 10%. The most common forms of external credit enhancement are (1) a corporate guarantee; (2) a letter of credit; (3) pool insurance; and (4) bond insurance.

Pool insurance policies cover losses resulting from defaults and foreclosures. Policies are typically written for a dollar amount of coverage that continues in force throughout the life of the pool. However, some policies are written so that the dollar amount of coverage declines as the pool seasons as long as two conditions are met: (1) The credit performance is better than expected; and (2) the rating agencies that rated the issue approve. Since only defaults and foreclosures are covered, additional insurance must be obtained to cover losses resulting from bankruptcy (i.e., court-mandated modification of mortgage debt—"cramdown"), fraud arising in the origination process, and special hazards (i.e., losses resulting from events not covered by a standard homeowner's insurance policy).

Bond insurance provides the same function as in municipal bond structures. Typically, bond insurance is not used as the primary protection but to supplement other forms of credit enhancement.

A nonagency security with external credit support is subject to the credit risk of the third-party guarantor. If the third-party guarantor is downgraded, the issue itself could be subject to downgrade even if the structure is performing as expected.

External credit enhancements do not materially alter the cash flow characteristics of a CMO structure except in the form of prepayment. In case of a default resulting in net losses within the guarantee level, investors will receive the principal amount as if a prepayment has occurred. If the net losses exceed the guarantee level, investors will realize a shortfall in the cash flows.

Internal Credit Enhancements   Internal credit enhancements come in more complicated forms than external credit enhancements and may alter the cash flow characteristics of the loans even in the absence of default. The most common forms of internal credit enhancements are reserve funds, overcollateralization, and senior-subordinated structures.

Reserve funds come in two forms: cash reserve funds and excess servicing spread. *Cash reserve funds* are straight deposits of cash generated from issuance proceeds. In this case, part of the underwriting profits from the deal are deposited into a fund, which typically invests in money market instruments. Cash reserve funds are typically used in conjunction with some form of external credit enhancement.

Excess servicing spread accounts involve the allocation of excess spread or cash into a separate reserve account after paying out the net coupon, servicing fee, and all other expenses on a monthly basis. For example, suppose that the gross weighted-average coupon (gross WAC) is 7.75%, the servicing and other fees are 0.25%, and the net weighted-average coupon (net WAC) is 7.25%. This means that there is an excess servicing spread of 0.25%. The amount in the reserve account will gradually increase and can be used to pay for possible future losses.

With *overcollateralization*, the value of the collateral exceeds the value of the structure's obligations. For example, if a structure has two tranches with a par value of $300 million, then that is the amount of the liability. The amount of the collateral backing the structure must be at least equal to the amount of the liability. If the amount of the collateral exceeds the amount of the liability of the structure, the deal is said to be overcollateralized. The amount of overcollateralization represents a form of internal credit enhancement because it can be used to absorb losses. For example, if the liability of the structure is $300 million and the collateral's value is $320 million, then the structure is overcollateralized by $20 million. Thus, the first $20 million of losses will not result in a loss to any of the tranches in the structure.

In a *senior-subordinated structure* there is a senior tranche and at least one junior or subordinated tranche. The credit enhancement for the senior tranches comes from the junior tranches.

The basic concern in the senior-subordinated structure is that while the subordinated tranches provide a certain level of credit protection for the senior tranche at the closing of the deal, the level of protection changes over time due to prepayments. The objective after the deal closes is to distribute any prepayments such that the credit protection for the senior tranche does not deteriorate over time.

There is a well-developed mechanism used to address this concern called the *shifting interest mechanism*. Here is how it works. The percentage of the principal balance of the subordinated tranche to that of the principal balance for the entire deal is called the *level of subordination* or the *subordinate interest*. The higher the percentage, the greater the level of protection for the senior tranches. The subordinate interest changes after the deal is closed due to prepayments.

That is, the subordinate interest shifts (hence the term "shifting interest"). The purpose of a shifting interest mechanism is to allocate prepayments so that the subordinate interest is maintained at an acceptable level to protect the senior tranche. In effect, by paying down the senior tranche more quickly, the amount of subordination is maintained at the desired level. The prospectus will provide the shifting interest percentage schedule.

Prepayments

Dealers involved in the underwriting and market making of nonagency mortgage-backed securities have developed prepayment models for these loans. Several firms have found that the key difference between the prepayment behavior of borrowers of nonconforming mortgages and conforming mortgages is the important role played by the credit characteristics of the borrower.

Borrower characteristics and the seasoning process must be kept in mind when trying to assess prepayments for a particular deal. In the prospectus of an offering, a base-case prepayment assumption is made—the initial speed and the amount of time until the collateral is seasoned. The prepayment benchmark can be expressed as a percent of the PSA curve or may be issuer specific. The prospectus may spell out a *prospectus prepayment curve* or PPC. As with the PSA benchmark described earlier in this chapter, slower or faster prepayment speeds are a multiple of the PPC

Unlike the PSA prepayment benchmark, the PPC is not generic. By this it is meant that the PPC is issuer specific. In contrast, the PSA prepayment benchmark applies to any type of collateral issued by an agency for any type of loan design. This feature of the PPC is important for an investor to keep in mind when comparing the prepayment characteristics and investment characteristics of the collateral between issuers and issues (new and seasoned).

NAS and PAC Tranches

Tranches have been structured to give some senior tranches greater prepayment protection than other senior tranches. The two types of structures that do this are the planned amortization class (PAC) tranche discussed earlier and the *nonaccelerating senior* (NAS) tranche. An NAS tranche receives principal payments according to a schedule. The schedule is not a dollar amount. Rather, it is a principal schedule that shows for a given month the share of pro rata principal that must be distributed to the NAS tranche. The NAS tranche usually receives no principal payments for a preset number of years.

RESIDENTIAL REAL ESTATE ASSET-BACKED SECURITIES

Two major sectors of the asset-backed securities market in which the collateral is residential real estate are home equity loan backed securities and manufactured housing-backed securities. What is described here about credit enhancement and prepayment measurement in terms of PPC for nonagency MBS apply equally to these two ABS products. Both sectors are described below.

Home Equity Loan-Backed Securities

A home equity loan (HEL) is a loan backed by residential property. At one time, the loan was typically a second lien on property that was already pledged to secure a first lien. In some cases, the lien was a third lien. In recent years, the character of a home equity loan has changed. Today, a home equity loan is often a first lien on property where the borrower has either an impaired credit history and/or the payment-to-income ratio is too high for the loan to qualify as a conforming loan for securitization by Ginnie Mae, Fannie Mae, or Freddie Mac; that is, the home equity market is comprised primarily of subprime first liens. Typically, the borrower used a home equity loan to consolidate consumer debt using the current home as collateral rather than to obtain funds to purchase a new home.

Home equity loans can be either closed end or open end. Most home equity loan-backed deals have been backed by closed-end HELs. A closed-end HEL is designed the same way as a fully amortizing residential mortgage loan. That is, it has a fixed maturity and the payments are structured to fully amortize the loan by the maturity date.

There are both fixed-rate and variable-rate closed-end HELs. Typically, variable-rate loans have a reference rate of 6-month LIBOR and have periodic caps and lifetime caps. (A periodic cap limits the change in the mortgage rate from the previous time the mortgage rate was reset; a lifetime cap sets a maximum that the mortgage rate can ever be for the loan.) The cash flow of a pool of closed-end HELs is comprised of interest, regularly scheduled principal repayments, and pre-payments, just as with mortgage-backed securities. Thus, it is necessary to have a prepayment model and a default model to forecast cash flows. The prepayment speed is measured in terms of a conditional prepayment rate (CPR).

Borrower characteristics and the seasoning process must be kept in mind when trying to assess prepayments for a particular deal. In the prospectus of an offering, a base-case prepayment assumption is made—the initial speed and the amount of time until the collateral is expected to be sea-soned. Thus, the prepayment benchmark is issuer specific. As explained earlier in this chapter, the benchmark speed in the prospectus is called the prospectus prepayment curve or PPC. Slower or faster prepayments speeds are a multiple of the PPC.

The securities backed by the adjustable-rate (or variable-rate) HELs are called HEL floaters. Institutional investors who seek securities that better match their floating-rate funding costs are attracted to securities that offer a floating-rate coupon such as HEL floaters. To increase the attractiveness of home equity loan-backed securities to such investors, the securities typically have been created in which the reference rate is 1-month LIBOR. Because of (1) the mismatch between the reference rate on the underlying loans (typically 6-month LIBOR) and that of the HEL floater (1-month LIBOR) and (2) the periodic and life caps of the underlying loans, there is a cap on the coupon rate for the HEL floater. Unlike a typical floater, which has a cap that is fixed throughout the security's life, the effective cap of an HEL floater is variable. The effective cap, referred to as the available funds cap, will depend on the amount of funds generated by the net coupon on the principal, less any fees.

As with nonagency MBSs, a HEL-backed deal can include planned amortization class (PAC) and nonaccelerated senior (NAS) tranches.

Manufactured Housing-Backed Securities

Manufactured housing-backed securities are backed by loans for manufactured homes. In contrast to site-built homes, manufactured homes are built at a factory and then transported to a manufactured home community or private land. The loan may be either a mortgage loan (for both the land and the home) or a consumer retail installment loan.

Manufactured housing-backed securities are issued by Ginnie Mae and private entities. The former securities are guaranteed by the full faith and credit of the U.S. government. The manufactured housing loans that are collateral for the securities issued and guaranteed by Ginnie Mae are loans guaranteed by the Federal Housing Administration (FHA) or Veterans Administration (VA). Loans not backed by the FHA or VA are called *conventional loans*. Manufactured housing-backed securities that are backed by such loans are called *conventional manufactured housing-backed securities*. These securities are issued by private entities.

The typical loan for a manufactured home is 15 to 20 years. The loan repayment is structured to fully amortize the amount borrowed. Therefore, as with residential mortgage loans and HELs, the cash flow consists of net interest, regularly scheduled principal, and prepayments. However, prepayments are more stable for manufactured housing-backed securities because they are not sensitive to refinancing. There are several reasons for this. First, the loan balances are typically small so that there is no significant dollar savings from refinancing. Second, the rate of depreciation of mobile homes may be such that in the earlier years depreciation is greater than the amount of the loan paid off. This makes it difficult to refinance the loan. Finally, borrowers are typically of lower credit quality and therefore find it difficult to obtain funds to refinance.

COMMERCIAL MORTGAGE-BACKED SECURITIES

Commercial mortgage-backed securities (CMBSs) are backed by a pool of commercial mortgage loans on income-producing property—multifamily properties (i.e., apartment buildings), office buildings, industrial properties (including warehouses), shopping centers, hotels, and health care facilities (i.e., senior housing care facilities). There are three types of CMBS deal structures that have been of interest to bond investors: (1) liquidating trusts; (2) multiproperty single borrower; and (3) multiproperty conduit. The liquidating or nonperforming trusts are a small segment of the CMBS market. This segment, as the name implies, represents CMBS deals backed by nonperforming mortgage loans. The fastest growing segment of the CMBS is conduit-originated transactions. Conduits are commercial-lending entities that are established for the sole purpose of generating collateral to securitize.

Credit Risk

Unlike residential mortgage loans where the lender relies on the ability of the borrower to repay and has recourse to the borrower if the payment terms are not satisfied, commercial mortgage loans are nonrecourse loans. This means that the lender can only look to the income-producing property backing the loan for interest and principal repayment. If there is a default, the lender looks to the proceeds from the sale of the property for repayment and has no recourse to the borrower for any unpaid balance. Basically, this means that the lender must view each property as a standalone business and evaluate each property using measures that have been found useful in assessing credit risk.

While fundamental principles of assessing credit risk apply to all property types, traditional approaches to assessing the credit risk of the collateral differs for CMBS than for nonagency MBS and real estate-backed ABS discussed earlier. For MBS and ABS backed by residential property, typically the loans are lumped into buckets based on certain loan characteristics and then assumptions regarding default rates are made regarding each bucket. In contrast, for commercial mortgage loans, the unique economic characteristics of each income-producing property in a pool backing a CMBS requires that credit analysis be performed on a loan-by-loan basis not only at the time of issuance, but monitored on an ongoing basis.

Regardless of the property type, the two measures that have been found to be key indicators of the potential credit performance is the debt-to-service coverage ratio and the loan-to-value ratio.

The *debt-to-service coverage* (DSC) ratio is the ratio of the property's net operating income (NOI) divided by the debt service. The NOI is defined as the rental income reduced by cash operating expenses (adjusted for a replacement reserve). A ratio greater than 1 means that the cash flow from the property is sufficient to cover debt servicing. The higher the ratio, the more likely that the borrower will be able to meet debt servicing from the property's cash flow.

For all properties backing a CMBS deal, a weighted-average DSC ratio is computed. An analysis of the credit quality of an issue will also look at the dispersion of the DSC ratios for the underlying loans. For example, one might look at the percentage of a deal with a DSC ratio below a certain value.

Studies of residential mortgage loans have found that the key determinant of default is the loan-to-value (LTV) ratio. The figure used for "value" in this ratio is either market value or appraised value. In valuing commercial property, there can be considerable variation in the estimates of the property's market value. Thus, analysts tend to be skeptical about estimates of market value and the resulting LTVs reported for properties. The lower the LTV, the greater the protection afforded the lender.

Another characteristic of the underlying loans that is used in gauging the quality of a CMBS deal is the prepayment protection provisions. We discuss these provisions later. Finally, there are characteristics of the property that affect quality. Specifically, analysts and rating agencies look at the concentration of loans by property type and by geographical location.

Basic CMBS Structure

As with any structured finance transaction, sizing will determine the necessary level of credit enhancement to achieve a desired rating level. For example, if certain DSC and LTV ratios are needed, and these ratios cannot be met at the loan level, then subordination is used to achieve these levels.

The rating agencies will require that the CMBS transaction be retired sequentially, with the highest-rated bonds paying off first. Therefore, any return of principal caused by amortization, prepayment, or default will be used to repay the highest-rated tranche.

Interest on principal outstanding will be paid to all tranches. In the event of a delinquency resulting in insufficient cash to make all scheduled payments, the transaction's servicer will advance both principal and interest. Advancing will continue from the servicer for as long as these amounts are deemed recoverable.

Losses arising from loan defaults will be charged against the principal balance of the lowest-rated CMBS tranche outstanding. The total loss charged will include the amount previously advanced as well as the actual loss incurred in the sale of the loan's underlying property.

The investor must be sure to understand the cash flow priority of any prepayment penalties and/or yield maintenance provisions because this can impact a particular bond's average life and overall performance.

Structural Call Protection

The degree of call protection available to a CMBS investor is a function of the following two characteristics: call protection available at the loan level and call protection afforded from the actual CMBS structure. At the commercial loan level, call protection can take the following forms: prepayment lockout, defeasance, prepayment penalty points, and yield maintenance charges.

A *prepayment lockout* is a contractual agreement that prohibits any prepayments during a specified period of time, called the lockout period. The lockout period at issuance can be from two to five years.

After the lockout period, call protection comes in the form of either prepayment penalty points or yield maintenance charges. With *defeasance*, rather than prepaying a loan, the borrower provides sufficient funds for the servicer to invest in a portfolio of Treasury securities that replicates the cash flows that would exist in the absence of prepayments. *Prepayment penalty points* are predetermined penalties that must be paid by the borrower if the borrower wishes to refinance. *Yield maintenance charge*, in its simplest terms, is designed to make the lender indifferent as to the timing of prepayments. The yield maintenance charge, called the "make-whole charge" in the corporate area, makes it uneconomical to refinance solely to get a lower mortgage rate.

The other type of call protection available in CMBS transactions is structural. That is, because the CMBS bond structures are sequential-pay (by rating), the AA-rated tranche cannot pay down until the AAA is completely retired, and the

AA-rated bonds must be paid off before the A-rated bonds, and so on. However, principal losses due to defaults are impacted from the bottom of the structure upward.

Call provision at both the loan and structure level make contraction risk less likely. Therefore unlike some of the mortgage assets described earlier, they are not likely to exhibit negative convexity.

Balloon Maturity Provisions

Many commercial loans backing CMBS transactions are balloon loans that require substantial principal payment at the end of the term of the loan. If the borrower fails to make the balloon payment, the borrower is in default. The lender may extend the loan, and in so doing may modify the original loan terms. During the workout period for the loan, a higher interest rate will be charged, the default interest rate.

The risk that a borrower will not be able to make the balloon payment because either the borrower cannot arrange for refinancing at the balloon payment date or cannot sell the property to generate sufficient funds to pay off the balloon balance is called *balloon risk*. Since the term of the loan will be extended by the lender during the workout period, balloon risk is also referred to as extension risk.

REAL ESTATE INVESTMENT TRUST DEBT

Real estate investment trust (REITs) are companies that buy, develop, manage, and sell real estate assets. One special feature of REITs is that they qualify as passthrough entities and are therefore free from taxation at the corporate level. REITs must comply with a number of Internal Revenue Code provisions to qualify for that tax-free status. In particular, REITs must pay dividends equaling at least 90% of their taxable income, and more than 75% of total investment assets must be in real estate assets. Their major business activity is the generation of property income, and no more than 30% of gross income can come from the sale of real estate property held for less than four years. So they are clearly "buy and operate" entities, not flippers or tradesters.

REIT Taxonomy

REITs fall into three broad categories: equity REITs, mortgage REITs, and hybrid REITs.

Equity REITs are the dominant category, representing about 95% of total market capitalization. Their revenues are derived principally from rents. Equity REITs invest in and own properties (and are thus responsible for the equity or value of their real estate assets). Equity REITs differ by specialization. Some focus on a specific geographic area (a specific region, state or metropolitan area), others focus on a specific property type (such as retail properties, industrial facilities, strip malls, office buildings, apartments or health-care facilities). Still other REITs have a broad focus, and invest in a variety of assets across a wide spectrum of loca-tions. The most important asset holdings are retail proper-ties, residential properties, and industrial offices.

Mortgage REITs represent between 3% and 4% of total REIT market capitalization. These REITs provide mortgage money to owners of real estate, and purchase existing mort-gages and mortgage-backed securities. Their revenues are generated primarily by interest they earn on the mortgage loans. Mortgage REITs have become a considerably less important part of the market over time. In 1990, they had represented about 29% of total REIT market capitalization.

Hybrid REITS represent less than 2% of the market. They combine the investment strategies of equity REITs and mortgage REITS by investing in both properties and mort-gages.

Mortgage REITs are rarely used in CDO deals. CDO managers are interested exclusively in equity REITs. This is because recovery assumptions for mortgage REITs are much more stringent than for equity REITs. In SF CDO deals, recovery assumptions are dependent on the bond's percentage representation of initial capital ("the thickness of the slice of the deal"). Recovery rates on typical subordinated CMBS/ABS/MBS assets are 30–35%. For equity REITs, Moody's assumes a recovery rate of 40%, which reflects the strong covenant packages that we will discuss later. Thus assumed recovery rates for equity REITs are very similar to those on subordinate CMBS/ABS/MBS assets. By contrast, on healthcare REITs, which carry special risks due to significant government regulation of their ownership and operation, and mortgage REITs, which tend to be highly leveraged, Moody's assumes a 10% recovery rate.

REIT Capitalization

The REIT capital structure consists of secured bank loans, unsecured debentures, preferred stock, and equity. Since an equity REIT can buy and sell assets and change financial ratios, debt covenants are one of the most important protections available for holders of unsecured REIT debt.

Here we look more closely at REIT debt covenants, and learn how minimum ratios compare to those on CMBS. We will find BBB rated REIT debt has ratios very similar to single A rated CMBS debt. We will also learn that, in practice, REITs hold ratios even much higher than those provided by the covenants.

REIT Debt Covenants

Investors in REIT debt will find the covenants quite significant in providing protection. Standard covenants are shown in Exhibit 4.1. A typical REIT covenant package includes the following:

1. Total debt cannot exceed 60% of total assets.
2. Unencumbered assets must represent at least 150% of unsecured debt.
3. Secured debt cannot exceed 40% of total assets.
4. Interest coverage must be greater than 1.5×.

EXHIBIT 4.1   Senior Unsecured REIT Debt: Comparison to CMBS

Covenant	Required Ratio	Comparable CMBS Ratio
Debt/Adjusted total assets	No more than 60%	LTV
Total unencumbered assets/Unsecured debt	At least 150%	LTV
Secured debt/Adjusted total assets	No more than 40%	Percent of debt that is senior
Consolidated income available for debt service/Annual debt service	At least 1.5×	DSCR

While these look very different from levels that mortgage market junkies are accustomed to, they are easily translated. In fact, they parallel very closely A ratings for CMBS. Let's look of each of these more closely.

The debt/adjusted total assets ratio is very close to an LTV in the CMBS market: It measures the value of the loan versus the value of the property. This ratio must be no more than 60%. In fact, for singe A rated CMBS debt, the implied LTV is generally in the range of 60–65%. Generally in a CMBS conduit deal, total LTV is 75%. However, approximately 15% of the deal is subordinated to the single A tranche, so we can multiply the LTV on the deal by 0.85. This gives 64% LTV (0.75×0.85).

The total unencumbered assets/unsecured debt ratio must be at least 150% in a REIT. This leverage ratio is actually a very close relative of LTV measures used in CMBS. It says that unsecured debt cannot be more than 66% of total unencumbered assets. Again, these levels are very similar to the LTVs for single A rated CMBS debt.

The next ratio is secured debt/adjusted total assets. Since REIT debt is senior, but unsecured, this ratio measures the percent of debt ahead of the bondholder in a REIT capital structure. That ratio must be no greater than 40%. In a CMBS deal, there is approximately 25% subordination under the AAA. The AA and A are generally about 5% each. So the single A rated CMBS bond has 80% of the deal ahead of it. Thus, the BBB rated REIT has a much lower percent of the deal with a prior claim on the assets, which provides a heavy measure of protection.

The final ratio, consolidated income available for debt service/annual debt service, is very close to a debt service coverage ratio (DSCR). This measures how much income cushion there is to pay bondholders the interest due them. This ratio must be at least 1.5× on a REIT deal. For a single A class on a CMBS deal, it is right around the same level. That is, the deal typically has a 1.25× DSCR at the whole loan level. With 85% of the deal senior, or *pari passu*, to the single A (15% subordination), we obtain a DSCR of 1.47× (1.25/0.85) on the single A CMBS.

Reasons for Tough Ratings

The minimum covenant restrictions for BBB rated REIT debt are very close to the ratios that are required for a single A rating in the CMBS market. Moody's acknowledges this by saying "REIT ratings tend to run several grades lower than commercial mortgage backed securities (CMBS) ratings for pools with comparable asset classes and financial ratios."[2] The reasons for the tougher grading scale for REIT debt are fourfold.

- REITS may substantially alter the composition of their portfolio assets unlike a CMBS, which involves fixed pools. So REIT assets can be purchased and sold, while CMBS assets can only leave the pool, and none can be added.[3]
- Financial ratios of a REIT can change over time, but the capital structure of a CMBS is permanent. REIT covenants typically allow significantly greater leverage than the capital structure currently in place. This gives REITs more financial flexibility, but could jeopardize bondholders.
- REIT debt is unsecured, whereas first mortgage positions of CMBS are secured.

---

[2] See Moody's Investors Service, "Credit Rating Evaluation of REITs" (December 9, 1994).

[3] In a FASIT structure, substitutions are permissible.

■ And finally, REIT debt is in the form of bonds, while most CMBS debt is in passthroughs. Thus the REIT debt must be paid in full on a specific day, which is a more stringent hurdle than that for a passthrough completing payment by a stated final maturity.

Investors should realize that not only are covenants in a REIT extremely conservative, but most BBB rated REITs have ratios far more conservative than what covenants actually permit.

Reasons REITs Are Included in CDOs

REITs have become a very important part of structured finance CDOs, comprising 10–50% of total assets on a number of deals. REIT debt is included because

■ REITs do not have negative convexity and hence help minimize the negative convexity for the CDO.
■ REITs provide valuable diversification for CDO deals.
■ REIT yields are somewhat higher than CMBS yields for assets with similar ratings.

Minimizing Negative Convexity

REIT debt generally has 10–12 year final maturities and excellent call protection. The call protection occurs because the securities are noncallable bullets or have yield maintenance provisions. The yield maintenance provisions (or "make whole" provisions) are very similar to those found in CMBS deals, with most deals using a discount rate of Treasuries plus 25 basis points. If a deal carrying yield maintenance provisions is called, bondholders will be owed the difference between the value of the cash flows, discounted at Treasuries plus 25 basis points, and par. Calling yield maintenance deals usually represents a windfall to the investor.

To illustrate, assume an investor hypothetically purchased a new par REIT bond, with a 10-year maturity and a coupon of 8.35%, selling exactly at par. (Also assume that the 10-year

Treasury note is 5.85%, implying the REIT debt has a spread of 250 bps to the 10-year.) If the bond is called immediately, its value (at a Treasury plus 25 basis points discount rate) is $116.66. Thus, investors receive a $16.66 windfall. If interest rates have fallen, the value of the bond is even larger. In practice, this means that REIT debt is rarely called. It is totally noneconomic to refinance, as bondholders receive more than the savings from any refinancing following lower rates.

This call protection is important because both residential, mortgage-backed securities and mortgage-related ABS have some amount of negative convexity. The convexity problem is minimized in any CDO by limiting the amount of negative convex paper in that deal. Thus the deals must use a heavy component of non-mortgage-related ABS paper, CMBS paper, and REIT paper.

Diversification

REIT paper provides valuable diversification for CDO deals. CDO ratings are derived by reducing the asset pool to a set of nearly homogenous, uncorrelated assets. Structured finance-backed CDOs generally have much lower diversity scores than do high-yield CDOs, since there are substantially fewer categories. On a structured finance deal, a typical diversity score is 15–20, compared to the typical 50–60 on a high-yield deal. So for convexity purposes, it is important to include nonmortgage-related assets, as well as CMBS and REITs. However, availability of nonmortgage-related subordinated tranches is very limited, and Moody's has only three CMBS categories. By contrast, there are 8 REIT categories, as shown in Exhibit 4.2. Thus, REITs turn out to be a very valuable source of diversification for CDO deals.

Some Yield Pick-Up to CMBS

Investors are able to obtain this diversification and collateral availability advantage without giving up yield. In fact, REITs actually yield more than do comparably rated CMBS.

EXHIBIT 4.2   Moody's Industry Classifications

Industry Classifications	Category
CMBS	
Conduit	1
Credit Tenant Leases	2
Large Loan	3
REIT	
Hotel & Leisure	4
Residential	5
Office	6
Retail	7
Industrial	8
Healthcare	9
Diversified	10
Self Storage	11

Source: Moody's Investors Service, "The Inclusion of Commercial Real Estate Assets in CDOs," October 8, 1999.

One would think that with such conservative rating methodology on ratios, REITs would tend to trade tighter than CMBS. In fact, the reverse is the case. REITs tend to trade wider at each rating level. Industrial and residential REITs generally tend to trade 5–10 basis points wider than equivalently rated CMBS debt at the BBB and BB levels. And retail/storage REITs tend to trade about 30–35 basis points wider.

A number of investors have expressed frustration that REIT spreads do not follow the same patterns as those on other corporate bonds. Yet, in fact, REIT debt tends to track CMBS debt very closely in the BBB categories.

A Final Advantage

In addition to giving managers a wider choice of available assets, we have argued that REITs add diversification to CDO deals. We also have explained that REIT covenants are approximately as conservative at the BBB level as are CMBS ratios at the single A level. Moreover, most REITs tend to have actual financial ratios far more conservative than what their covenants allow. The final advantage stems from the fact that REITs are actually wider in yield than comparably rated CMBS debt. In short, REIT exposure should be looked at as a "plus" within the context of a structured finance REIT.

CREDIT CARD RECEIVABLE-BACKED SECURITIES

A major sector of the ABS market is that of securities backed by credit card receivables. Credit cards are issued by banks (e.g., Visa and MasterCard), retailers (e.g., JC Penney and Sears), and travel and entertainment companies (e.g., American Express). Credit card deals are structured as a master trust. With a master trust the issuer can sell several series from the same trust.

Cash Flow

For a pool of credit card receivables, the cash flow consists of finance charges collected, fees, and principal. Finance charges collected represent the periodic interest the credit card borrower is charged based on the unpaid balance after the grace period. Fees include late payment fees and any annual membership fees.

Interest to security holders is paid periodically (e.g., monthly, quarterly, or semiannually). The interest rate may be fixed or floating—roughly half of the securities are floaters. The floating rate is uncapped.

A credit card receivable-backed security is a nonamortizing security. For a specified period of time, referred to as the lockout period or revolving period, the principal payments made by credit card borrowers comprising the pool are retained by the trustee and reinvested in additional receivables to maintain the size of the pool. The lockout period can vary from 18 months to 10 years. So, during the lockout period, the cash flow that is paid out to security holders is based on finance charges collected and fees.

After the lockout period, the principal is no longer reinvested but paid to investors. This period is referred to as the principal-amortization period, and the various types of structures are described later.

Performance of the Portfolio of Receivables

Several concepts must be understood in order to assess the performance of the portfolio of receivables and the ability of the issuer to meet its interest obligation and repay principal as scheduled.

The gross yield includes finance charges collected and fees. Charge-offs represent the accounts charged off as uncollectible. Net portfolio yield is equal to gross portfolio yield minus charge-offs. The net portfolio yield is important because it is from this yield that the bondholders will be paid. So, for example, if the average yield (WAC) that must be paid to the various tranches in the structure is 5% and the net portfolio yield for the month is only 4.5%, there is the risk that the bondholder obligations will not be satisfied.

Delinquencies are the percentages of receivables that are past due for a specified number of months, usually 30, 60, and 90 days. They are considered an indicator of potential future charge-offs.

The monthly payment rate (MPR) expresses the monthly payment (which includes finance charges, fees, and any principal repayment) of a credit card receivable portfolio as a percentage of credit card debt outstanding in the previous month. For example, suppose a $500 million credit card receivable portfolio in January realized $50 million of payments in February. The MPR would then be 10% ($50 million divided by $500 million).

There are two reasons why the MPR is important. First, if the MPR reaches an extremely low level, there is a chance that there will be extension risk with respect to the principal payments on the bonds. Second, if the MPR is very low, then there is a chance that there will not be sufficient cash flows to pay off principal. This is one of the events that could trigger early amortization of the principal (described as follows).

At issuance, portfolio yield, charge-offs, delinquency, and MPR information are provided in the prospectus. Information about portfolio performance is thereafter available from various sources.

Early Amortization Triggers

There are provisions in credit card receivable-backed securities that require early amortization of the principal if certain events occur. Such provisions, which are referred to as either early amortization or rapid amortization, are included to safeguard the credit quality of the issue. The only way that the principal cash flows can be altered is by triggering the early amortization provision.

Typically, early amortization allows for the rapid return of principal in the event that the 3-month average excess spread earned on the receivables falls to zero or less. When early amortization occurs, the credit card tranches are retired sequentially (i.e., first the AAA bond, then the AA rated bond, and so on). This is accomplished by paying the principal payments made by the credit card borrowers to the investors instead of using them to purchase more receivables. The length of time until the return of principal is largely a function of the monthly payment rate. For example, suppose that a AAA tranche is 82% of the overall deal. If the monthly payment rate is 11%, then the AAA tranche would return principal over a 7.5-month period (82%/11%). An 18% monthly payment rate would return principal over a 4.5-month period (82%/18%).

Several services publish monthly each deal's trigger formula and base rate. The trigger formula is the formula that shows the condition under which the rapid amortization will be triggered. The base rate is the minimum payment rate that a trust must be able to maintain to avoid early amortization.

AUTO-LOAN BACKED SECURITIES[4]

Auto loan-backed securities represents one of the oldest and most familiar sectors of the ABS market. A key factor in the appeal of auto ABS securities is the historically strong credit quality of the underlying collateral. Of the most active sectors in the ABS arena—autos, credit cards, home equity loans (HELs)—autos are generally considered to have the strongest credit quality (that is, before credit enhancement brings virtually all senior securities across sectors to a triple-A rating).

Auto ABS are issued by:

1. the financial subsidiaries of auto manufacturers (domestic and foreign);
2. commercial banks; and
3. independent finance companies and small financial institutions specializing in auto loans.

Prime auto loans are of fundamentally high credit quality for the following reasons. First, they are a secured form of lending (credit cards are unsecured lending). Second, they begin to repay principal immediately through amortization (credit cards require only a minimum payment). Third, they are short-term in nature (HELs have 15–30 year maturities). Finally, for the most part, major issuers of auto loans have tended to follow reasonably prudent underwriting standards.

Unlike the subprime mortgage industry, there is less consistency on what actually constitutes various categories of prime and subprime auto loans. According to Moody's, the *prime* market is composed of issuers typically having cumulative losses (on a static pool basis) of less than 3%; *near-prime* issuers that have cumulative losses of 3–7%; and subprime issuers with losses exceeding 7%.

---

[4] The ABS products discussed in the balance of this chapter draws from Frank J. Fabozzi and Thomas A. Zimmerman, "Non-Real Estate Backed ABS," in Frank J. Fabozzi (ed.), *The Handbook of Financial Instruments* (New York: John Wiley & Sons, Inc., 2002).

Cash Flows and Prepayments

The cash flow for auto loan-backed securities consists of regularly scheduled monthly loan payments (interest and scheduled principal repayments) and any prepayments. For securities backed by auto loans, prepayments result from

1. sales and trade-ins requiring full payoff of the loan
2. repossession and subsequent resale of the automobile
3. loss or destruction of the vehicle
4. payoff of the loan with cash to save on the interest cost
5. refinancing of the loan at a lower interest cost

While refinancings may be a major reason for prepayments of mortgage loans, they are of minor importance for automobile loans. Moreover, the interest rates for the automobile loans underlying some deals are substantially below market rates since they are offered by manufacturers as part of a sales promotion.

Prepayments for auto loan-backed securities are measured in terms of the absolute prepayment speed (ABS). The ABS is the monthly prepayment expressed as a percentage of the original collateral amount. As explained earlier, the single monthly mortality rate (SMM) is a monthly conditional prepayment rate (CPR) that expresses prepayments based on the prior month's balance.

Structures

There have been several interesting developments in auto ABS structures in recent years. First was the introduction of a soft-bullet in late-1999, a structure that had been the norm in credit cards for many years. Second was the shift towards greater floating-rate issuance, a sharp contrast to the long-term convention of fixed-rate auto ABS. The final change was use of an initial revolving period, which extends the average life of the securities.

Soft Bullets

Perhaps the most interesting innovation was the introduction of the soft bullet structure. Since the inception of auto ABS in the mid-1980s, auto ABS securities have been structured with amortizing principal payments. This cash flow structure of the security mirrors underlying payments on the collateral, which typically are 4- to 5-year amortizing loans. Although the owner trust structure allowed for prioritization of cash flows across different classes, the amortization of principal had not been dealt with until 2001

The Capital Auto Receivables Asset Trust (CARAT) 1999-2 issue by GMAC in August 1999 marked the first time that investors were able to buy auto loan ABS with a soft bullet maturity. This structure was able to offer soft bullet classes instead of amortizing classes, because it included a new type of security that could (1) absorb the amortizing principal cash flows prior to the bullet date and (2) provide the cash flow to meet the bullet principal payment at maturity.

In the CARAT structure this security was christened a "variable pay term note" (VPTN). At origination, the deal contained a VPTN-1 class that received all principal payments until class A-1 targeted final maturity date, at which point the VPTN-1 class would be paid down. At that point the trust would issue a new VPTN-2 class, the proceeds from which would be used to pay-down the A1 class. During the next period, principal payments would go to pay down the VPTN-2 class. On the maturity date of the A2 class, a new class, VPTN-3, would be issued; the proceeds would pay off the A2 bullet class. This process of creating new variable notes and paying them down continues until all the bullet securities are paid off.

Beginning with the CARAT 2000-2 deal, GMAC modified its soft-bullet structure by using a single variable pay note rather than a series of notes. At the maturity date of each bullet class, the VTPN in this revised structure is increased by the amount needed to pay off the bullet class. Then the enlarged variable pay note is paid down until the next bullet maturity date.

Ford's soft bullet deals utilized a structure similar to that in the early CARAT deals. The first such Ford deal, Ford 2000-B, was issued in April 2000.

Since the initial CARAT soft bullet deal, the use of the soft bullet structure has been irregular. So far, only GMAC (via CARAT deals) and Ford have used the structure. Ford used it on three deals in 2000: Ford Credit Auto Owner Trusts 2000-B, 2000-D, and 2000-F. However, so far in 2001, Ford has not revisited the soft bullet structure. On the other hand, GMAC has used it exclusively since the initial CARAT 1999-2.

Floating-Rate Autos

The second major change in the auto sector was the increased issuance of floaters. In response to the volatile environment for corporates in 2001 and early 2002, the auto ABS market experienced a dramatic increase in floater issuance. Until that time, auto loans were almost exclusively a fixed-rate product. Floating-rate issuance in 2000 accounted for only 4.3% of total auto ABS issuance. In the first half of 2001, however, that percentage shot up to 25.5%.

An example of a floating-rate auto loan ABS is the Toyota Motor Credit of May 2001 (Toyota Auto Receivables 2001-B Owner Trust), the first auto deal entirely comprised of floating-rate tranches.[5] This $1.5 billion issue was divided into four tranches, three of which were sold publicly. The fourth tranche, a $418 million money-market class, was placed privately.

---

[5] In order to provide floating-rate tranches, the Trust entered into a swap agreement with Toyota Motor Credit Corporation (TMCC) in which TMCC receives the fixed-rate payments from the collateral and pays a floating-rate to the Trust (net of fees). The Trust is then able to pay the floating-rate coupon to investors. However, because the deal contains a fixed-to-floating swap, the ratings of the deal are subject to the counterparty risk of TMCC. Unlike the bullet structure, it is easy for most issuers to incorporate a swap into their deals and to issue floaters.

EXHIBIT 4.3 Average Life: Revolving versus Non-Revolving

	No Revolving Period Ford 2001-D	Revolving Period Ford 2001-F
A1	0.47	2.00
A2	0.97	2.50
A3	1.47	3.00
A4	1.97	3.50
A5	2.47	4.00

Revolving Period

Another recent innovation, introduced in the Ford 2000-F deal, is an initial revolving period during which the securities receive no principal payments. Instead, during this time, collateral payments are used to purchase additional receivables. After the revolving period ends, the securities pay down in sequential order. The revolving period in this deal added 1.5 years to the average life of each class. We can see this in Exhibit 4.3, which compares average lives of Ford 2000-F tranches with those from Ford 2000-D, a deal typical of other Ford soft bullet deals. The advantage to investors is that they can purchase an auto ABS with a longer average life than found in other auto deals. However to our knowledge, this is the only public auto deal using this technique, which suggests that demand for this structure was not great enough to encourage a follow-up deal.[6]

STUDENT LOAN-BACKED SECURITIES

Student loans are made to cover college cost (undergraduate, graduate, and professional programs such as medical school and law school) and tuition for a wide range of vocational and trade schools. Securities backed by student loans are popularly referred to as SLABS (student loan asset-backed securities).

---

[6] However, the revolving structure has been used in several 144a deals.

The student loans that have been most commonly securitized are those that are made under the Federal Family Education Loan Program (FFELP). Under this program, the government makes loans to students via private lenders. The decision by private lenders to extend a loan to a student is not based on the applicant's ability to repay the loan. If a default of a loan occurs and the loan has been properly serviced, then the government will guarantee up to 98% of the principal plus accrued interest.

Loans that are not part of a government guarantee program are called *alternative loans*. These loans are basically consumer loans, and the lender's decision to extend an alternative loan will be based on the ability of the applicant to repay the loan. Alternative loans have been securitized.

Congress created Fannie Mae and Freddie Mac to provide liquidity in the mortgage market by allowing these government-sponsored enterprises to buy mortgage loans in the secondary market. Congress created the Student Loan Marketing Association (Sallie Mae) as a government-sponsored enterprise to purchase student loans in the secondary market and to securitize pools of student loans. Sallie Mae is the major issuer of SLABS, and its issues are viewed as the benchmark issues. Other entities that issue SLABS are either traditional corporate entities (e.g., the Money Store and PNC Bank) or nonprofit organizations (Michigan Higher Education Loan Authority and the California Educational Facilities Authority). The SLABS of the latter typically are issued as tax-exempt securities and therefore trade in the municipal market.

Collateral

There are different types of student loans under the FFELP, including subsidized and unsubsidized Stafford loans, Parental Loans for Undergraduate Students (PLUS), and Supplemental Loans to Students (SLS). These loans involve three periods with respect to the borrower's payments-deferment period, grace period, and loan repayment period. Typically, student loans work as follows. While a student is in school, no payments are made by the student on the loan. This is the *deferment period*. Upon leaving school, the student is extended a *grace period* of usually six months when no payments on the loan must be made. After this period, payments are made on the loan by the borrower.

Prepayments typically occur due to defaults or loan consolidation. Even if there is no loss of principal faced by the investor when defaults occur, the investor is still exposed to contraction risk. This is the risk that the investor must reinvest the proceeds at a lower spread and, in the case of a bond purchased at a premium, the premium will be lost. Studies have shown student loan prepayments are insensitive to the level of interest rates. Consolidation of a loan occurs when the student who has loans over several years combines them into a single loan. The proceeds from the consolidation are distributed to the original lender and, in turn, distributed to the bondholders.

Structures

Structures on student loan floaters have experienced more than the usual amount of change since 2000. The reason for this is quite simple. The underlying collateral—student loans—is exclusively indexed to three-month Treasury bills, while a large percentage of securities are issued as LIBOR floaters. This creates an inherent mismatch between the collateral and the securities.

Issuers have dealt with the mismatch in a variety of ways. Some issued Treasury bill floaters which eliminates the mismatch, others issued hedged or unhedged LIBOR floaters, while others switched back and forth between the two. Recently, some have issued both Treasury and LIBOR floaters in the same transaction.[7]

---

[7] Also in conjunction with the choice of index, issuers have incorporated a variety of basis swaps and/or have bought cap protection from third parties, while some have used internal structures to deal with the risk.

It is important to bear in mind that when an ABS structure contains a basis mismatch, it is not only the investor, but the issuer that bears a risk. Student loan deals (like deals in many other ABS classes) have excess spread, i.e., roughly the difference between the net coupon on the collateral and the coupon on the bonds.

In mortgage-related ABS, the excess spread is much larger than in the student loan sector, and is used to absorb monthly losses. Since losses in federally guaranteed student loans are relatively small, the vast majority of the excess spread flows back to the issuer. Hence, the Treasury bill/LIBOR-basis risk is of major concern to issuers. When an issuer incorporates a swap in the deal, it not only reduces the risk to the investor (by eliminating the effect of an available funds cap) but reduces risk to the issuer by protecting a level of excess spread. When a cap is purchased, it is primarily for the benefit of the investor, because the cap only comes into play once the excess spread in the deal has been effectively reduced to zero.

The indices used on private and public student loan ABS transactions since the earliest deals in 1993 have changed over time (even though throughout this period, the index on the underlying loans was always three-month Treasury bills). During 1993–1995, most issuers, with the notable exception of Sallie Mae, used one-month LIBOR, which indicated strong investor preference for LIBOR floaters. By contrast, from Sallie Mae's first deal in late 1995-on, that issuer chose to issue Treasury bill floaters to minimize interest rate mismatch risk.

SBA LOAN-BACKED SECURITIES

The Small Business Administration (SBA) is an agency of the U.S. government empowered to guarantee loans made by approved SBA lenders to qualified borrowers. The loans are backed by the full faith and credit of the government. Most SBA loans are variable-rate loans where the reference rate is the prime rate. The rate on the loan is reset monthly on the first of the month or quarterly on the first of January, April, July, and October. SBA regulations specify the maximum coupon allowable in the secondary market. Newly originated loans have maturities between five and 25 years.

The Small Business Secondary Market Improvement Act passed in 1984 permitted the pooling of SBA loans. When pooled, the underlying loans must have similar terms and features. The maturities typically used for pooling loans are 7, 10, 15, 20, and 25 years. Loans without caps are not pooled with loans that have caps.

Most variable-rate SBA loans make monthly payments consisting of interest and principal repayment. The amount of the monthly payment for an individual loan is determined as follows. Given the coupon formula of the prime rate plus the loan's quoted margin, the interest rate is determined for each loan. Given the interest rate, a level payment amortization schedule is determined. This level payment is paid until the coupon rate is reset.

The monthly cash flow that the investor in an SBA-backed security receives consists of:

- The coupon interest based on the coupon rate set for the period
- The scheduled principal repayment (i.e., scheduled amortization)
- Prepayments

Prepayments for SBA-backed securities are measured in terms of CPR. Voluntary prepayments can be made by the borrower without any penalty. There are several factors contributing to the prepayment speed of a pool of SBA loans. A factor affecting prepayments is the maturity date of the loan. It has been found that the fastest speeds on SBA loans and pools occur for shorter maturities. The purpose of the loan also affects prepayments. There are loans for working capital purposes and loans to finance real estate construction or acquisition. It has been observed that SBA pools with maturities of 10 years or less made for working capital purposes tend to prepay at the fastest speed. In contrast, loans backed by real estate that are long maturities tend to prepay at a slow speed. All other factors constant, pools that have capped loans tend to prepay more slowly than pools of uncapped loans.

AIRCRAFT LEASE-BACKED SECURITIES

Aircraft financing has gone thorough an evolution over the past several years. It started with mainly bank financing, then moved to equipment trust certificates (ETCs), then to enhanced ETCs (EETCs), and finally to aircraft ABS. Today, both EETCs and aircraft ABS are widely used.

EETCs are corporate bonds that share some of the features of structured products, such as credit tranching and liquidity facilities. Aircraft ABS differ from EETCs in that they are not corporate bonds, and they are backed by leases to a number of airlines instead being tied to a single airline. The rating of aircraft ABS is based on the cash flow from their pool of aircraft leases or loans and the collateral value of that aircraft, not on the rating of lessee airlines.

One of the major characteristics that set aircraft ABS apart from other forms of aircraft financing is their diversification. ETCs and EETCs finance aircraft from a single airline. An aircraft ABS is usually backed by leases from a number of different airlines, located in a number of different countries and flying a variety of aircraft types. This diversification is a major attraction for investors. In essence, they are investing in a portfolio of airlines and aircraft types rather than a single airline— as in the case of an airline corporate bond. Diversification also is one of the main criteria that rating agencies look for in an aircraft securitization. The greater the diversification, the higher the credit rating, all else being equal.

Aircraft Leasing

Although there are various forms of financing that might appear in an aircraft ABS deal—including operating leases, financing leases, loans or mortgages—to date, the vast majority of the collateral in aircraft deals has been operating leases. In fact, all of the largest deals have been issued by aircraft leasing companies. This does not mean that a diversified finance company or an airline itself might not at some point bring a lease-backed or other aircraft ABS deal. It just means that so far, aircraft ABS have been mainly the province of leasing companies. Airlines, on the other hand, are active issuers of EETCs.

Aircraft leasing differs from general equipment leasing in that the useful life of an aircraft is much longer than most pieces of industrial or commercial equipment. In a typical equipment lease deal, cash flow from a particular lease on a particular piece of equipment only contributes to the ABS deal for the life of the lease. There is no assumption that the lease will be renewed. In aircraft leasing, the equipment usually has an original useful life of 20+ years, but leases run for only around 4–5 years. This means that the aircraft will have to be re-leased on expiration of the original leases. Hence, in the rating agencies' review, there's a great deal of focus on risks associated with re-leasing the aircraft.

The risk of being able to put the plane back out on an attractive lease can be broken down into three components: (1) the time it takes to re-lease the craft; (2) the lease rate; and (3) the lease term. Factors that can affect releasing include the general health of the economy, the health of the airline industry, obsolescence, and type of aircraft.

Servicing

Servicing is important in many ABS sectors, but it is crucial in a lease-backed aircraft deal, especially when the craft must be re-marketed when their lease terms expire before term on the aircraft ABS. It is the servicer's responsibility to re-lease the aircraft. To fulfill that function in a timely and efficient manner, the servicer must be both well-established and well-regarded by the industry.

As Moody's states, the servicer "should have a large and diverse presence in the global aircraft marketplace in terms of the number of aircraft controlled. Market share drives the ability of a servicer to meet aircraft market demand and deal with distressed airlines."

The servicer is also the key to maintaining value of the aircraft, through monitoring usage of the craft by lessees. If a lessee is not maintaining an aircraft properly, it is the servicer's responsibility to correct that situation. Because of servicers' vital role to the securitization, the rating agencies spend a great deal of effort ascertaining how well a servicer is likely to perform.

Defaults

In addition to the risk from needing to re-lease craft, rating agencies are also concerned about possible defaults. Because of protections under Section 1110 of the U.S. Bankruptcy Code, and international statutes that favor aircraft creditors, there is relatively little risk of losing an aircraft. There are, however, repossession costs, plus the loss of revenues during the time it takes to repossess and restore the aircraft to generating lease income.

The rating agencies will "stress" an aircraft financing by assuming a default rate, a period of time and cost for repossessing the aircraft. A major input into base default assumptions is the credit rating of airline lessees. For this part of the review, the ABS rating analyst relies on the corporate rating of the airline.

While there is little risk of not recovering the aircraft in event of a default, the rating agencies do carefully review the legal and political risks that the aircraft may be exposed to, and evaluate the ease with which the aircraft can be repossessed in the event of a default, especially if any of the lessees are in developing countries.

Enhancement Levels

In aircraft ABS, as in every other ABS sector, the rating agencies attempt to set enhancement levels that are consistent across asset types. That is, the risk of not receiving interest or principal in a aircraft deal rated a particular credit level should be the same as in a credit card or home equity deal (or, for that matter, even for a corporate bond) of the same rating. The total enhancement ranges from 34% to 47%.

Since the early deals, there has been a change in enhancement levels. Early deals depended largely on the sale of aircraft to meet principal payments on the bonds. Since then, the aircraft ABS relied more on lease revenue. Since lease revenue is more robust than sales revenue, the enhancement levels have declined. To understand why a "sales" deal requires more enhancement than a "lease" deal, consider the following. If an aircraft is sold during a recession, the deal suffers that entire decline in market value. On the other hand, if a lease rate declines during a recession, the deal sustains only the loss on the re-lease rate.

FRANCHISE-LOAN BACKED SECURITIES

Franchise loan securities are a hybrid between the commercial mortgage-backed securities (CMBS) and ABS markets. They are often backed by real estate, as in CMBS, but the deal structures are more akin to ABS. Also, franchise loans resemble Small Business Administration (SBA) loans and CDOs more than they do consumer loan-backed ABS securities. Greater reliance is placed on examining each franchise loan within the pool than on using aggregate statistics. In a pool of 100–200 loans (typical franchise loan group sizing) each loan is significant. By contrast within the consumer sector, any individual loan from a pool of 10,000 loans (as in home equity deals) does not represent as large a percentage, thus is not considered quite as important.

Franchise loans are similar to SBA loans in average size, maturity and end use. But whereas most SBA loans are floating rate loans indexed to the prime rate, most securitized franchise loans are fixed rate; if they are floating, they are likely to be LIBOR-linked. Franchise loans are used to fund working capital, expansion, acquisitions and renovation of existing franchise facilities.

The typical securitized deal borrower owns a large number of units, as opposed to being a small individual owner of a single franchise unit. However, individual loans are usually made on a single unit, secured either by the real estate, the building, or the equipment in the franchise.

The consolidation within the industry and the emergence of large operators of numerous franchise units has improved industry credit performance. A company owning 10 to 100 units is in a better position to weather a financial setback than is the owner of a single franchise location.

Loans can also be either fixed- or floating-rate, and are typically closed-end, fully amortizing with maturities of 7–20 years. If secured by equipment, maturities range from 7–10 years. If they are secured by real estate, maturities usually extend 15–20 years. Interest rates ranges from 8–11%, depending on maturity and risk parameters.

Security Characteristics

Because franchise loan collateral is relatively new to the ABS market, and deal size is small, most of these securitized packages have been issued as a 144a. Issuers also prefer the 144a execution for competitive reasons, because they are reluctant to publicly disclose details of their transactions.

Deals typically range from $100–$300 million, and are customarily backed by 150 to 200 loans. Average loan size is around $500,000, while individuals loans may range from $15,000–$2,000,000.

Most deals are structured as sequential-pay bonds with a senior/subordinate credit enhancement. Prepayments can occur if a franchise unit closes or is acquired by another franchisor. However, few prepayments have been experienced within securitized deals as of this writing, and most loans carry steep prepayment penalties that effectively discourage rate refinancing. Those penalties often equal 1% of the original balance of the loan.

Major Sectors

The vast majority of franchise operations consist of three types of retail establishments: restaurants, specialty retail stores (e.g., convenience stores, Blockbusters, 7-11s, Jiffy Lube, and Meineke Muffler), and retail energy outlets (e.g., Texaco and Shell). The restaurant category has three major subsectors: quick-service restaurants (e.g., McDonald's, Burger King, Wendy's, and Pizza Hut), casual restaurants (e.g., T.G.I. Fridays, Red Lobster, and Don Pablo's), and family restaurants (e.g., Denny's, Perkins, and Friendly's).

A "concept" is simply another name for a particular franchise idea, since each franchise seeks to differentiate itself from its competitors. Hence, even though Burger King and Wendy's are both QSRs specializing in sandwiches, their menu and style of service are sufficiently different that each has its own business/marketing plan—or "concept." For example, Wendy's has long promoted the "fresh" market, because the firm mandated fresh (not frozen) beef patties in their hamburgers, and helped pioneer the industry's salad bars. Burger King is noted for its "flame broiled" burgers, and doing it "your way."

In addition to segmenting the industry by functional types, it is also segmented by credit grades. For example, Fitch developed a credit tiering system based on expected recoveries of defaulted loans. Tier I concepts have a much lower expected default level than Tier II concepts, and so on. Many financial and operational variables go into these tiered ratings, including number of outlets nationwide (larger, successful concepts benefit from better exposure, national advertising, and the like); concept "seasoning" (especially if it has weathered a recession); and viability in today's competitive environment. (Yesterday's darlings may have become over saturated, or unable to respond to changing tastes or trends by revamping and updating!)

Risk Considerations

There are several risk factors to be aware of when comparing franchise loan pools, and the following are some of the most important.

Number of Loans/Average Size

High concentrations of larger loans represent increased risk, just as in any other pool of securitized loans.

Loan-to-Value Ratio

LTVs can be based on either real estate or business values. It is important to determine which is being used in a particular deal in order to make a valid comparison with other franchise issues. Note that when business value is used to compute LTV, it is common for a nationally recognized accounting firm to provide the valuation estimate.

Fixed Charge Coverage Ratio

The fixed charge coverage ratio (FCCR) is calculated as follows:

$$FCCR = \frac{\text{Adjusted free cash flow less occupancy costs}}{\text{Occupancy costs plus debt service}}$$

Typical FCCRs range from 1.00–3.00, and average around 1.5. A deal with most unit FCCRs below 1.5 would be viewed as having greater risk than average, while one with most FCCRs above 1.5 would be perceived as having less risk than average.

Diversification

As in all ABS sectors, a primary risk factor is the degree of diversification. In a franchise loan deal important areas for diversification include franchise owner, concept and location.

A typical franchise pool includes loans to 10–15 franchisees, each having taken out loans on 5–20 individual units. A large concentration of loans to any single franchise operator might increase deal risk. However, such concentration is sometimes allowed, and rating agencies will not penalize extensively if that particular franchisee has a very strong record and the individual franchise units have strong financials. It might even be better to have a high concentration of high-quality loans than a more diverse pool of weaker credits.

Concept diversification is also important. Franchise loans extend for 10–20 years, and a profitable concept today may become unprofitable as the loans mature.

It is not as important that pooled loans include representation across several major sectors (such as more than one restaurant subsector, or loans from all three major groups). Many finance companies specialize in one or two segments of the industry, and know their area well. Thus a deal from only one of the major sectors does not add any measurable risk as long as there is diversification by franchisee and concept.

Geographical diversification is also important, as it reduces risk associated with regional economic recessions.

Control of Collateral

A key factor in the event of borrower (franchisee) default is control of the collateral. If a franchise loan is secured by a fee simple mortgage, the lender controls disposition of collateral in a bankruptcy. However, if that collateral is a leasehold interest (especially if the lessor is a third party and not the franchisor), the lender may not be able to control disposition in the event of default.

RATE REDUCTION BONDS

The concept of *rate reduction bonds* (RRBs)—also known as *stranded costs* or *stranded assets*—grew out of the movement to deregulate the electric utility industry and bring about a competitive market environment for electric power. Deregulating the electric utility market was complicated by large amounts of "stranded assets" already on the books of many electric utilities. These stranded assets were commitments that had been undertaken by utilities at an earlier time with the understanding that they would be recoverable in utility rates to be approved by the states' utility commissions. However, in a competitive environment for electricity, these assets would likely become uneconomic, and utilities would no longer be assured that they could charge a high enough rate to recover the costs. To compensate investors of these utilities, a special tariff was proposed. This tariff, which would be collected over a specified period of time, would allow the utility to recover its stranded costs.

This tariff, which is commonly known as the *competitive transition charge* (or CTC), is created through legislation. State legislatures allow utilities to levy a fee, which is collected from its customers. Although there is an incremental fee to the consumer, the presumed benefit is that the utility can charge a lower rate as a result of deregulation. This reduction in rates would more than offset the competitive transition charge. In order to facilitate the securitization of these fees, legislation typically designates the revenue stream from these fees as a statutory property right. These rights may be sold to an SPV, which may then issue securities backed by future cash flows from the tariff.

The result is a structured security similar in many ways to other ABS products, but different in one critical aspect: The underlying asset in a RRB deal is created by legislation, which is not the case for other ABS products.

In the first quarter of 2001 there was a good deal of concern regarding RRBs. The sector came under intense scrutiny as a result of the financial problems experienced by California's major utilities. Yet despite the bankruptcy motion filed by Pacific Gas and Electric (PG&E) in 2001—a bellwether issuer of RRBs—rating agencies maintained their triple-A ratings on California's existing RRB issues. This is not the first time the RRB sector had found itself in turmoil. Over much of 1998, the sector was roiled by a movement in California to overturn the existing legislation that had been created specifically for RRB securitization. This put existing RRB issues in jeopardy. However, the ultimate result—a voter initiative was defeated—proved to be positive for this product. The ability of this asset class to retain its rating despite a significant credit crisis at an underlying utility, as well as a serious challenge to the legislation that allows for the creation of these securities, speaks volumes for the soundness of the structures of RRB deals.

Structure

As noted above, state regulatory authorities and/or state legislatures must take the first step in creating RRB issues. State regulatory commissions decide how much, if any, of a specific utility's stranded assets will be recaptured via securitization. They will also decide upon an acceptable time frame and collection formula to be used to calculate the tariff (the CTC). When this legislation is finalized, the utility is free to proceed with the securitization process.

The basic structure of an RRB issue is straightforward. The utility sells its rights to future CTC cash flows to an SPV created for the sole purpose of purchasing these assets and issuing debt to finance this purchase. In most cases, the utility itself will act as the servicer since it collects the CTC payment from its customer base along with the typical electric utility bill. Upon issuance, the utility receives the proceeds of the securitization (less the fees associated with issuing a deal), effectively reimbursing the utility for its stranded costs immediately.

RRBs usually have a "true-up" mechanism. This mechanism allows the utility to recalculate the CTC on a periodic basis over the term of the deal. Because the CTC is initially calculated based on projections of utility usage and the ability of the servicer to collect revenues, actual collection experience may differ from initial projections. In most cases, the utility can reexamine actual collections, and if the variance is large enough (generally a 2% difference), the utility will be allowed to revise the CTC charge. This true-up mechanism provides cash flow stability as well as credit enhancement to the bondholder.

Enhancement Levels

Credit enhancement levels required by the rating agencies for RRB deals are very low relative to other ABS asset classes. Although exact amounts and forms of credit enhancement may vary by deal, most transactions require little credit enhancement because the underlying asset (the CTC) is a statutory asset and is not directly affected by economic factors or other exogenous variables. Furthermore, the true-up mechanism virtually assures cash-flow stability to the bondholder.

As an example, the Detroit Edison Securitization Funding 1 issued in March 2001 was structured with 0.50% initial cash enhancement (funded at closing) and 0.50% overcollateralization (to be funded in equal semi-annual increments over the terms of the transactions). This total of 1% credit enhancement is minuscule in comparison to credit cards, for example, which typically require credit enhancement in the 12–15% range for large bank issuers.

Unique Risks

RRBs are subject to risks that are very different from those associated with more traditional structured products (e.g., credit cards, HELs, and so on). For example, risks involving underwriting standards do not exist in the RRB sector, since the underlying asset is an artificial construct. Underwriting standards are a critical factor in evaluating the credit of most other ABS. Also, factors that tend to affect the credit-worthiness of many other ABS products—such as levels of consumer credit or the economic environment—generally do not have a direct effect RRBs. Instead, other unique factors that must be considered when evaluating this sector. The most critical risks revolve around the legislative process and environment plus the long-term ability of the trust to collect future revenues to support the security's cash flows.

CHAPTER 5

Structured Finance Cash Flow CDOs

The collateral pool for structured finance (SF) cash flow CDO deals have used almost the entire spectrum of structured finance products in the market reviewed in the previous chapter. Within the mortgage-related sector, cash flow CDO deals have used a combination of BBB rated residential mortgage-backed securities (RMBS), commercial mortgage-backed securities (CMBS), and real estate investment trust (REIT) debt. There are no cash flow mortgage deals to date that employ more than 33% RMBS assets. Most of the assets used for these deals are BBB rated CMBS, REIT debt, or asset-backed securities (ABS). The decision as to which types of products to include is based on several considerations, but spreads play a key role as one would expect. Another key factor is the asset manager's expectation as to the future performance of a sector of the ABS/MBS market.

The first CDO that contained structured finance debt tranches came out in 1995. This premier issuance, as well as most SF CDOs over the next four years, was an arbitrage-purpose, market value structure that issued commercial paper backed by short-term RMBS. But SF CDOs became much more diversified in 1998. That year saw the first cash

---

This chapter was coauthored with Douglas Lucas and Tom Zimmerman of UBS Warburg.

flow structure, the first use of ABS and CMBS as collateral, the first balance sheet transaction, and the first use of a credit default swap referencing structured finance assets.

In 2001, about $16 billion of structured finance debt resecuritized in CDOs was issued. That brought total issuance over for the years 1995–2001 years to $54 billion. Almost all of 2001 of SF CDOs were done with cash collateral (as opposed to credit default swaps), used U.S. collateral, and were done for arbitrage purposes. Significantly, as of the first quarter of 2002, no SF CDO tranche has been downgraded or put on watch for downgrade (although some tranches were under pressure at that time). So SF CDO performance has established itself quite positively relative to other CDO categories.

In this chapter, we look at these SF CDO structures. Many investors consider SF cash flow CDOs to be a very different animal from high-yield cash flow CDOs. In fact, however, current cash flow deals utilizing structured finance assets are quite similar to those using high-yield assets. In this chapter we learn the similarities and differences between cash flow deals backed by structured finance assets versus those supported by high-yield corporate assets. We then look at the relative credit quality of structured finance debt versus corporate debt as CDO collateral. By using the same criteria to rate all types of CDOs, it will be shown that the rating agencies impose an extra burden on those backed by structured finance collateral. As a result, the ratings are conservative and offer investors relative value. Finally, we look at a few structuring issues.

SF CDOS VERSUS HIGH-YIELD CDOS

There are many similarities between the cash flow CDOs backed by structured financial assets and those backed by high-yield assets. The reasons are:

1. They are structured similarly
2. The rating methodology is similar

3. Both share similar protections via overcollateralization and interest coverage tests

However, there are minor differences that generally stem from the fact that the credit quality of a SF CDO is much higher than in a high-yield CDO, which permits lower equity levels in SF CDO structures. The two effects should offset, theoretically producing similar expected losses at each rating level.

Deal Structure

In a cash flow CDO, ability to service the rated notes is based on the interest and principal cash flows of portfolio assets. Both high-yield and SF CDO deals typically have a 5- to 10-year average life, and an 8- to 14-year expected maturity.

One small difference is that SF deals tend to have very long legal final maturities compared to high-yield deals. The legal final reflects the underlying legal final of the last cash flow in the portfolio. For example, the manager of a SF cash flow CDO deal done in mid-2002, with a 5-year revolving period, must be able to purchase a 30-year structured finance product at the end of the revolving period. That creates a 2037 legal final. By contrast, in a high-yield deal the longest securities that can be purchased are 12 to 14 years. This will be discussed further in this chapter when we look at extension risk.

Liability structure is very similar in all cash flow deals, regardless of the underlying assets. It consists of senior notes, mezzanine notes, and equity. If the underlying assets are fixed and the liabilities are floating, interest rate swaps are used in both cases. One major difference is that credit quality (average rating) of the structured finance assets tends to be considerably higher, which allows less equity in SF CDO structures than in high-yield CD structures.

For example, a typical 100% high-yield deal will have an average rating of B1 to B2, and equity will average 13–15% of the deal amount. By contrast, a typical ABS/MBS deal will have average credit quality of Baa2 or Baa3, with equity averaging only 4–6% of the deal. This is shown in Exhibit 5.1.

EXHIBIT 5.1   Liability Structure of Cash Flow Deals

	High-Yield Bond Deal	High-Yield Loan Deal	SF Deal
Aaa	73–75	75–80	78–83
Mezzanine	10–14	10–15	13–16
Equity	13–15	8–10	4–6

It is interesting to note that while equity is much lower in the SF CDO deals, the Aaa rated bonds constitute a very similar percentage of both types of deals. In a 100% high-yield bond deal containing Aaa, Baa, and unrated tranches, Aaa rated bonds will constitute 73–75% of the deal, equity will be 13–15%, with the remainder in Baa rated bonds. In a high-yield loan deal, Aaa rated bonds will be 75–80% of the deal, Baa rated bonds 10–15%, and equity 8–10%. In a ABS/MBS deal, Aaa rated bonds will be 78–83%, equity will be 5%, and mezzanine bonds will represent the remainder. SF CDO deals typically have a number of mezzanine tranches, including a sizeable Aa rated tranche.

Another consequence of the higher credit quality on the SF CDO is that overcollateralization and interest coverage tests on the SF CDO are lower than on the high-yield deals. For example, in SF CDO deals, subordinate overcollateralization triggers are in the range of 100–105, much lower than the 105–112 on CDOs backed by high-yield bonds. Again, this is a natural consequence of the higher quality of the underlying collateral and the lower equity requirements.

RELATIVE CREDIT QUALITY: STRUCTURED FINANCE DEBT VERSUS CORPORATE DEBT

Compared to corporate bond default studies, those in the structured finance default arena have been pretty feeble. Defaults among corporate obligations have been studied for over 40 years and these studies are reviewed in Chapter 3. They started with the auspicious, and now classic, W. Braddock Hickman study (published in 1958) of pre-World War II defaults. Beginning in 1985, Edward Altman of New York University created annual corporate bond default studies. In 1997, Moody's expanded its database to include corporate defaults retroactive to 1919, and that rating agency now banks data on the default histories of 16,000 corporate issuers.

By contrast, the structured finance market cannot provide such a rich or lengthy history of default experience, since the market only began in the mid-1980s. The quality of structured finance default data is also hampered by differences between the structured and corporate debt markets.

In *corporate default* studies, the unit of study is usually an *issuer.* The simplifying assumption made in corporate studies is that if an issuer defaults, all of that issuer's other obligations will also default. That assumption is not too big a reach, as real life corporate defaults almost always turn out that way. So in tracking defaults over time, corporate default researchers keep track of debt *issuers*, not individual debt *issues*. The advantage of such an approach is that as particular issues mature or are called, a corporate issuer almost always has other debt outstanding, which helps provide a continuous history of performance and rating at the issuer level.

In contrast, interest about default and default rates in the *structured finance* market is at the *tranche* level. And different tranches of the same special purpose vehicle are specifically designed to go into default at separate points in time or upon separate sets of events. For this reason we are interested in the default performance of, and the default rates of, for example, triple-A tranches versus single-B tranches, even if they are issues of the same special purpose vehicle.

This major difference between corporate defaults and structured finance defaults will hamper an analysis of relative credit quality between the two (but we will do our best). First, we will examine the structured finance default data that does exist and try to relate it to corporate bond default studies. Then, as a measure of credit quality volatility, we will look at structured finance rating transition studies and compare them to corporate bond rating transition studies.

Lifetime Approach to Structured Default Rates

Fitch took what could be called a "lifetime approach" to the problem. This rating agency examined all the structured finance debt they had rated from 1989 to mid-2000. It identified the dollar amount of defaulted debt through 2000 and compared it to the total dollar amount of structured finance debt.[1] Fitch's calculated ratios are shown in Exhibit 5.2

In an article on structured finance recoveries, S&P provided the necessary data for computing lifetime default statistics on the basis of the number of S&P rated tranches.[2] The statistics we derived from S&P's report are shown in Exhibit 5.3.

EXHIBIT 5.2 Fitch Structured Finance Lifetime Default Rates (By Dollar Amount)

ABS	0.07%
RMBS	0.02%
CMBS	0.04%
All structured finance	0.05%

EXHIBIT 5.3 S&P Structured Finance Lifetime Default Rates (By Number of Tranches)

ABS	0.37%
RMBS	1.30%
CMBS	0.71%
All structured finance	0.86%

---

[1] David R. Howard, *et al.*, "Structured Finance Default Study," Fitch IBCA, Duff & Phelps (1/8/2001).
[2] Joseph Hu, *et al.*, "Life After Death: Recoveries of Defaulted U.S. Structured Finance Securities," Standard & Poor's (September 4, 2001).

The difference in results for comparable asset classes between the two exhibits is eye-catching, as the S&P lifetime default rates are so many times higher than the Fitch rates. Part of that discrepancy may be due to the longer time periods included in S&P's report. Data in the Fitch study only began in 1989, while S&P's extended back to 1985 for ABS and CBMS and 1978 for RMBS. It might also be the case that S&P had rated more lower-quality tranches (and presumably more lower-rated tranches) than did Fitch.

It is most likely, however, that the difference between Fitch's dollar-weight statistics and S&P's tranche-weighted statistics is due to the fact that highly rated senior tranches tend to be many times the dollar size of lower rated junior tranches. Thus, Fitch more heavily weights the large dollar size senior tranches, while S&P-derived statistics more heavily weight smaller but numerous junior tranches.

Challenges in Applying Lifetime Default Statistics

Neither set of lifetime default statistics can be interpreted as default rates over a specific period of time (e.g., a 1-year default rate or a 5-year default rate). For example, structured finance deals rated by Fitch in 1989 and the early 1990s have probably matured already. But their inclusion in the statistics contributes a default rate over the entire life of those deals. In theory, Fitch-rated structured debt issued in 1989 had up to 12 years of performance history. So those tranches could contribute a 12-year default rate to Exhibit 5.2.

But structured finance deals rated by the agencies in 2000 provide only a few months of history. Since the quantity of structured finance tranches rated each year by Fitch and S&P has grown over time, we can assume that the default rates in Exhibits 5.2 and 5.3 are skewed toward recent issues and shorter-term histories. We do not exactly know the average maturity or experience of the structured finance tranches included in Exhibits 5.2 and 5.3. A good guess is four to seven years.

EXHIBIT 5.4   Investment Grade Corporate Default Rates

	One Year	Two Years	Five Years
Moody's	1.08%	2.23%	5.26%
S&P	1.38%	2.75%	6.20%

The other item of interest hidden in these statistics is the variability of default rates by rating category. We would expect higher rated structured finance tranches to have a lower default rate than lower rated tranches. We would expect triple-A and double-A default rates to be near zero. These tranches also make up the majority of structured finance debt structures. But combining highly rated tranches with lower-rated tranches obscures the individual characteristics of tranches.

To compare the Fitch dollar-weighted structured statistics to corporate bond defaults, some penalizing assumptions have been made about the structured finance statistics. First, even though there is some dollar amount of speculative grade tranches incorporated in Fitch's statistics ratings, we can compare them to investment grade corporate defaults. Second, the average time incorporated in the structured statistics was very short. In Exhibit 5.4, investment grade corporate default rates are shown for selected short maturities.[3]

Note that most of Fitch's structured default rates in Exhibit 5.2 are smaller than the 1-year investment grade corporate default rates from either S&P or Moody's. And all of Fitch's structured default rates are smaller than the 2-year investment grade corporate default rates. By contrast, Moody's and S&P's 5-year (a much more realistic estimation of the average structured tenor in the Fitch data) corporate default rates are respectively a whopping 16 and 18 times higher than the structured default rate.

---

[3] Brooks Brady and Roger J. Bos, "Record Defaults in 2001 the Result of Poor Credit Quality and a Weak Economy," Standard and Poor's (February 2002); and David T. Hamilton, Greg Gupton, and Alexandra Berthault, "Default and Recovery Rates of Corporate Bond Issuers: 2000," Moody's Investors Service (February 2001).

EXHIBIT 5.5   75% Investment Grade /25% Speculative Grade
Corporate Default Rates

	One Year	Two Years	Five Years
Moody's	0.05%	0.17%	0.82%
S&P	0.10%	0.24%	0.91%

To compare the S&P-derived structured default rates in Exhibit 5.3 to corporate default rates, the higher weighting of speculative grade tranches in S&P's data had to be considered. The ratio of speculative grade to investment grade tranches in the data was then conservatively estimated at 1:3. So, in Exhibit 5.5, that was paralleled with blended weighting of 75% investment grade and 25% speculative grade corporate default rates.

Note that every default rate derived from S&P data in Exhibit 5.3 is smaller than the 1-year corporate default rates.

S&P Ratings Lifetime Default Method

S&P also provides lifetime default statistics by rating grade for ABS and CMBS debt tranches.[4] Again, S&P's default rates are calculated on the basis of number of tranches as opposed to Fitch's dollar amount method. But while these S&P statistics still suffer from the problem of combining tranches with different tenors, they do control for rating. In Exhibit 5.6 the lifetime structured finance default rates are presented alongside 5- and 7-year corporate default rates.

Note that the lifetime structured finance default rates are, with one exception, all smaller than the 7-year corporate default rates. And with two exceptions, they are all smaller than the 5-year corporate default rates. The difference is often significant, especially for the BBB and lower ratings.

---

[4] Joseph Hu, *et al.*, "Rating Transition 2001: U.S. ABS Credit Ratings Endure the Test of Recession," Standard & Poor's (January 14, 2001); and Peter P. Kozel and Roy Chun, "Rating Transition 2001: CMBS Continues to Show Strong Credit Performance," Standard & Poor's (January 29, 2002).

EXHIBIT 5.6   S&P Default Rates

Rating	ABS Lifetime	CMBS Lifetime	Corporate 5 Year	Corporate 7 Year
AAA	0.00%	0.00%	0.11%	0.31%
AA	0.00%	0.67%	0.26%	0.56%
A	0.83%	0.59%	0.64%	1.08%
BBB	0.96%	0.00%	2.26%	3.67%
BB	2.28%	0.82%	11.90%	16.79%
B	3.79%	2.42%	29.12%	34.58%

EXHIBIT 5.7   Annual Default Rates

Rating	CMBS	Moody's Corporate	S&P Corporate
Investment grade	0.06%	0.05%	0.10%
Speculative grade	0.14%	4.15%	5.20%

All Rating Agency CMBS Lifetime Default Rates

Fitch has also computed 1-year CMBS default rates by dollar amount for investment grade and speculative grade issues.[5] CMBS issues are divided into investment grade or speculative grade categories based on their lowest rating agency rating. While the study does not take into account differences in the distribution of ratings within the broad investment grade and speculative grade categories, CMBS compares favorably with annual corporate default rates, as shown in Exhibit 5.7.

Structured Finance Rating Transitions

S&P provide 1-year rating transition matrices for their ABS, CMBS, and RMBS ratings.[6] These allow us to examine *short-term ratings volatility*, and, by proxy, *short-term credit*

---

[5] Diane M. Lans and Janet G. Price, "Comparing CMBS and Corporate Bond Defaults," Fitch IBCA, Duff & Phelps (November 17, 2000).

[6] Hu, *et al.*, "Rating Transition 2001: U.S. ABS Credit Ratings Endure the Test of Recession;" Hu, *et al.*, "Rating Transition 2001: U.S. RMBS Credit Ratings Show Continued Resiliency;" and, Kozel and Chun, "Rating Transition 2001: CMBS Continues to Show Strong Credit Performance."

quality volatility. We can then compare these results to those of corporate bonds.

In Exhibits 5.8, 5.9, and 5.10, S&P 1-year transition matrices for ABS, CMBS, and RMBS are shown side-by-side with their corporate 1-year transition matrix. In all cases, there are significantly fewer structured finance downgrades than corporate downgrades. The highest downgrade rate for any of the three types of structured finance transactions in any investment grade rating category is 5.3%. The lowest downgrade rate for corporate credits in any investment grade rating category is 10.5%. That makes for a big difference in downgrade experience and performance!

We conclude that corporate credits are a lot more volatile than structured finance credits, as measured by their ratings volatility. Also, rating downgrades can be seen as a very sensitive measure of credit deterioration and default risk. In some ways, investment grade rating downgrades are actually more reliable than default rates, because the rarity of defaults limits the pool of data and thus makes default statistics unreliable.

EXHIBIT 5.8 S&P One-Year Rating Transition Matrix—ABS

Rating	ABS			Corporates		
	Up	Stable	Down	Up	Stable	Down
AAA	0.0%	99.7%	0.3%	0.0%	93.3%	6.7%
AA	1.6%	96.1%	2.3%	0.6%	91.6%	7.7%
A	1.1%	96.0%	3.0%	2.3%	91.8%	6.0%
BBB	2.2%	92.6%	5.3%	4.9%	89.4%	5.7%

EXHIBIT 5.9 S&P One-Year Rating Transition Matrix—CMBS

Rating	CMBS			Corporates		
	Up	Stable	Down	Up	Stable	Down
AAA	0.0%	99.3%	0.7%	0.0%	93.3%	6.7%
AA	3.0%	95.9%	1.1%	0.6%	91.6%	7.7%
A	3.8%	94.9%	1.3%	2.3%	91.8%	6.0%
BBB	3.7%	93.7%	2.6%	4.9%	89.4%	5.7%

EXHIBIT 5.10   S&P One-Year Rating Transition Matrix—RMBS

	RMBS			Corporates		
Rating	Up	Stable	Down	Up	Stable	Down
AAA	0.0%	99.8%	0.2%	0.0%	93.3%	6.7%
AA	6.4%	91.4%	2.2%	0.6%	91.6%	7.7%
A	7.5%	90.3%	2.2%	2.3%	91.8%	6.0%
BBB	7.5%	89.0%	3.5%	4.9%	89.4%	5.7%

EXHIBIT 5.11   Moody's One-Year Rating Transition Matrix

	Corporates			ABS		
Rating	Up	Stable	Down	Up	Stable	Down
Aaa	0.0%	99.7%	0.3%	0.0%	90.6%	9.4%
Aa1	3.0%	88.8%	8.3%	2.8%	80.4%	16.8%
Aa2	2.2%	95.9%	2.0%	3.7%	81.1%	15.2%
Aa3	2.4%	94.2%	3.5%	3.5%	81.9%	14.6%
A1	10.4%	88.2%	1.5%	5.6%	81.5%	12.9%
A2	4.8%	95.0%	0.8%	6.1%	81.0%	12.9%
A3	2.5%	93.6%	3.9%	9.8%	76.3%	13.9%
Baa1	2.0%	88.6%	9.4%	10.5%	75.6%	13.9%
Baa2	1.0%	95.3%	3.7%	11.4%	76.4%	12.2%
Baa3	1.7%	87.0%	11.3%	14.7%	71.6%	13.7%

Moody's Transition Matrix

Moody's provides a 1-year ABS transition matrix specific to the 1s, 2s, and 3s the rating agency uses to modify their letter rating categories.[7] In the same article, Moody's provides a corporate bond transition matrix, averaged from 1986 through 2001 (the same time period as the ABS matrix). As shown in Exhibit 5.11, Moody's results echo those of S&P. The instances of investment grade ABS tranche downgrade ranged from 0.3 to 11.3%, while those of corporate debt downgrades ranged from 9.4% to 16.8%.

---

[7] Julia Tung, "Rating Changes in the U.S. Asset-Backed Securities Market: 2001 Transition Matrix Update," Moody's Investors Service (January 25, 2002).

Again, we conclude that corporate credit is a lot more volatile than structured finance credit, and that rating downgrades are a reliable way of measuring credit risk among investment grade assets.

Default Severity

Defaulted corporate bonds have a wide distribution of recoveries, but historically their loss upon default has averaged about 72% of par. Defaulted structured finance tranches, however, should exhibit much higher rates of recovery and lower loss rates because they are backed by a portfolio of underlying assets.

Suppose, for example, that a structured finance vehicle holds 500 individual consumer loans of some particular type. An investment grade tranche issued by the structured finance vehicle might itself default if 100 of the underlying consumer loans defaulted. At that point, the severity of the default might be such that the investment grade tranche would experience a small diminution of IRR.

However, there is probably a greater chance of 100 of the underlying consumer loans defaulting than of 101 loans defaulting. Higher defaults among an underlying consumer loan portfolio become more and more unlikely. So, for the investment grade tranche, there is a greater chance of losing a little than of losing a lot. That's directly opposite the documented experience of corporate bonds in default.

The scant empirical work on structured finance tranche losses in the event of default bears out our theory. Compared to the 72% loss for corporate bonds, defaulted ABS tranches have historically lost 71%, defaulted RMBS tranches 39%, and defaulted CMBS tranches 34%. Those heavy losses among ABS tranches, which nearly equal the corporate bond loss rate, are driven by instances of fraud in credit card-backed ABS. Without such human-augmented defaults, losses upon default for ABS shrink to 39%. So in general, losses in the event of default for structured finance tranches have been half that of corporate bonds.

RATING AGENCIES ON STRUCTURED FINANCE CDOs

The rating agency approach to the credit quality of collateral in SF CDOs has been more pessimistic than the default studies reviewed above. Moody's notes that "unlike corporate bonds, defaults for structured securities have been rare." However, the rating agencies worry that this phenomena is due to the relatively short history of structured finance rather than to any intrinsic difference in the credit quality of structured finance tranches. In any event, the rating agencies treat SF CDO collateral like equally rated corporate debt with respect to credit quality.[8]

Perhaps this conservatism is due to the short history of the structured finance market. However, we must also realize that the rating agencies seek to present their ratings as common measures of credit quality across the corporate, public, sovereign, structured finance debt markets, and even across different jurisdictions around the world. They could not market their opinions that way if they admitted, for example, that a structured single-A had the same credit quality as a corporate triple-A.

In any event, Moody's treats structured finance collateral as if it had the same combination of default probability and default severity potential as corporate debt. This means that SF CDO tranches benefit from the same protective credit enhancement requirements that are demanded on corporate debt collateral that has historically had higher default rates and greater default severity.

As we shall see, the rating agencies also tend to treat SF CDOs conservatively with respect to the assessment of their *collateral diversity* and response to *collateral distress*.

---

[8] Jeremy Gluck and Helen Remeza, "Moody's Approach to Rating Multisector CDOs," Moody's Investors Service (September 15, 2000).

Collateral Diversity

The diversity of a CDO collateral pool is an important rating consideration and it bears directly on the amount of credit enhancement a CDO tranche must have to achieve a particular rating. Rating agency treatment of diversity in a SF CDO adds a conservative bias to their ratings of SF CDO tranches. Diversity refers to the *default correlation* of assets in the CDO's portfolio, or the propensity of CDO assets to default at the same time.

Suppose we know that each asset in a CDO's portfolio has a 10% probability of default over the lifetime of the CDO. Does that mean that exactly 10% of the portfolio will default, or does it mean that there is a 10% chance that 100% of the portfolio will default? In both scenarios, there is a 10% probability of default. But the first scenario illustrates extreme *negative* default correlation while the second displays extreme *positive* default correlation.

As seen by this example, positive default correlation creates wide swings in a portfolio's experienced default rate. In our example of extreme positive default correlation, 90% of the time no assets default and 10% of the time all assets default. The credit quality and rating consequences are obvious. If defaults are so correlated that 10% of the time the whole portfolio defaults, then credit enhancement will have to address the significant probability that the entire portfolio will default. At the other extreme, if defaults are so negatively correlated that 10% and only 10% of the portfolio will ever default, the CDO only has to protect against the 10% defaults that are bound to occur.

So in a rational rating world, CDO portfolios with high positive default correlation must have extra credit enhancement against their inbred potential for very high defaults. With respect to the diversity of SF CDOs, the rating agencies hold the view that defaults among structured finance tranches are *more* correlated than corporate defaults.

The magic and mysteries of default correlation, and the methods used by the rating agencies to assess it in SF CDO portfolios, are discussed in other chapters of this book. For our purposes here, it is important to understand that the typical Moody's diversity score (the method Moody's uses to quantify a portfolio's diversity) is usually a minimum of 40–50 for a corporate debt-backed portfolio. For a SF CDO, the diversity score is typically a minimum of 18–20.

The lower diversity score on SF CDOs raises the required credit enhancement, perhaps by as much as 40%. But typically the weighted average rating factor (WARF) for a SF CDO is lower (the average rating quality of the SF CDO assets is higher) than for a corporate investment grade bond-backed CDO. A SF CDO with a WARF of 400–500 might require 4% equity while an investment grade bond-backed CDO with a WARF of 600 might require only 3% equity. And, do not forget, the structured finance assets have higher credit spreads and historically lower default rates than corporate debt. The higher required equity comes from the rating agency's conservative view of structured finance diversity.

Underlying Collateral Distress

The identification of a collateral default in a SF CDO also adds a conservative feature to SF CDOs. Identifying a corporate debt default in a corporate debt-backed CDO is usually pretty straightforward. The issuer is typically in bankruptcy or has missed an interest or principal payment. When corporate debt defaults in a corporate debt-backed CDO, its par is taken out of overcollateralization tests and its coupon is taken out of interest coverage tests. This may cause the corporate-backed CDO to withhold cash flow from one or more subordinated tranches and instead pay down its most senior tranche. This protective measure lowers leverage and protects senior debt tranches.

Unlike corporate debt collateral, structured finance tranches are susceptible to being "written down" in part as well as in whole. This happens as losses have occurred in the underlying assets of the structured finance collateral pool and those losses are allocated to specific deal tranches. Such a written down tranche in a SF CDO would be penalized in the calculation of the SF CDO's overcollateralization and interest coverage tests. First, the written down portion of the tranche and its associate interest, are eliminated for the SF CDO's overcollateralization and interest coverage tests. But second, the unwritten down portion of the structured security is multiplied by the lower of market value or a conservative rating agency recovery assumption in the tests. Redirection of cash flow to the senior SF CDO tranche might then occur. This treatment is conservative because, unlike a defaulted corporate bond, the unwritten down structured finance tranche is still performing. The structured security might also be written back up over time because of the effects of excess spread in the structured finance transaction.

Timing of Credit Losses

Let's look at the disadvantage created by the rating agencies' assumptions regarding the timing of credit losses. Briefly, the rating agencies utilize a loss distribution curve more front-loaded than historical loss experience on structured finance collateral would suggest. Losses on ABS, RMBS, and CMBS bonds have different distributions than those on investment-grade and high-yield corporates. Yet, the same loss distribution tests are applied to all CDO collateral categories. And while the approach may be appropriate for high-yield and other types of CDOs, it certainly penalizes SF CDO transactions.

Moody's Approach

As explained in Chapter 2, Moody's approach to rating cash flow CDOs involves several steps. These include developing a diversity score; calculating a weighted average rating factor;

using the binomial distribution to determine the probability of a specific number of defaults; and finally, calculating the impact of those defaults on bonds within the CDO structure. One element needed to calculate that impact is a distribution of defaults and losses across time. It is this distribution defaults and losses that we are addressing.

Moody's stresses the tranches via the six different loss distributions shown in Exhibit 2.9 of Chapter 2, and a tranche must pass each test. The agency's basic approach assumes 50% of the losses will occur at a single point in time, and that remaining losses are evenly distributed over a 5-year period. This single 50% loss is assumed to occur at a different point in each of the six tests. For example, Test 1 assumes that the single 50% loss occurs at the beginning of the deal. Tests 1, 2, and 3 are the hardest for SF CDO structures to pass and for that reason really determine ratings on the CDO tranches. But, in fact, actual SF CDO losses are more akin to those set up in Tests 4 and 5. If these latter two tests were the toughest criteria used by the rating agency, then a lower cost structure could be used for the SF CDO tranches. The result might be that some receive a higher rating, since it is easier for an SF CDO tranche to pass Tests 4 and 5. A similar argument does not apply to corporate and high-yield CDOs; their losses are more front-loaded, and the general CDO rating approach (emphasizing diversity scores) is designed for those securities.

SF Collateral Default and Bond Loss Curves

We now show that typical loss curves for ABS and MBS collateral are less front-loaded than either high-yield losses or the losses assumed in Moody's loss distribution tests. To illustrate, Exhibit 5.12 shows default curves for four types of collateral found frequently in SF CDOs. (The appendix to this chapter provides a summary of how the default curves were derived.) This can be compared with the last column in Exhibit 5.12, which shows defaults on speculative-grade corporate bonds.

EXHIBIT 5.12 SF CDO Collateral Default and Loss Curves

Year	MH	Jumbo WL	CMBS	Home Equities	Avg. Collateral Defaults	Avg. Collateral Losses	BBB SF Bond Losses	Spec.-Grade Corp. Losses
1	7	5	3	3	4.5	0.0	0.0	13.2
2	19	14	9	12	13.5	4.5	0.0	13.5
3	22	20	13	23	19.5	13.5	4.5	12.7
4	19	18	14	25	19.0	19.5	13.5	11.5
5	13	15	14	15	14.3	19.0	19.5	10.6
6	9	11	15	10	11.3	14.3	19.0	9.2
7	5	8	13	8	8.5	11.3	14.3	8.1
8	3	5	8	4	5.0	8.5	11.3	7.6
9	3	3	7	0	3.3	5.0	8.5	6.7
10	0	1	4	0	1.3	3.3	5.0	6.8
Total	100	100	100	100	100.0	—	—	—

Defaults on mortgage-related collateral typically increase for several years, level off, and then decline. Peak defaults usually occur between Years 3 and 5. There are several reasons why there are few defaults in the first year or two. For example, in the residential sector, most homeowners cannot receive a loan unless they meet strict underwriting criteria. Once a homeowner passes that credit scrutiny, it typically takes a while for their financial position to deteriorate to the point where a default becomes a real possibility.

Also, when comparing loss curves in Exhibit 5.12, bear in mind that these only tell when losses occur, not their magnitudes. For example, in certain market environments, home equity deals can easily generate total losses of 4–5%, whereas jumbo whole loans produce losses of only 25–30 basis points. That is a ratio of 15 or 20 to 1. Of course, to offset those higher loss rates, home equity deals carry much greater credit enhancement in the form of excess spread, overcollateralization, and either subordinated bonds or monoline insurance.

As shown in Exhibit 5.12, defaults in the CMBS sector are distributed over a longer period than in residential loans, and peak defaults come a little later. The manufactured housing (MH) curve in Exhibit 5.12 is a little more front-loaded than other mortgage-related curves. Buyers of manufactured houses typically have less disposable income than site-built home buyers, and if financial difficulty (sickness, divorce, death, and the like) develops they are less able to maintain payments than the average homeowner. This means that manufactured housing losses occur somewhat faster than in other sectors.

We calculated an aggregate default curve from the individual curves presented in Exhibit 5.12. This involved taking a simple average of the four curves on the assumption that each type of collateral appears in CDO deals in roughly the same percentages. The resulting aggregate default curve is then converted into a loss curve by pushing each period's defaults forward one year.

In both the jumbo and home equity sectors, this is a good approximation of how long it takes to move a defaulted loan from foreclosure to liquidation. It admittedly can be longer in some states, and shorter in others. In the CMBS market, the time from default to liquidation can be longer than in the residential mortgage market (roughly 1.5–2 years). In contrast, in manufactured housing and some other sectors that are often included in ABS CDOs, default-to-liquidation periods are shorter than one year. Hence, using a one-year period for an overall average seems to be a good approximation. The collateral loss curve generated from this approach peaks in Years 4 and 5. The collateral default curve appears as column 5 in Exhibit 5.12 and the collateral loss curve appears as column 6.

Once a collateral loss curve is developed, the question remains of how these losses filter through into losses on the structured bonds. Excess spread, overcollateralization, and other subordinated bonds stand between collateral losses and the bonds that go into a CDO. This protective structuring clearly pushes the bond loss curve out further than the collateral loss curve.

Estimating a bond loss curve for each collateral type requires an enormous number of calculations across many scenarios. In lieu of doing this for the collateral types in our example, we illustrate by showing how long it would take a BBB home equity tranche to experience a loss of principal under various stress scenarios. We selected the BF1 (BBB) class from Saxon 2000–3. That deal had an original WAC of 11.36% and a WAM of 238 months. A loss curve is then used that would produce total cumulative losses of 4.5% over the life of the deal. This is in line with losses experienced on most home equity deals originated today. Collateral characteristics are quite similar to loans created over the several prior years at the time of the analysis, which, on average, have total losses trending towards the 4–5% level. We distributed the losses using the standard loss curve we use for stressing home equity bonds. This is a more conservative (i.e., more front-loaded) distribution than the one used in Exhibit 5.12.

The BBB bond did not get hit until losses reached 250% of the base loss curve (i.e., until cumulative losses reached 11.25%), and that initial hit did not occur until 53 months (4.4 years). Once the peak loss period was past, excess spread became positive again and the bond recovered its lost principal. When the loss curve was raised to 300% of the base loss curve (i.e., total cumulative losses reached 13.5%) the BBB bond was hit at 37 months (3.1 years). For a deal to experience losses three times the "normal" curve, the economy must experience an extreme recession. That is very low probability event.

This exercise suggests that actual bond losses, as opposed to collateral loses, extend from around three years out to five or six years, with very few losses occurring in years one or two.

While a full distribution of bond losses has not been developed here, we believe a conservative approach is to simply move the collateral loss curve in Exhibit 5.12 forward one year to represent a bond loss curve. This gives no bond losses in Years 1 and 2 and very few in Year 3, which agrees with our BBB bond example and our understanding of how infrequently structured BBB bonds experience problems in the first several years.[9]

SF ASSETS' NEGATIVE CONVEXITY

Thus far, we have talked about similarities in determining expected defaults among rating methodologies. There is still a nagging concern that we missed something. It is the property of negative convexity, which is potentially a problem for structured finance assets but not for high-yield assets. In most discussions of structured finance products, negative convexity is front and center.[10] Should investors in SF CDOs be concerned with negative convexity?

There is no reason for concern. The reason is that there are no SF cash flow deals to date that employ more than 33% residential MBS assets. As indicated at the outset of this chapter, most of the assets used for these deals are CMBS, ABS, or REIT debt. As explained when we reviewed CMBS in Chapter 4, these assets have excellent call protection, and most have yield maintenance provisions, which make investors whole in the event of early redemption. Similarly, REIT debt is typically either a noncall bullet security or call-protected by yield main-

---

[9] To further support this line of reasoning, we note that the rating agencies awarded BBB ratings to two-year home equity net interest margins (NIMs). That is, they are giving a BBB rating to the first two years of cash flow from an unrated stream of cash flows because collateral losses are statistically very low in the first years of the deal.

[10] In an option-free bond or a bond whose call option value has very little value, the price performance of a bond is such that for a large change in interest rates, the price appreciation is greater than the price depreciation. For example, for a 100 basis point change in interest rates, the price appreciation might be 20% while the price decline might be only 14%. A bond that exhibits this characteristic is said to exhibit "positive convexity." A bond that exhibits a characteristic whereby for a large change in interest rates the gain is less than the loss is said to be "negatively convex." A concern of an investor when acquiring a bond that exhibits negative convexity is that when interest rates decline, the price performance of that bond will be inferior to that of an otherwise similar duration bond that exhibits positive convexity.

tenance provisions. ABS backed by residential mortgages such as home equity loans and manufactured housing have much less negative convexity than residential mortgage paper.

Moreover, subordinated residential mortgage paper tends to have better call protection than does the underlying collateral. Subordinated mortgage paper typically has a 5-year lockout and a shifting interest structure for the next five years. This paper does not actually receive a pro-rata share of prepayments until Year 10.

Finally, investors should realize that high-yield bonds and loans backing CDOs do not have absolute call protection. High-yield bonds with a 10-year maturity typically have a lockout for 3–5 years, and then are callable at a premium, which declines over time. By Year 7, the paper is typically callable at par. Loans are generally floating rate, with little call protection. If spreads narrow, borrowers often refinance.

EXTENSION RISK

Extension risk often arises in discussing SF CDOs. SF CDOs might have a "legal final" maturity of 30 years but an "expected final" maturity of 10 or 12 years. The earlier maturity is based on the successful auction of assets in the SF CDO portfolio at the expected final date. If proceeds from the sale of SF CDO assets at the expected final date would not be enough to repay all outstanding debt tranches, no sale is made, the assets are retained, and the SF CDO continues on. Auctions are held every three to six months until aggregate bids on the SF CDO's assets are enough to retire all outstanding debt tranches.

Extension risk comes from the possibility that successive auctions fail to attract high enough bids. Even though almost all SF CDO tranches are floating-rate instruments, many investors have maturity restrictions or cash flow considerations, so they view any extension of their investment beyond the expected maturity as a bad thing.

Extension Risk in Perspective

So what are the chances an SF CDO will extend, and how bad can it be? We will base our observations on a hypothetical, but broadly characteristic, CDO. Suppose that two-thirds of a SF CDO portfolio is made up of assets that can extend and that SF CDO tranches are scheduled to mature at 10 years. Given very slow prepayment rates, where actual prepayments are half that of pricing prepayment speeds, and rating agency expected default rates on underlying assets, the AAA tranche might be paid down to 38% of its original balance at year 10. Given that the AAA tranche was originally 82% of the SF CDO's capital structure, over half of the CDO's debt tranche principal has been amortized.

The effect of this is to decrease equity's leverage in the transaction. Equity's share of the SF CDO's capital structure would double in this scenario from 4% to 8%. This would mean that the hurdle for retiring the SF CDO's debt tranches is an average asset price of 92%. Note that at this point, the remaining weighted average life of the SF CDO's assets is quite short, so it is more likely the auction is successful.

But if a clearing price is never reached on the serial auctions, the AAA tranche will still completely retire in 16 years under these assumptions. And its average life extends only one and a half years, from eight years to nine and a half years. Not that all investors would see extension as a bad thing. After the expected final maturity, if the auction fails to clear, SF CDO debt tranches coupons are often increased or "stepped up." Some triple-A tranches step up, often 50 basis points. Almost all subordinated tranches step up, usually by considerably more than 50 basis points.

Extension Risk versus Default Risk

Many investors confuse default risk and extension risk. It is clear that severely poor collateral performance will cause the SF CDO to fail its auction test and extend. But extension due to default is not a phenomena limited to SF CDOs.

Any security, whether a corporate bond or loan or corporate debt-backed CDO, will probably extend if it defaults. In the corporate debt world, a default often involves a debt restructuring, which leads to the issuance of a replacement security that might incorporate a lower coupon, lower par, and a longer maturity.

For the reasons enumerated above, SF CDO tranches are less likely to default than corporate debt and corporate-backed CDOs. Also, a defaulted SF CDO tranche is likely to recover more than corporate debt. So with respect to default risk or extension risk associated with default risk, an SF CDO tranche is a happier story than corporate debt or corporate debt-backed CDOs. The unique risk of extension in a SF CDO, as distinct from default risk, is limited to the extension risk of an otherwise healthy security.

And the extension of a SF CDO tranche can be positive. This is because at the end of the life of the corporate bond-backed CDO, the asset manager is required to sell the collateral for whatever he or she can get. In the SF CDO, the asset manager is able to hold the collateral if he or she thinks higher recoveries are likely. Meanwhile, the SF CDO investor always has the option of selling the extended offending tranche. Thus, the asset manager is no worse off and probably better off than in the case of the corporate bond-backed CDO.

CONCLUSION

Many investors view CDOs backed by structured finance asset collateral as completely different in character than CDOs backed by high-yield collateral. The two major differences are that the SF cash flow deals tend to employ higher rated assets and require less capital to support the liabilities. Investor motivation to look at SF CDOs can be summarized concisely: SF CDO tranches have high credit quality underlying assets, tough structuring requirements, and high tranche spreads.

The survey in this chapter of rating agency default studies showed lower default rates and lower ratings volatility for structured finance collateral when compared to corporate debt. We also found lower default severity for structured debt than corporate credits. Finally, we noted that the rating agencies do not give benefit for this better credit quality when they rate SF CDOs; rating agencies demand credit enhancement on SF CDOs equivalent to corporate debt-backed CDOs.

Meanwhile, spreads on SF CDOs are quite attractive. Triple-A spreads average five basis points higher, and triple-B spreads average 30 basis points higher than the already high spreads on high yield bond-backed CDOs.

Extension risk on SF CDOs is addressed via coupon step-ups and collateral auctions. Underlying collateral performance is addressed with rules detailing the treatment of written down collateral.

The conclusion is that SF CDOs offer investors attractive relative yields for quite superior credits.

APPENDIX

Exhibit 5.12 presented an SF CDO collateral default and loss curves. This appendix explains how these curves were derived for CMBS, home equities, and jumbo nonagency whole loans.

CMBS

The CMBS default curve in Exhibit 5.12 is based on a 1999 study of commercial mortgage defaults by Esaki, L'Heureux, and Snyderman.[11] The study covered over 15,000 commercial real estate loans originated by life insurance companies between 1972 and 1992. We used this series

---

[11] Howard Esaki, Steven L'Heureux, and Mark Snyderman, "Commercial Mortgage Defaults: An Update," *Real Estate Finance* (Spring 1999).

because the CMBS conduit market is too new to have sufficient data from which to construct a loss curve. Also, there is no comprehensive record of default data from the S&L industry. The conduit business essentially took over the role of S&Ls in the commercial mortgage industry. That role was to provide smaller loans to slightly less creditworthy borrowers than did traditional insurance companies. Hence, default rates from the Esaki-L'Heureux-Snyderman study, which are based on life insurance data, may underestimate total defaults that one might expect from a conduit program. However, the timing of conduit defaults should differ little from those found in the Esaki-L'Heureux-Snyderman default curve.

The data in Exhibit 5.12 are for the first 10 years of the commercial mortgage default curve, and as such, are slightly more front loaded than in the Esaki-L'Heureux-Snyderman study.

Home Equities

The home equity default curve is shown in Exhibit 5.12 was obtained as follows. To get a better picture of an actual home equity loan default curve, Moody's historical home equity credit performance indices were used to calculate actual loss curves for vintages 1993–1994, 1995, 1996, 1997, and 1998. The data are shown in Exhibit 5.A1. Only 1993–1994 data were sufficiently seasoned at the time of the analysis to give an accurate picture of an entire loss curve. For that vintage, losses peaked in Years 4, 5, and 6 (when 20.6–24.8% of total losses occurred annually). While vintage years 1995–1998 were not sufficiently seasoned to show a complete curve, it is clear from Moody's data that there was a sharp increase in losses between Years 3 and 4, just as there was in the 1993–1994 data. Because the 1995–1998 vintage years behaved similarly to 1993–1994 loans, using 1993–1994 experience seems accurate as a basis for our home equity loss curve.

EXHIBIT 5.A1   Historical Home Equity Loss Curves (Moody's Indices)

Year	Date	Cum Loss	Annual Loss	Annual as Percent of Total Loss
1993–1994 Originations				
1	12/94	0.02	0.02	0.80
2	95	0.09	0.07	2.70
3	96	0.39	0.30	11.50
4	97	1.00	0.61	23.30
5	98	1.65	0.65	24.80
6	99	2.19	0.54	20.60
7*	00	2.62	0.43	16.40
1995 Originations				
1	12/95	0.00	0.00	
2	96	0.13	0.13	
3	97	0.78	0.65	
4	98	1.90	1.12	
5	99	3.10	1.20	
6*	00	4.38	1.28	
1996 Originations				
1	12/96	0.01	0.01	
2	97	0.16	0.15	
3	98	0.84	0.68	
4	99	2.27	1.43	
5*	00	3.73	1.46	
1997 Originations				
1	12/97	0.01	0.01	
2	98	0.25	0.24	
3	99	1.37	1.12	
4*	00	4.11	1.73	
1998 Originations				
1	12/98	0.01	0.01	
2	99	0.29	0.28	
3*	00	1.92	1.03	

*Estimated from seven months of data.

EXHIBIT 5.A2   Jumbo Nonagency Default Curve

Year	SDA Curve			225 PSA Percent of 10-yr Loss	S&P
	200 PSA	225 PSA	250 PSA		
1	4.5	4.8	5.0	4.8%	7.9
2	13.6	14.2	14.7	14.4%	8.4
3	19.3	19.9	20.4	20.2%	10.1
4	17.4	17.6	17.7	17.8%	13.0
5	15.0	15.0	14.9	15.2%	12.0
6	11.7	11.4	11.1	11.6%	9.7
7	7.9	7.6	7.3	7.7%	8.9
8	5.0	4.7	4.4	4.8%	7.3
9	2.7	2.6	2.4	2.6%	7.0
10	1.0	0.9	0.8	0.9%	5.6
11	0.3	0.3	0.2		4.2
12	0.3	0.2	0.2		2.8
13	0.2	0.2	0.2		1.8
14	0.2	0.2	0.2		1.4
15+	0.9	0.7	0.5		
Total	100.0	100.0	100.0	100.0%	100.0

Note that the data in Exhibit 5.A1 are loss data, not default data. Since the overall comparisons in Exhibit 5.A1 were made using default data, the home equity loss data was converted to default data by lagging it a year (to account for the average time a home equity loan is in foreclosure and REO).

Jumbo Nonagency

The jumbo nonagency default numbers in Exhibit 5.A2 come from the PSA Standard Default Assumption (SDA) curve. Even though the SDA curve is not a perfect representation of nonagency default patterns, several studies have shown it to be fairly accurate. The jumbo default curve shown in Exhibit 5.12 is based on a PSA speed of 225. Assuming a faster speed would push the defaults forward, but a 50 PSA change in speed has only a modest impact on the default distribution.

Exhibit 5.A2 shows the basic SDA data used. It also shows a loss curve sometimes used by S&P for jumbo loans. Note that the S&P curve spreads the losses over a longer period than does the SDA curve. In this way the S&P curve is actually less conservative than the SDA curve used in the analysis. In fact, the S&P jumbo loss curve looks a lot like the one for CMBS. However, since the SDA curve is used so widely in jumbo security evaluations, it was chosen for this analysis.

CHAPTER 6

Emerging Market CDOs

Many portfolio managers have invested a substantial amount of time and energy in understanding CDO structures. Most have become comfortable with CDO deals backed by both high-yield bonds and bank loans. However, these same portfolio managers are still quite uneasy about any CDO backed primarily by sovereign emerging markets bonds, as they believe that all emerging market debt is tainted by high default experience.

In this chapter, we shed some light on the differences that matter between emerging markets and high-yield deals. The picture that "emerges" (pun intended!) may surprise you—positively, that is—for the following reasons:

- There have actually been few defaults on U.S. dollar denominated sovereign Emerging Market (EM) bonds. The negative bias of many investors against EM CDOs is because they do not fully appreciate the differences between EM sovereign bank loans and EM sovereign bonds.

- Rating agencies are far more conservative in their assumptions when rating emerging markets deals than in rating high-yield deals, as performance data on EM bonds is far more limited. So there is an extra credit cushion already built into comparable credit levels.

■ EM CDOs generally provide much greater structural protection, as the average portfolio credit quality is higher, resulting in a lower probability of default on the underlying portfolio. Subordination on EM deals is also much higher, hence the equity itself is much less leveraged.

We will examine each of these points in turn and find that EM CDOs are no more risky than high-yield CDOs, and the rated debt often yields much more.

EM SOVEREIGN BOND DEFAULTS

EM debt has developed a bad rap. This tainted reputation stems from the fact that many potential investors do not distinguish between EM sovereign foreign currency bank loans and sovereign foreign currency bonds. In fact, the historical record on EM sovereign foreign currency bonds is very favorable. Sovereigns are far more likely to default on foreign currency bank loans than on foreign currency bond debt.

Let's look at the asset record, compiled in a Standard & Poor's study released in December 1999, which covers both public and private debt.[1] Exhibit 6.1 shows that out of a universe of 201 sovereign issuers, 13.9% of the issuers are currently in default. This includes defaults on foreign currency debt (both bank loans and bonds) as well as in local currency debt. Note that 11.9% of the issuers are in default within the category of total foreign currency debt, which includes both bank loans and bonds. But a separate break-out of just the sovereign foreign currency bonds indicates that most of these issuers are in default only on their bank loans. In fact, Column (6) of Exhibit 6.1 shows that in 1999 only 2.5% of the issuers were in default on their foreign currency bonds! Note that the 2.5% default on foreign currency bonds is even lower than the 3.5% default on local currency debt.

---

[1] See David T. Beers and Ashok Bhatia, "Sovereign Defaults: Hiatus in 2000?" *Standard & Poor's Credit Week* (December 22, 1999).

EXHIBIT 6.1   Sovereign Default Rates

(Percent of All Sovereign Issuers)	Number of Issuers	All Issuers in Default (%)	New Issuers in Default (%)	All Foreign Currency Debt* (%)	Foreign Currency Bonds (%)	Local Currency (%)
1975	164	2.4	N.A.	1.2	0.6	1.2
1976	165	2.4	0.6	2.4	0.6	0.6
1977	166	2.4	0.0	1.8	0.6	0.6
1978	169	4.7	2.3	4.1	0.6	0.6
1979	173	6.4	2.3	5.8	0.6	1.2
1980	174	6.3	1.7	5.7	0.6	0.6
1981	176	10.2	6.3	9.1	0.0	1.1
1982	176	15.9	5.7	15.3	0.0	1.7
1983	177	24.9	10.2	23.7	0.0	1.1
1984	178	25.3	1.1	23.6	0.6	1.7
1985	178	24.7	2.8	24.2	0.6	1.1
1986	179	28.5	5.6	27.9	0.6	1.7
1987	179	30.7	3.3	29.1	1.1	2.2
1988	179	30.2	1.7	29.6	1.1	1.1
1989	179	30.2	1.7	29.1	2.2	1.7
1990	178	30.9	4.2	29.8	1.1	2.8
1991	198	27.3	3.0	26.8	1.0	1.5
1992	198	29.3	3.5	28.8	2.0	1.5
1993	200	27.0	0.5	26.5	1.5	2.0
1994	201	24.4	0.0	23.9	1.5	2.0
1995	201	22.9	1.5	21.9	1.5	3.0
1996	201	21.4	0.5	19.9	1.5	3.5
1997	201	15.9	0.0	14.9	1.5	2.0
1998	201	15.9	2.5	13.9	2.5	3.5
1999	201	13.9	0.5	11.9	2.5	3.5

N.A. = Not available.
* Bonds and bank debt.
Source: Standard & Poor's.

This 2.5% default rate amounts to only five issuers out of 201 issuers (sovereign borrowers). They consist of Ecuador, Ukraine, the former Yugoslavia, Pakistan, and Russia.[2] Ecuador was the only new issuer to default in 1999. That country first blew the whistle that it might not meet payments on its

---

[2] On January 6, 2000, after the S&P study was published, the Ivory Coast announced it was suspended foreign currency debt payments indefinitely. It is clear that the country's bank loans will be impacted. It is unclear if their Eurobonds would be affected as well.

Brady debt during the summer, and then proceeded to default on the bonds. This shook the markets, since it was the first time that Brady debt had defaulted. However, realize that there was no contagion—other Latin American countries continued to make timely payments on their Brady bonds. Investors should realize that a sovereign can default on some bonds, while remaining timely on others. This would be reflected in Exhibit 6.1 as a default. For example, while Russia has defaulted on some of its bonds, it has continued to service on a timely basis its large public issues, including the Russian Federation's "CCC" rated Eurobonds. It is also keeping current four other Ministry of Finance foreign currency bonds.

Cumulatively, since 1975, Standard and Poor's has identified a total of 78 issuers (38.8% of all sovereigns) that defaulted on their foreign currency bond and bank loans since 1975. (This constitutes a much smaller percent of all foreign currency debt in default.) Defaults usually took the form of late payments of principal and/or interest on bank loans. In fact, there were 75 bank debt defaults since 1975, and some sovereigns defaulted more than once. By contrast, only 14 issuers defaulted on foreign currency bonds in that same period. In most of these cases, the defaulted bonds had been issued by smaller countries which had little total debt outstanding. The bonds that the countries defaulted on tended to be held by banks, rather than being public issues held by a broad cross sector of investors.

This has been independently confirmed in a 1995 study by Moody's rating service. The Moody's study noted that "a review of worldwide sovereign default experience since World War II shows that when sovereign nations have defaulted on any of their foreign currency obligations...they have been more likely to default on bank loans than on sovereign bonds or notes."[3]

---

[3] Vincent Truglia, David Levey and Christopher Mahoney, "Sovereign Risk: Bank Deposits Versus Bonds," Moody's Investors Service, Global Credit Research (October 1995).

WHY THE BETTER TRACK RECORD?

There are four reasons that EM sovereign bonds have a better track record than sovereign bank loans. First, there is a strong disincentive for a sovereign to default on foreign currency bonds: it will restrict capital market access going forward. The consequences of defaulting on (or rescheduling) bank loans has been more predictable, and far less detrimental to a nation's interest than defaulting on its bonds. Defaulting on bonds could essentially bar a country from the international capital markets for a considerable period of time and will result in much higher borrowing costs when that country is finally able to enter. Most of the developing nations depend on external financing for their growth, and hampering access to capital markets could sacrifice medium-term growth.

Second, more sovereigns have access to cross-border bank financing than have access to bond issuance in the international capital markets. International bond markets have been receptive to issuance by speculative grade rated sovereign credits since the early 1990s. But relative credit sanity has prevailed, as there have been barriers to entry by sovereigns of less credit quality, notably those from sub-Saharan Africa.

Third, it is far easier to renegotiate debt held by a few banking institutions rather than a bond issuance held by large numbers of international investors. For one, identification of creditors in advance is not always easy. By definition, there are a large number of creditors, some of which may have relatively small holdings. All of which makes restructuring more complex. Also, any one of even the smallest creditors can potentially bring legal proceedings against an issuer in a number of jurisdictions, depending on the security's documentation. The possibility of asset attachments is greater, simply because of the number of potential court cases.

The fourth and final major difference between bank loans and bond debt is that banks have multifaceted relationships with borrowers, and usually receive sizeable fees for a variety of services. Banks often keep their long-term relationship with the borrower in perspective when agreeing to reschedule. Bondholders are not relationship-driven, and there are no business consequences for the bondholders in trying to extract the last possible dollar. The net result is this: Sovereign default rates on bonds are much lower than on bank loans. Unfortunately, many investors do not distinguish between the two and keep looking at sovereign debt as a homogeneous category, which clearly, it is not.

CDO RATING DIFFERENCES: EM VERSUS HIGH YIELD

The rating methodology for cash flow CDOs involves looking at the expected loss on the various tranches under various default scenarios, and probability weighting the results. This in turn requires making assumptions on how diversified the collateral is, how likely it is to default, and how much will be recovered if any default occurs. It is much harder for the rating agencies to feel comfortable with the parameters that they are using for EM bonds than U.S. high-yield bonds. Let's look at why.

First, consider EM sovereign debt. Default rate statistics on EM sovereign bonds are very limited. Moreover, EM economies are subject to greater economic instability than those of more developed countries. Corporate debt in EM countries is even more problematic for the rating agencies. Clearly, there is generally less publicly available information about companies in EM countries than about issuers in developed countries. Moreover, financial reporting in many foreign countries is often not subject to uniform reporting and disclosure requirements. Finally and most importantly, the actions of local governments are far more likely to affect the ability or willingness of EM corporates to service their debt.

Given the issues that were mentioned above, the rating agencies react by rating EM assets in a more conservative manner than other collateral. As a result, additional levels of credit protection are built into EM CDOs beyond that which is structured into high-yield CDOs. We now review some major differences in those assumptions.

Recovery Rates

The rating agencies typically assume 30% recovery rates for high-yield debt and 50% on bank loans. For sovereign debt, Moody's assumes that base case recovery rates are 30% of the market value, or 25% of par, whichever is lower. For EM corporate debt, Moody's assumes that recovery rates are 20% of market value (15% of par value) if the issuer is domiciled in an investment grade country, and 15% of market value (10% of par value) if the issuer is domiciled in a noninvestment-grade country. Bonds of countries that face unusually adverse political or economic conditions are treated as having a lower recovery rate, which in some cases, can be as low as zero.

In point of fact, historical recovery rates on sovereign bonds have proved far more favorable. A September 1998 Standard and Poor's study showed that since 1975, the recovery rate on foreign currency bonds has been around 75%.[4] It was higher in the majority of cases in which the defaults were cured quickly though the issuance of new debt. It was lower on bonds that remained in default for longer periods of time. Even for bonds that remained in default for longer periods, most of the recovery rates were just under 50%—far higher than the recovery assumptions made by the rating agencies. The 75% overall recovery rate on sovereign foreign currency bonds is well above the 60% recovery rate on foreign currency bank loans.

---

[4] See David T. Beers, "Sovereign Defaults Continue to Decline," Standard and Poor's (September 1998).

EXHIBIT 6.2   Moody's Diversity Score Table for CDOs

No. of Companies (Regions)	Diversity Score	Diversity Score for Latin America*
1.0	1.00	1.00
1.5	1.20	1.10
2.0	1.50	1.25
2.5	1.80	1.40
3.0	2.00	1.50
3.5	2.20	1.60
4.0	2.30	1.65
4.5	2.50	1.75
5.0	2.70	1.85
5.5	2.80	1.90
6.0	3.00	2.00

*Diversity = 1 + (Standard Diversity Score − 1) × 0.5
Source: Moody's Investors Service.

Moreover, even though the rating agencies are more generous in the recovery rates they assume for U.S. high-yield borrowers than for sovereign borrowers, actual recovery rates for sovereign borrowers have been higher. A Moody's study showed that the recovery rates on senior unsecured U.S. corporate debt in the 1977–1988 period average 51.31%.[5] Compare this with the 75% recovery rate on the sovereign bonds.

Diversity Scores

Each rating agency has its own set of tools for measuring the diversity of underlying collateral. Moody's methodology has become the industry standard. This treatment reduces the pool of assets to a set of homogenous, uncorrelated assets. For CDOs backed by high-yield or bank loans, a diversity score is calculated by dividing the bonds into 1 of 33 industry groupings, and each industry group is assumed to be uncorrelated. (See Exhibit 6.2.)

---

[5] C. Keenan, Igor Shtogrin, and Jorge Sobehart, "Historical Default Rates of Corporate Bond Issuers, 1920–1998," Moody's Investors Service (January 1999).

Assumptions are more conservative for EM bonds, reflecting rating agency fears of "contagion." Countries that carry an investment-grade sovereign rating from Moody's are each treated as a separate industry. Bonds from non-investment-grade EM issuers are grouped into six geographic regions. These are Latin America, the Caribbean, Eastern Europe, Africa, East Asia, and West Asia. The latter includes the Middle East. Each region constitutes a single "industry." All bonds from a region, regardless of the industry they represent, are taken as part of the same group. Thus, the value of including corporate EM borrowers, which would customarily be seen as providing greater diversity and reduced risk from that diversification, is discounted entirely. In point of fact, many EM deals include up to 20% of the portfolio in corporate form.

For all regions except Latin America, the diversity score is the standard table used by Moody's, which relies on the assumption that defaults on bonds in the same region or industry have a correlation coefficient of approximately 30%. This is shown in the first two columns of Exhibit 6.2. For example, if there were equal amounts of debt from each of four Caribbean countries, the diversity score is 2.3. That is, the deal would be credited as if there were 2.3 uncorrelated assets. For Latin American it is assumed the correlation is about 60%, and the diversity score is shown in the third column of Exhibit 6.2. If there were four Latin American issuers, the diversity score would be 1.65. Thus, combining four Caribbean issuers and four Latin American issuers in equal amounts would "count" as 3.95 uncorrelated issuers.

To be even more conservative, all bonds from a particular EM country are taken as constituting one issue. Essentially, 100% correlation is assumed within each country. In effect, EM collateral does not receive diversity score "credit" for having multiple corporate issuers or industries. Thus, if one compares the diversity score on a pool of 100% emerging markets collateral with a pool of U.S. high-yield assets with similar industry diversification, the EM collateral would have a substantially lower diversity score.

Structural Protections

We have thus far focused on how Moody's deals with limited historical experience (by making more conservative assumptions). In practice, these more conservative assumptions mean several forms of additional built-in protection for the CDO buyer. First, the average credit quality is higher on a EM CDO than on a high-yield CDO. Second, subordination levels are also generally higher on an EM CDO than on a high-yield CDO.

Higher Average Credit Quality

The conservative approach used by Moody's means that average credit quality of an EM CDO deal is much higher than on a high-yield CDO. That is, CDO managers will generally choose to include higher credit quality bonds to compensate for the lower diversity scores and the more stringent recovery assumptions. Most EM deals have average credit qualities of Ba2 or Ba3. By contrast, most high-yield deals have an average credit quality of B1 or B2.

This difference is highly significant, as shown in Exhibit 6.3. The exhibit shows Moody's data for the average cumulative default rates by letter rating after 10 years. This groups corporate bonds with a given initial rating, and tracks those bonds through time. Data for the period 1970–1998 are included. The exhibit is used to highlight cumulative default rates after 10 years, as that roughly corresponds to the average lives of CDO deals. The findings show that default rates tend to rise exponentially as credit letter ratings fall. Of the bonds that started out life with a Baa rating, 4.39% had defaulted by the end of 10 years. Bonds with an initial rating of Ba had a cumulative default rate of 20.63%, while bonds initially rated B had a cumulative default of 43.91%. While numbers on sovereign debt are unavailable, the results are indicative that higher rated bonds actually default much less than do their lower-rated brethren. Bottom line: The higher initial portfolio quality on sovereign EM CDOs is highly significant.

EXHIBIT 6.3 Cumulative Default Rates After 10 Years as a Function of Credit Quality

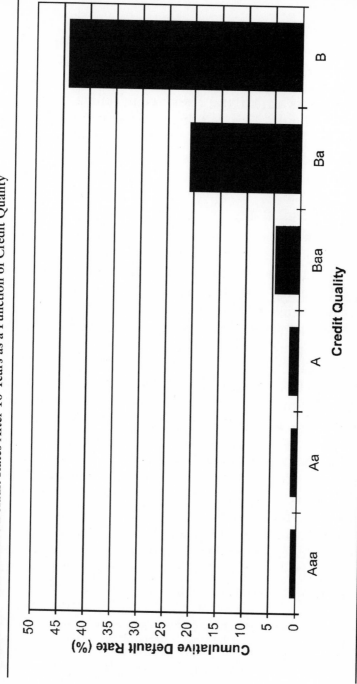

Source: Moody's Investors Service.

Moreover, actual EM portfolio quality may be slightly higher than even that indicated by the overall rating. EM corporate bonds (generally 5–20% of the deal) can generally receive a rating no higher than the country in which it is based.[6] This is called the "sovereign ceiling." Thus, if a company is rated Aa2 based on "standalone" fundamentals, but is based in a country rated Ba2, the company itself can generally only receive that same Ba2 rating. This same methodology and rating effect is reflected throughout the overall portfolio.

More Subordination

The more conservative rating methodology also means that the rating agencies require higher subordination levels. In particular, equity tranches are usually much larger on EM deals than in high-yield deals. Exhibit 6.4 shows a representative high-yield deal versus a representative sovereign EM deal, both brought to market at approximately the same time. Note that the equity tranche is 7.9% on the high-yield deal versus 18% on the EM deal. More generally, the investment grade bonds receive much more protection on the EM deal than they do on the high-yield deal. In the EM deal, 22.2% of the deal is subordinated to the investment grade bonds, on the high-yield deal only 11.9% is subordinated.

The yields for each tranche are higher on the EM CDO than for the corresponding tranche on the high-yield CDO, in spite of the fact that the rating is as high or higher on the EM debt. The AAA rated bond on the EM deal is priced at 68 discounted margin (DM), versus 57 DM on the high-yield deal. The A rated EM tranche is priced at +250/10-year Treasury, versus +225/10-year Treasury for a lower

---

[6] There have been a few CDOs backed primarily by Asian corporate bonds. These CDOs are "story bonds" driven by local investors, and have take advantage of brief "windows of opportunity." This chapter focuses on CDOs backed by diversified sovereign EM bonds. In practice, the rating agencies criteria is such that it has never been economic to include more than 20% EM corporate bonds in a sovereign EM deal.

rated (A–) tranche of the high-yield deal. This translates into roughly a 50 b.p. differential, as the credit quality differential is worth 25 b.p. The Ba1 mezzanine bond in the EM deal is priced at +800/10-year, versus +700/10-year for the BB– tranche of the high yield deal. Here the EM investor is receiving a 100 b.p. higher spread, as well as higher credit quality. The equity on the EM deal is the only exception to this. It may yield slightly less than on high-yield deals, as the equity is far less leveraged. The difference in the leverage can be seen by the fact that the EM equity is 18% of the deal versus 7.9% of the high-yield deal.

EXHIBIT 6.4 Comparison of Emerging Market and High-Yield Deal Structure

Class	Ratings Moody's/S&P/D&P	Amount ($M)	Percent of Deal	Percent Sub	Current Pricing Info
Representative Emerging Market Deal					
A1	Aaa/AAA/NR	163.00	68.6%	31.4%	+68 DM*
A2	A2/A/NR	22.00	9.3%	22.2%	+250/10yr Tsy
Mezz	Ba1/NR/NR	10.00	4.2%	18.0%	+800/10yr Tsy
Equity	NR	42.74	18.0%	—	—
Total		237.74			
Representative High Yield Deal					
A1	Aaa/AAA/AAA	344.50	68.2%	31.8%	+57 DM*
A2	NR/A-/A-	79.00	15.6%	16.2%	+225/10yr Tsy
Mezz 1	NR/NR/BBB-	22.00	4.4%	11.8%	+360/10yr Tsy
Mezz 2	NR/NR/BB-	20.00	4.0%	7.9%	+700/10yr Tsy
Equity	NR	39.79	7.9%	—	—
Total		505.29			

* DM = discounted margin.

CONCLUSION

It is unfortunate that many investors may be reluctant to look at CDOs backed by EM collateral because of general misimpressions about the collateral. In this chapter, we have shown that there have been few actual defaults on sovereign EM bonds, which is the collateral used to back many EM CDOs. Many investors do not realize this, as they tend to clump together the experiences of both sovereign bank loans and sovereign bonds. Sovereign bank loans have clearly experienced more significant level of defaults. Moreover, when there is a default, the recovery rates are higher on the sovereign bonds than on the bank loans.

Realize that because of the limited history of sovereign bonds, the rating agencies are far more conservative in their ratings. They are particularly harsh in the assumptions they make about recoveries and on diversity characteristics. This more conservative rating methodology means that the average credit quality of bonds is higher in the EM deal. Finally, EM CDOs have more subordination. This extra structural protection is clearly not priced in. EM CDOs trade wider than high-yield CDOs for every rated tranche.

CHAPTER 7

Market Value CDOs

As explained in Chapter 1, there are cash flow and market value collateralized debt obligations. Many investors look suspiciously at the senior and mezzanine tranches of market value CDOs. Their concern is that this deal structure gives the manager the same latitude to manage a portfolio as a hedge fund manager. That view is wrong. It is based on a misconception about how market value CDOs are really structured and the protection they provide investors.

While market value deals are a distinct minority of CDOs, they are the structure of choice for certain types of collateral, where the cash flows are not predictable. It is very difficult to use unpredictable cash flows within the confines of a cash flow structure. Moreover, market value structures may also appeal to managers and equity buyers who like the greater trading flexibility inherent in these deals. Finally, market value transactions also facilitate the purchase of assets that mature beyond the life of the transaction, because the price volatility associated with the forced sale of these assets is explicitly considered.

This chapter provides an overview of the differences between cash flow and market value structures. It also examines the mechanics of market value CDOs, focusing on the advance rates (i.e., the percentage of a particular asset that may be issued as rated debt)—the key to protecting the debt holders. Then we look at some volatility numbers, which indicate how conservative the advance rates used by the rating agencies are.

CASH FLOW VERSUS MARKET VALUE DEALS

Cash flow deals are dependent on the ability of the collateral to generate sufficient current cash flow to pay interest and principal on rated notes issued by the CDO. The ratings are based on the effect of collateral defaults and recoveries on the receipt of timely interest and principal payments from the collateral. The manager focuses on controlling defaults and recoveries. Overcollateralization, as measured on the basis of the par value of the portfolio, provides important structural protection for the bondholders. If overcollateralization tests are not met, then cash flow is diverted from mezzanine and subordinated classes to pay down senior notes, or cash flow is trapped in a reserve account. There are no forced collateral liquidations.

Market value transactions depend upon the ability of the fund manager to maintain and improve the market value of the collateral. Funds to be used for liability principal payments are obtained from liquidating the collateral. Liability interest payments can be made from collateral interest receipts, as well as collateral liquidation proceeds. Ratings are based on collateral price volatility, liquidity, and market value. The manager focuses on maximizing total return while minimizing volatility.

Market overcollateralization tests are conducted regularly. These require that the market value of assets multiplied by the advance rates (discussed later) must be greater than or equal to debt outstanding. If that is not the case, collateral sales and liability redemptions may be required to bring overcollateralization ratios back into compliance. Market value deals have diversity, concentration and other portfolio constraints, albeit less than cash flow transactions. For example, in a cash flow transaction if there is a constraint that the asset manager may not hold more than $20 million par value in a particular industry, then if $15 million is currently in the portfolio and the manager would like to invest in $10 million more in that industry, that cannot be done. The manager may only invest in an additional $5 million. In contrast, in a market value transaction, the same manager facing a $20 million constraint could invest an additional $10 million, but when the overcollateralization test is performed, the manager would only be permitted to use $20 million, not $25 million.

Exhibit 7.1 summarizes the salient features of cash flow versus market value deals.

THE RATING PROCESS

The credit enhancement for a market value deal is the cushion between the current market value of the collateral and the face value of the structure's obligations. Within this framework, the collateral must normally be liquidated (either in whole or in part) if the ratio of the market value of the collateral to the debt obligations falls below a predetermined threshold. The liquidated collateral is used to pay down debt obligations, which brings the structure back into compliance.

The biggest risk in a market value transaction is a sudden decline in the value of the collateral pool. Thus, the rating agencies focus on the price volatility and liquidity of the assets that may be incorporated into these structures. Volatility and liquidity are assumed to be reflected in a set of advance rates that are designed to provide a cushion against market risk, and represent adjustments to the value of each asset.

Let's first look at how a market value deal really works. We then take up the methodology used by rating agencies to determine the advance rate. Finally, we look at how conservative those advance rates are relative to the actual price volatility of these instruments.

EXHIBIT 7.1 Comparison of Cash Flow and Market Value CDOs

	Cash Flow Deal	Market Value Deal
Objective	Cash flow deals depend on the ability of the collateral to generate sufficient current cash to pay interest and principal on rated notes issued by the CDO.	Market value transactions depend on the ability of the fund manager to maintain and improve the market value of the collateral.
Rating Focus	The ratings are based on the effect of collateral defaults and recoveries on the timely payment of interest and principal from the collateral	Ratings are based on collateral price volatility, liquidity, and market value.
Manager Focus	Manager focuses on controlling defaults and recoveries.	Manager focuses on maximizing total return while minimizing volatility.
Structural Protection	Overcollateralization is measured on the basis of the portfolio's par value. If overcollateralization tests are failed, then cash flow is diverted from the mezzanine and subordinated classes to pay down senior notes, or cash flow is trapped in a reserve account. There are no forced collateral liquidations.	Market value overcollateralization tests are conducted regularly. The market value of assets multiplied by the advance rates must be greater than or equal to the debt outstanding*; otherwise collateral sales and liability redemptions may be required to bring overcollateralization ratios back into compliance.
Diversity and Concentration Limits	Very strict.	Substantial diversification is required. More is "encouraged" by the structure of advance rates.
Trading Limitations	There are limitations on portfolio trading.	There is greater portfolio trading flexibility.
Collateral	Typical cash flow assets include bank loans, high-yield bonds, emerging market bonds/loans, and project finance.	Typical market value assets include assets eligible for inclusion in cash flow CDOs as well as distressed debt, equities, and convertibles

* Advance rate is the percentage of the market value of a particular asset that may be issued as rated debt. Advance rates depend upon the price volatility and quality of price/return data and the liquidity of the assets. Assets with lower price volatility and greater liquidity are typically assigned higher advance rates.

EXHIBIT 7.2   Moody's Asset Types

High-Yield Bonds
High-Yield Loans
Distressed Bonds
Distressed Loans
Distressed Equity

Source: Yvonne Fu Falcone and Jeremy Gluck, "Moody's Approach to Market-Value CDOs," Special Report, *Structured Finance* (April 8, 1998). Reprinted with permission from Moody's Investors Service.

EXHIBIT 7.3   Fitch Asset Types

High-Yield Bank Loans
BB High-Yield Bonds
Emerging Market Bonds
Equity
Distressed Debt

Source: "Market-Value CBO/CLO Rating Criteria," Fitch (June 1999).

EXHIBIT 7.4   S&P Asset Types

High-Yield Bond
Distressed Bond
Emerging Markets Bond
Bank Loan
Public Equity

Source: Erkan Erturk and Soody Nelson, "Structured Market-Value Transactions: A Quantitative Enhancement Approach," Standard & Poor's (August 1999).

Advance Rates and Overcollateralization Tests

A market value deal simply requires that the market value of the collateral times the advance rate (the adjustment to the value of the assets to provide a cushion against market risk) be greater than the book value of the liabilities. The rating agencies use a set of advance rates to determine how much rated debt can be issued against the market value of an asset.

Later we learn how advance rates are derived. For now, it important to understand how advance rates are used for the overcollateralization tests. A rating agency assigns an advance rating by asset type. Exhibits 7.2, 7.3, and 7.4 show the asset types used by Moody's, Fitch, and S&P, respectively.

For each asset type there is an advance rate based on the desired rating for the debt issued based on (1) the structure of the transaction and (2) the portfolio composition. For example, Exhibit 7.5 shows Moody's advance rates for a more detailed breakdown of asset type assuming the following:

1. There is only one tranche in the transaction (i.e., there is no subordination, so the only protection is from the advance rates).
2. There is only one asset type in the portfolio.
3. The diversification constraints are as follows:
   a. the maximum allowable investment in one issuer is 5%;
   b. the maximum allowable investment in any one industry is 20%; and
   c. the least diversified portfolio consists of 20 issuers and 5 industries.

To see how to use the advance rates in Exhibit 7.5, suppose (1) a portfolio consists of performing high-yield bonds rated B and (2) the deal is carved only into a bond rated A2 and equity (i.e., there is only one rated tranche). As can be seen from Exhibit 7.5, Moody's advance rate would be 0.79. Thus, the market value of the deal times the advance rate (0.79 in this case) must be greater than the par value of the liabilities (the A2 rated bonds). So, suppose that a deal has assets with a market value of $500 million and liabilities with a par value of $375 million, then the overcollateralization test would involve first calculating the "adjusted market value of the assets." With an advance rate of 0.79 and a market value for the assets of $500 million, the adjusted market value is

$$\text{Adjusted market value} = 0.79 \times \$500 \text{ million} = \$395 \text{ million}$$

The adjusted market value exceeds the par value of the liabilities of $375 million. Therefore, the overcollateralization test is passed.

The advance rates are higher for greater diversification. This can be seen by comparing the advance rates in Exhibit 7.6 based on 40 issuers and 10 industries and the advance rates in Exhibit 7.5 based on 20 issuers in five industries.

EXHIBIT 7.5 Moody's Advance Rates for Different Asset Types by Target Rating: Single Tranche Transaction with One Asset Type (20 Issuers and 5 Industries)

Asset Type	Target Rating									
	Aaa	Aa1	Aa2	Aa3	A1	A2	A3	Baa1	Baa2	Baa3
Performing bank loans valued $0.90 and above	0.870	0.890	0.895	0.900	0.905	0.910	0.915	0.930	0.935	9.400
Distressed bank loans valued $0.85 and above	0.760	0.780	0.790	0.795	0.810	0.815	0.820	0.830	0.840	0.870
Performing high-yield bonds rated Baa	0.76	0.79	0.80	0.81	0.83	0.84	0.85	0.87	0.88	0.90
Performing high-yield bonds rated B	0.72	0.75	0.76	0.77	0.78	0.79	0.80	0.82	0.83	0.85
Distressed bank loans valued below $0.85	0.58	0.62	0.63	0.64	0.67	0.68	0.69	0.71	0.72	0.74
Performing high-yield valued below Caa	0.45	0.49	0.50	0.51	0.56	0.58	0.60	0.62	0.64	0.67
Distressed bonds	0.35	0.39	0.40	0.41	0.47	0.48	0.50	0.54	0.56	0.57
Reorganized equities	0.31	0.37	0.38	0.39	0.44	0.46	0.47	0.51	0.52	0.54

Source: Table Yvonne Fu Falcone and Jeremy Gluck, "Moody's Approach to Market-Value CDOs," Special Report, Structured Finance (April 8, 1998), p. 9. Reprinted with permission from Moody's Investors Service.

EXHIBIT 7.6 Moody's Advance Rates for Different Asset Types by Target Rating; Single Tranche Transaction with One Asset Types (40 Issuers and 10 Industries)

Asset Type	Target Rating									
	Aaa	Aa1	Aa2	Aa3	A1	A2	A3	Baa1	Baa2	Baa3
Performing bank loans valued $0.90 and above	0.880	0.895	0.900	0.905	0.910	0.915	0.920	0.930	0.935	0.940
Distressed bank loans valued $0.85 and above	0.790	0.805	0.810	0.815	0.820	0.825	0.830	0.840	0.850	0.870
Performing high-yield bonds rated Ba	0.81	0.84	0.85	0.86	0.87	0.88	0.89	0.90	0.91	0.92
Performing high-yield bonds rated B	0.74	0.78	0.79	0.80	0.81	0.82	0.83	0.84	0.85	0.87
Distressed bank loans valued below $0.85	0.62	0.66	0.67	0.68	0.69	0.70	0.71	0.73	0.74	0.76
Performing high-yield bonds rated Caa	0.50	0.56	0.57	0.58	0.61	0.62	0.64	0.67	0.68	0.70
Distressed bonds	0.43	0.47	0.48	0.49	0.52	0.53	0.54	0.58	0.59	0.61
Reorganized equities	0.41	0.45	0.46	0.47	0.49	0.50	0.51	0.54	0.55	0.56

Source: Table A4 in Yvonne Fu Falcone and Jeremy Gluck, "Moody's Approach to Market-Value CDOs," Special Report, *Structured Finance* (April 8, 1998), p. 13. Reprinted with permission from Moody's Investors Service.

The advance rates in Exhibit 7.5 and 7.6 are for deals with a single tranche and only one asset type. When there is more than one asset type the advance rates will be different depending on the correlation between the asset types. Specifically, if there is greater diversification within a deal, then the advance rates would be somewhat higher.

To demonstrate how the adjusted market value is computed for a tranche when there is more than one asset type, we will use the advance rates in Exhibit 7.5 *for illustrative purposes only.* The deal has a $375 million rated tranche and $125 million equity. The portfolio composition is shown in Exhibit 7.7. The rating for the tranche is A2, so the advance rates are those shown in Exhibit 7.5 for an A2 rating. Notice that the adjusted market value is $394.9 million which exceeds the $375 million par value of the tranche. Thus, the overcollateralization test is passed.

If a deal has several tranches, then the senior tranches are being provided protection by more than the advance rates.[1] The advance rates will be different from those shown in Exhibits 7.5 and 7.6 and there will be an overcollateralization test applied to each tranche. In the case of a deal with one senior tranche, one subordinated tranche, and an equity tranche, there will be an overcollateralization test for the senior tranche and the subordinated tranche. The former test compares the adjusted market value of the portfolio (based on the advance rates for the senior tranche) to the par value of the senior tranche outstanding. The test is passed when the adjusted market value exceeds the par value of the senior tranche. The overcollateralization for the subordinated tranche compares the adjusted market value (based on the advance rates for the subordinated tranche) to the par value of the subordinated tranche outstanding. If the adjusted market value exceeds the par value of the subordinated tranche, the overcollateralization test is passed.

---

[1] For an explanation of how subordination impacts the advance rates in the Moody's rating methodology, see Exhibit C in Yvonne Fu Falcone and Jeremy Gluck, "Moody's Approach to Market-Value CDOs," Special Report, *Structured Finance* (April 8, 1998), pp, 14–15.

EXHIBIT 7.7 Example of Adjusted Market Value Calculation with More than One Asset Type

	Asset Type ($ millions)	Market Value Portfolio	For A2 Rated(*)	
			Percent of Rate	Advance of Assets
Performing bank loans valued $0.90 and above	$110	22.00	0.91	$100.10
Distressed bank loans valued $0.85 and above	97	19.40	0.815	79.06
Performing high-yield bonds rated Baa	106	21.20	0.84	89.04
Performing high-yield bonds rated B	84	16.80	0.79	66.36
Distressed bank loans valued below $0.85	35	7.00	0.68	23.80
Performing high-yield valued below Caa	39	7.80	0.58	22.62
Distressed bonds	29	5.80	0.48	13.92
Reorganized equities	0	0.00	0.46	0.00
Total	$500	100.00		$394.90

* Assumes advance rates in Exhibit 7.5.

A Simple Example of Deal Mechanics

In an effort to illustrate and deal test mechanics, we created a sample deal using the advance rates in Exhibit 7.5 and looked at the effect of an unrealistically rapid asset value deterioration on this deal. The deal originally consisted of $500 million in assets, with $375 million of bonds rated A2 and $125 million of equity (shown in Exhibit 7.8). Initially, the value of the assets times the advance rate is $395 million (in Exhibit 7.8, the column labeled "Adjusted" MV of Assets). This is obviously greater than the $375 million in bonds. The deal has 25% equity to begin ($125 million /$500 million).

We assume that the assets earn 1% per month, and that the value of the assets declines by 3% per month. The net result is that the value of the assets is declining by 2% per month. In addition, the rated debt holders are paid 0.66% per month. For simplicity, we assume all interest payments on the collateral are collected monthly, and the interest payments on the debt are disbursed monthly. After month 3 of declining market prices, the value of the assets is $463.32 million. Applying the 0.79 advance rate, the "adjusted" market value of the assets is $366.02 million, against $375 million of bonds. The structure fails the overcollateralized (market value) test: the adjusted market value of the securities is less than the par value of the bonds. The deal must begin to liquidate.

Let's walk through the process. The shortfall between the adjusted market value of assets and debt is $8.98 million (shown in Exhibit 7.8, the column labeled "Difference"). Since the advance rate is 0.79, each dollar of liquidation is the equivalent of curing only $0.21 of the shortfall. To bring the new adjusted MV of assets into line with the bonds, we must liquidate assets to cure the shortfall. The amount that must be liquidated is determined as follows:

Collateral to be liquidated = [Shortfall/(1 – Advance rate)]

EXHIBIT 7.8 Illustration of Market Value Deal Mechanics

Assumptions:
1. 3% Drop in market value per month.
2. Assets yield 1% per month.
3. 0.66% income paid per month on A2 bonds).

$Million

Month	Market Value of Assets	"Adjusted" MV of Assets*	Par Value of Bonds Rated A2	Diff	Liq	New MV of Assets	New AMV of Assets	New Par on Bond	% Equity Before Liq	% Equity After Liq	New Par on Bond
0	500.00	395.00	375.00	20.00	0.00	500.00	395.00	375.00	0.25	0.25	375.00
1**	487.53	385.14	375.00	10.14	0.00	487.53	385.14	375.00	0.23	0.23	375.00
2	475.30	375.49	375.00	0.49	0.00	475.30	375.49	375.00	0.21	0.21	375.00
3	463.32	366.02	375.00	-8.98	42.75	420.56	332.25	332.25	0.19	0.21	332.25
4	409.96	323.87	332.25	-8.38	39.89	370.07	292.35	292.35	0.19	0.21	292.35
5	360.74	284.98	292.35	-7.37	35.10	325.64	257.25	257.25	0.19	0.21	257.25
6	317.43	250.77	257.25	-6.49	30.89	286.54	226.36	226.36	0.19	0.21	226.36
7	279.31	220.66	226.36	-5.71	27.18	252.13	199.19	199.19	0.19	0.21	199.19
8	245.78	194.16	199.19	-5.02	23.92	221.86	175.27	175.27	0.19	0.21	175.27
9	216.27	170.85	175.27	-4.42	21.04	195.22	154.23	154.23	0.19	0.21	154.23
10	190.30	150.34	154.23	-3.89	18.52	171.78	135.71	135.71	0.19	0.21	135.71

* Adjusted MV of assets = MV of assets × 0.79

** To illustrate calculations:

Market value of assets = +500 million × 0.97 = +485 million
+500 million × 0.01 = +5 million
−375 million × 0.66% = −2.475
= 487.53

In our example, since the shortfall is $8.98 million and the advance rate is 0.79

$$\text{Collateral to be liquidated} = [\$8.89 \text{ million}/(1 - 0.79)]$$
$$= \$42.75$$

Thus, the new market value of the assets is $420.56 million, and the new adjusted market value of the assets is $332.25 million. This is identical to the post liquidation par value of the liabilities.

Assume in the following month that the assets again earn 1%, their value again declines by 3%, and bondholders are again paid 0.66%. There will be another shortfall, this time of $8.38 million. Thus, $39.89 million must be liquidated to bring the new adjusted market value of the assets in line with the par value of the bonds.

There are a number of things to note from this example. First, the deal liquidates very quickly in an environment of unfavorable performance. In this simplified example, the par value of the bonds has amortized down to $154.23 million after 10 months. However, despite a very quick deterioration in market value, the rated debt holders have completely received 100% return of principal and timely payment of interest. Second, there is always a very hefty capital cushion. In this example, the equity before liquidation never drops lower than 19%. By definition, the equity after liquidation must be a minimum of (1 – the advance rate), or 21% in this case.

Market value deals are actually marked-to-market no less frequently than once a week, and the tests are applied at that time. Some are marked-to-market daily. When the test is failed, the excess indebtedness must be repaid within 10 to 15 business days.

Minimum Net Worth Test

In addition to the protection provided by advance rates, rating agencies also require a quarterly minimum net worth test to protect the rated debt. In our example, this requires that

60% of the original equity remains to protect the senior tranche, and 30% to protect the subordinated tranche. If the equity falls below that, noteholders of the senior tranche may vote to accelerate payment of the debt, at which point the asset manager must liquidate assets and fully pay down the debt related to the test that has failed. In the simple 1 bond CDO shown in Exhibit 7.8, assume that the rating agency requires a 50% minimum net worth. This would mean that if the equity falls below $62.5 million ($125 million × 50%), the noteholders could vote to liquidate the deal. In this example, this would happen at the end of month 6, where, after the adjustments required to pass the overcollateralization (market value) test, the value of the equity would be $60.18 million ($286.54 million – $226.36 million).

HOW ADVANCE RATES ARE DERIVED

Advance rates are the crucial variable in market value deals. It is useful to look more closely at how these are derived. Advance rates are actually a combination of three factors—price volatility of the securities, correlation among securities, and liquidity. It's interesting to look at how Moody's and Fitch, the two rating agencies that have rated the bulk of the market value transactions, view each of these variables.

Both Moody's and Fitch use historical volatility as the basis for deriving volatility estimates. This volatility is then stressed depending on the length of the historical record and the desired rating of the CDO tranche. Because there is a very complete record for the returns on high-yield bonds (that is, high-quality information collected over a large number of years) only a relatively small stress factor is applied to the historical volatility for this instrument. At the other end of the spectrum, a relatively large stress factor is applied to distressed instruments, especially reorganized equities. The higher the desired rating, the greater the stress factor, which reflects the fact that higher rated tranches are expected to hold up under greater standard deviations of stress. Fitch is very explicit on that final point. A security rated A must be able to sustain market value declines three times as large as needed for the security to obtain a single B rating. For an AAA rating, the security must be able to sustain market value declines five times as large as would be needed to obtain a B rating.

The choice of correlations is problematic. Historical correlations are useful, but correlations often rise sharply during periods of crisis. Thus, Moody's uses correlations that are higher than those prevailing during "normal" periods, but not as high as those observed during the most stressful periods. Moody's assumes correlation of 0.55 between firms within the same industry, and 0.40 among those in different industries.

For most securities, the bid-ask spread is small relative to ordinary price volatility. However, market value transactions lend themselves to using less liquid assets that also have irregular cash flows. For these securities, liquidity can become a key consideration, especially during periods of financial stress. Both Moody's and Fitch make assumptions as to what losses would be during periods of market stress. So, for performing high-yield bonds, Moody's assumes a 5% liquidity "haircut," while for distressed bonds, it's "crewcut" is 10%. For performing bank loans the haircut is 7%, while for distressed bank loans it is increased to 12.5%. Reorganized equities get scalped at 20%.

So these three factors—price volatility, correlation among securities and liquidity together—account for the advance rates shown in Exhibits 7.5 and 7.6.

Are Advance Rates Conservative?

To test how conservative advance rates actually are, we look at monthly performance for a readily available set of data—high-yield bonds. From Ryan Labs we obtain the performance of the Lehman and Merrill Lynch indices, from January 1985 to January 2002. These two indices plus Salomon are the three indices most commonly used by investors for measuring the performance of the high-yield sector. Since the Salomon data do not go back as far, we do not include that index in the analysis.

We use monthly observations because the market values are evaluated at least weekly, and a portfolio normally has 10 to 15 business days to liquidate assets to correct the deficiency. Thus, if the portfolio passes the test one period, and then the market value of the portfolio deteriorates, it could take a maximum of just over four weeks to find and correct the deficiency (1 week maximum until the next test, 15 business days to correct the deficiency). This suggests that monthly intervals are the correct benchmark period for looking at how conservative advance rates are.

Both indices include all publicly traded domestic debt with a fixed-rate coupon, a minimum maturity of one year, and a maximum credit quality of Ba1. Both indices exclude payment-in-kind (PIK) bonds, and Eurobonds. However, there are still a number of differences. Lehman requires a minimum of $100 million outstanding for inclusion, while Merrill only requires $10 million. Lehman does not have a minimum credit quality for inclusion, and includes securities in default, whereas Merrill does not include securities in default (rated DDD1 or less).

There are 193 observations in the period investigated. Exhibit 7.9 shows the 1-month returns as a histogram. The monthly return distributions are similar in that they are both representative of the market, and their returns are usually close. Note from this histogram that there was only 1 month in which the total return on the Lehman index was less than −7% (the worst single month was September 1990 at −7.30%). The worst month on the Merrill index was −6.41% in September 2001. Given that Lehman also includes defaulted securities and Merrill does not, we would expect that the Lehman index would display a higher variance of returns.

The worst three months on the indices were August, September, and October 1990. The Lehman index was down 5.69% in August, 7.30% in September, and 5.25% in October of 1990. During the worst three-month period in the history of the market, the total loss was 17.2%. The Merrill index also showed these to be the worst three consecutive months on record: down 3.83% in August, 4.35% in September, and 2.54% in October, for a cumulative decline of 10.35%. This period corresponded to the beginning of the recession. We showed earlier that the advance rates are meant to correspond to one-month price changes. However, the advance rates are more severe than the worst three-month period in the history of the market. Clearly, the advance rates are very conservative.

EXHIBIT 7.9 Monthly Return Distribution of Merrill Lynch and Lehman Brothers High-Yield Indices (January 1985–January 2002)

One-Month Return Range	Merrill Lynch	Lehman Brothers
−8 to −7	0	1
−7 to −6	1	1
−6 to −5	0	3
−5 to −4	2	0
−4 to −3	2	4
−3 to −2	5	6
−2 to −1	11	9
−1 to 0	18	17
0 to 1	60	60
1 to 2	62	51
2 to 3	21	23
3 to 4	6	12
4 to 5	4	4
5 to 6	0	1
6 to 7	0	0
7 to 8	1	0
8 to 9	0	0
9 to 10	0	0
10 to 11	0	1
11 to 12	0	0
Total Obs:	193	193
Mean	0.852	0.831

Source: Ryan Labs, Inc.

Further Evidence of Conservative Aspect of Advance Rates

Want proof of the extent of conservatism in the rating methodology? As of year end 2001, Moody's has never downgraded a single tranche of a market value CDO, whereas Fitch has downgraded tranches on only two deals. Many investors will find that particularly surprising in light of asset price volatility in the 1998–2001 period. Clearly, part of the answer is that the vast majority of CDOs have been of the cash flow variety. However, another part of the answer is that the advance rates are so conservative that price volatility in recent years is well within the range anticipated by the advance rates.

COMPARISON TO HEDGE FUNDS

Now that we all have such a good understanding of how market value deals work, it is useful to contrast them to hedge funds. From the bondholder's point of view, making an investment in a market value CDO is quite different from giving money to a hedge fund and betting on how well it will perform. First, note what happens to leverage in the two different investment situations. As the value of assets decline, hedge fund equity becomes smaller, and hence the asset package becomes more highly leveraged (to the extent allowed by bank lines of credit). In a market value CDO, the percent equity in the deal cannot fall below the threshold of one minus the advance rate. Thus, the minimum equity in the deal is a constant, prespecified percent, and the market value tests are designed to insure this minimum equity threshold. (We saw in Exhibit 7.8 that the percent equity in the deal after liquidation is never lower than 21%, with a 79% advance rate.)

Second, the equity financing in a CDO is permanent, whereas in a hedge fund, equity can leave, thus forcing liquidations. In a CDO, the only forced liquidations are those designed to protect the bondholders.

CONCLUSION

Many CDO investors have steered away from the debt in market value deals, believing that purchasing the debt is like making an investment in a hedge fund. As a result, market value deals trade at similar or slightly wider spreads than cash flow deals launched at the same time. The protections built into market value deals are quite powerful from the bondholder's point of view.

CHAPTER 8

Synthetic Balance Sheet CDOs

An increasingly important part of the CDO market is the synthetic CDO/credit derivative structure, or simply synthetic CDO. This structure is so named because the CDO does not actually own the pool of assets on which it has the economic risk. Stated differently, a synthetic CDO absorbs the economic risks, but not the legal ownership, of its reference credit exposures.

Historically, the dominant issuer of synthetic CDOs have been U.S. and European banks. The key motivation for the majority of synthetic CDOs issued by these entities has been to achieve ongoing regulatory capital relief. These structures are *synthetic balance sheet CDOs*. The delinking of ownership and the economic risk of the underlying assets provided by a synthetic CDO affords a bank, for example, substantial additional flexibility in balance sheet management. More specifically, a synthetic balance sheet CDO allows banks to reduce regulatory capital charges and reduce economic risk while retaining ownership of the attendant assets. Thus, the initial synthetic CDO deals were balance sheet deals.

Today, synthetic *arbitrage* deals dominate the market. Moreover, synthetic arbitrage CDOs are the fastest growing part of the CDO market. This should be expected to continue because of the many advantages of the synthetic structure over its cash counterpart.

EXHIBIT 8.1   Structure of a CLO

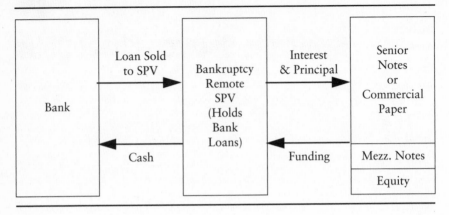

In this chapter and the next, our focus is on synthetic CDO structures. In this chapter we look at synthetic balance sheet CDOs. We look at basic structures and various structural nuances. We then learn the unique challenges confronting the rating agencies in evaluating these products and wrap up the chapter with the key differences between synthetic and nonsynthetic transactions. In the next chapter, we turn our attention to synthetic arbitrage deals, addressing the advantages of this structure over their cash counterparts.

CLOS FOR BALANCE SHEET MANAGEMENT

CLOs were the first vehicles to explicitly address the balance sheet needs of commercial banks. In a CLO, a bank sells a pool of loans to a special purpose vehicle (SPV), and takes back the first loss piece. There is a huge capital advantage to the bank using a CLO structure. If the bank held those loans directly in portfolio, it must then also hold risk-based capital equal to 8% of the loans. (Loans are a 100% risk weight item, capital charges of 8% are levied on these items.)

We have set out a typical CLO structure in Exhibit 8.1. Note that the loans have been transferred to the SPV, who funds these loans from the cash proceeds of the notes it has issued. The notes are credit-tranched. The senior notes (or commercial paper) are sold at a very tight spread. The mezzanine notes are sold in the marketplace to insurance companies, money managers, banks, and bank conduits. The equity is usually retained by the originating bank. Generally, the senior notes will be about 92% of the deal, the mezzanine notes 4%, with about 4% equity.

From the point of view of the originating bank, capital implications of this CLO structure are far more favorable than from holding the same loans outright. Banks are required to hold the lesser of (1) the capital charge on the unlevered amount, which would in this case be 8%, or (2) 100% of its liability. If 100% of a liability is the smaller number, as it generally will be in a CLO structure, we consider that institution subject to "low level recourse" requirements. In this case, the maximum liability of the originating bank is 4%. That is, a 100% capital charge on the 4% equity piece requires a 4% capital requirement. And this is precisely one half the 8% capital required if the bank alternatively held those same loans outright. This is shown in Exhibit 8.2, which we will refer to throughout this chapter.

BANK PROBLEMS USING CLO STRUCTURES

From the bank's point of view, CLO structures go a long way toward more efficient capital utilization. However, two problems still remain. First, there is a funding issue; and second, there is a confidentiality issue.

To address the first aspect, most banks are low-cost funders. It does not pay to transfer AAA risk from a low-cost funder to a higher cost funder, as that higher cost funder cannot profitably fund higher rated assets. Exhibit 8.3 shows us why. Assume that a high cost funder borrows at LIBOR + 30, while a low cost funder can achieve a funding cost of LIBOR − 5. Further assume a high-quality asset (loan) paying LIBOR + 35, with the cost of laying off the credit risk on this asset at 20 basis points. So after netting out credit risk, the asset yields LIBOR + 15. The high-cost funder could only finance this asset at a deficit of 15 basis points, while the low-cost funder carries the same asset at a surplus of 20 basis points.

EXHIBIT 8.2   Comparison of Capital Charges

Type of Security	Equity Retained	Capital Charge Methodology	Capital Charge Incurred
Hold loans on balance sheet	n.a.	100% risk weight, 8% risk-based capital (RBC) requirement	8%
CLO	4%	Low level recourse requirement: lesser of the capital charge on the unlevered amount or 100% of bank liability.	100% of 4% equity retained = 4%
Fully funded synthetic CLO	1%	Low level recourse requirement on equity. 20% risk weight on credit default swap if swap is with OECD institution. 0% risk weight if swap is with SPV and fully collateralized with 0% RBC securities (cash or cash substitutes or Treasuries).	If credit default swap is with an OECD institution: 100% of 1% equity + (20% × 8%) on swap = 2.6% $\quad$ If credit default swap is collateralized with 0% RBC securities: 100% of 1% equity + 0% on swap = 1%
Partially funded synthetic CLO	1% (10% junior credit default swap, 90% senior default swap, always with OECD institution)	For U.S. banks, the super senior piece always receives a 20% risk weight regardless of whether it is retained or laid off. Treatment on equity and junior credit default swap is the same as above.	If junior credit default swap is with OECD institution: 100% of 1% equity + (20% × 8% on swaps) = 2.6% $\quad$ If junior credit default swap is collateralized with 0% RBC securities: 100% of 1% equity + (0% × 10% junior swap) + (20% × 8% × 90% on super senior swap) = 2.44%

EXHIBIT 8.3 Transferring AAA Risk from Low-Cost Funder to High-Cost Funder

	Low-Cost Funder	High-Cost Funder
Yield on high-quality asset	LIBOR + 35	LIBOR + 35
Less funding cost	LIBOR – 5	LIBOR + 30
Less cost of laying off the credit risk	20 bps	20 bps
Net excess return	20 bps	–15 bps

That difference in funding costs is important, because CLO financing is relatively expensive. The AAA tranches sell for LIBOR + (35 – 45). Thus, efficiently managing regulatory capital can cause a bank to accept an inefficient means of financing. (But all is not gloom and doom. Realize that the CLO funding is *term funding*, which is more advantageous than funding which must be *rolled* over. It both guarantees availability and avoids the risk that credit spreads may widen.)

The second disadvantage of the CLO structure is one of confidentiality. If a loan is transferred into a special purpose vehicle for use as collateral for a CLO, borrower notification is always required, plus borrower consent often required. Banks believe it looks kind of shabby to sell customer loans. It is akin to selling your own kid's toys at a garage sale before they have outgrown them. Better that they do not know. So customer relationships understandably put an impediment on a bank's willingness to sell or transfer customer loan assets into outside pools. These disadvantages are shown in Exhibit 8.4.

A related disadvantage to the CLO structure is that terms and conditions of loan collateral cannot be modified within the structure. In order to modify any terms and conditions, that specified loan must be pulled out of the pool and another substituted. The substitution process required adds a substantial hassle factor.

EXHIBIT 8.4   Comparison of Bank Balance Sheet Management Techniques

Option	Achieve capital relief?	Achieve confidentiality?	Wide range of assets allowed?	Achieve favorable funding?
Leave assets on balance sheet	No	Yes	Yes	Yes
CLO	Yes	No	No	No
Fully funded CDO	Yes	Yes	Yes	No
Partially funded CDO	Yes	Yes	Yes	Yes

CREDIT DEFAULT SWAPS

The basis for synthetic securitizations are *credit default swaps*. These allow institutions to transfer the economic risk, but not legal ownership, of the underlying assets. This, in turn, permits those institutions to shed the economic risk of assets without having to notify borrowers or seek their consent. It also enables the securitization of the associated credit risk with a wider range of bank assets, including derivatives and receivables. Finally, it gives greater flexibility in modifying the terms and conditions of loans.

Credit default swaps are really quite simple—they are conceptually similar to insurance policies. The protection buyer is purchasing protection against default risk on a reference pool of assets. That reference pool can consist of loans, bonds or derivatives or receivables. In a credit default swap, the protection buyer pays a periodic fee in return for a contingent payment by the protection seller in the event of a "credit event" with respect to the reference entity. The fee or insurance premium paid by the protection buyer is typically expressed in basis points per annum, and is paid on the notional amount on the swap. The protection seller only makes a payment if that "credit event" occurs. This is illustrated in Exhibit 8.5.

EXHIBIT 8.5   Credit Default Swap

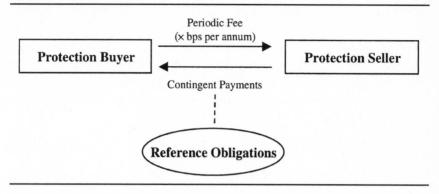

CREDIT EVENTS

In a credit default swap, a definition of a "credit event" is needed in order to determine when a loss has occurred. Typically, credit event definitions generally conform to the 1999 International Swaps and Derivatives Association (ISDA) credit derivative definitions including the supplemental amendments published by the ISDA. The ISDA credit events applicable to credit default swaps include

- Bankruptcy
- Failure to pay
- Obligation acceleration
- Repudiation/moratorium
- Restructuring

"Bankruptcy" is defined as a variety of events that are associated with bankruptcy or insolvency laws. The ISDA acknowledges that its definition of insolvency-related events is not the same as that used by rating agencies in their studies of corporate defaults. That is, in deriving ratings based on their studies of defaults, rating agency use a definition that is not as broad in scope as that used by the ISDA. As an example, suppose that at a board meeting a corporation considers the filing of a liquidation petition. While arguably this may be considered a credit event as defined by the ISDA, the rating agencies would not consider this a bankruptcy event.

A failure of the reference entity to make, when and where due, any payments under one or more obligations is defined as a "failure to pay." An "obligation acceleration" covers instances where the obligation becomes due and payable prior to the time when that obligation would otherwise have been due and payable and the payment was not made. A "default" for purposes of an obligation acceleration is a violation of a provision or term of the obligation by the reference entity. Generally, the credit default swap agreement will specify a minimum threshold (called the "default requirement") which the relevant sum being accelerated must exceed before the credit event occurs.

"Repudiation/moratorium" covers situations where the obligation is disaffirmed or challenged as to validity by the reference entity (or a governmental authority). "Restructuring" covers events in which the terms of the obligation are modified making them less favorable to the lender. Examples of such events are a reduction in the principal amount or interest payable, a postponement of payment or a change in ranking in priority of payment.

Restructuring has been the most controversial aspect of the ISDA's definition of credit events. Obviously, the protection seller (the investor, through the SPV) would prefer not to have restructuring as a "credit event," while the issuer has a preference to include it. In the wake of Conseco's restructuring in August 2000, in which the maturity of about $2.8 billion in debt was extended, which triggered payouts on credit default swaps, the dealer community has split widely over whether restructuring should be a "credit event." The concern was that even routine modifications that may be common in lending would trigger a credit event. Moreover, there was the fear that lenders (protection buyers in a constant default swap) had virtually nothing to lose by restructuring a reference entity's debt, triggering a payment by the protection seller. In April 2001, the ISDA revised its definition of restructuring specifying that to qualify as a restructuring there must be multiple lenders (at least three) and at least two-thirds of the lenders must agree to restructuring. Investors should be aware that restructuring is generally treated as a credit event and should be sure they understand what events can be considered "restructurings" when purchasing a synthetic CDO.

FULLY FUNDED SYNTHETIC CDOS

In a fully funded synthetic CDO, notes equal to approximately 100% of the reference pool of assets are issued by a special purpose vehicle (SPV). The notes are generally tranched by credit quality. The first fully funded synthetic CDO was Glacier Finance Ltd., done by Swiss Bank in August of 1997.

The proceeds of these notes are generally invested in a portfolio of high quality securities, which is used as collateral. These high-quality assets consist of government securities, repurchase agreements on government securities, or high-quality (AAA) asset-backed securities. Meanwhile, the originating bank enters into a credit default swap either directly or indirectly with the SPV. Essentially, the originating bank buys default protection in return for a premium that subsidizes the coupon to compensate the investor for the default risk on the reference credits. The mechanics of this are illustrated in Exhibit 8.6.

Intuitively, the investor is receiving an interest payment equal to the yield on the high-quality securities plus the credit default swap premium. The investor is, in turn, providing the credit protection to the bank portfolio, which allows the bank to reduce the regulatory capital it is required to maintain.

In synthetic CDOs, just as in the CLO structure, the originating bank retains a first-loss (equity) position. That's really the equivalent of an insurance deductible. That is, the originating institution generally absorbs the first 1–1.5% of losses. This is generally achieved by having the bottom tranche of securities be equity (retained by the originating institution).

EXHIBIT 8.6   Fully Funded Synthetic CDO Swap Directly Between Originating Bank and SPV

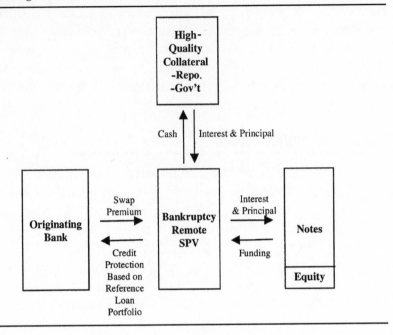

Using an example can make this clearer. Assume that the obligations of the SPV are comprised 95% of securities with an AAA rating, 2% of securities with a BBB rating, 2.0% of securities with a BB rating, and 1% as equity. Moreover, assume 2% of the notional amount of loans experiences a "credit event," and that payout on each credit event is 50%. The trustee would liquidate 1% of the high quality securities in the collateral account to pay off the originating bank. Interest payments to the equity holders would cease, and they would not receive any principal. If this were all the losses that arose in the course of the transaction, the rated noteholders would received all monies (both principal and interest) due them. If an additional 1% of loans in the portfolio experienced a credit event, also compensated at 50%, then an additional 0.5% of the high-quality securities in the collateral account would be liquidated, so the BB security would then take a hit.

EXHIBIT 8.7 Fully Funded Synthetic CDO Swap with OECD Bank as Intermediary

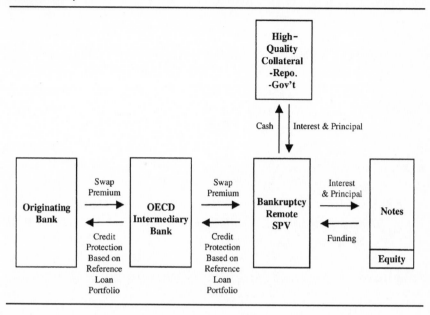

SWAP ARRANGEMENTS

The originating bank is usually the protection buyer, and the SPV is usually the protection seller. Thus, the credit default swap is done directly with the SPV. Alternatively, the credit default swap can done indirectly with the SPV, by introducing another OECD bank which acts as the counterparty on both sides. The originating bank (protection buyer) enters into a credit default swap with another OECD bank (protection seller). This OECD bank (the protection seller) offsets the risk on that first swap by entering into another swap with the SPV, with the OECD bank being the protection buyer and the SPV selling the protection. These back-to-back swaps have the economic effect of mitigating the risk for the OECD bank, and they leave the originating bank as the protection buyer and the SPV as the protection seller. This is illustrated in Exhibit 8.7.

While these structures are conceptually similar, there are subtle differences. If the swap is done directly with the SPV, then capital treatment for the originating bank will depend entirely on the risk weight of the investments of the SPV. That is, if the SPV invests the assets solely in cash, cash substitutes or Treasury securities, the risk-based capital charge associated with the swap is 0%. If the SPV invests in AAA assets with a current risk weight of 100%, risk-based capital charges then become a prohibitive 100%.

Introducing the intermediary bank changes the risk-based capital treatment. If the risk transference between the originating bank and the SPV is done indirectly, via introducing another OECD bank as an intermediary, the risk-based capital charge on the swap is 20%. Essentially, since the credit risk of the underlying asset has truly been transferred to the protection seller, the risk weighting of the underlying assets (the loans) is replaced with the risk weighting of the protection seller. Under BIS guidelines, the risk weighting of another OECD bank is defined as 20%.

Thus, when setting up the synthetic CDO, the originating bank must decide whether it is more favorable to (1) limit the collateral account to 0% risk weight assets, which will constrain the choice of high quality assets that can be used; or (2) introduce an OECD bank as intermediary and incur capital charges on a 20% risk weighted asset.

Capital Requirements

The equity that is retained by the originating bank will always carry a 100% risk weight. Assume this equity portion is 1%, as is shown in Exhibit 8.2. Additional capital requirements depend on whether there is an intermediary bank. Absent an intermediary bank, and if the SPV invests entirely in 0% risk weighted assets—then the capital charge on the swap is 0%, as mentioned above. Thus, the total capital charge on the CDO would just be the retained equity of, say, 1%. If there is an intermediary OECD bank, the risk-based capital requirement on the swap is 20% of 8% (equaling 1.6%) of the notional amount of the credit default swap. Thus, if a bank entered into a fully funded synthetic CDO with a 1% first-loss position, the capital requirement is 100% of the first-loss piece, plus the risk-based capital requirement on the credit default swap. This would mean a capital charge of 2.6%.

The U.S. Bank regultors allow for even lower capital charges for U.S. banks.[1] The regulators (the Federal Reserve and Office of the Comptroller of the Currency) describe two approaches, and require banks to use the higher of the two. The first approach is to hold a dollar for dollar loss against first loss position. On a 1% first loss position, this would be a 1% capital charge. The second approach would be to have this transaction treated as a direct credit substitute, and assessed an 8% capital charge against its face value of 1%. The second loss position, if collateral by Treasury securities would have no capital charge. If guaranteed by an intermediary bank the second loss position would be assigned to the 20% risk category. Thus, under this approach, using our example, the capital charge would be $(0.08 \times (0.01 + 0.2))$ or 1.68%. Since this is higher than the 1% charge under the first approach, it would be the applicable charge.

Advantages and Disadvantages

Now let's focus on the advantages of the synthetic fully funded CDO, as shown in Exhibit 8.4. First, the structure is confidential with respect to the bank's customers. None need be notified that their loan is being used within this structure, as the loan clearly stays with the bank. The names in the reference pool must be provided to the protection seller, but need not be publicly disclosed. For European banks, this point is particularly important, as selling a loan into an SPV is looked at by many as compromising a customer relationship. This explains the prevalence of the synthetic CLO structure there. Second, the bank has the flexibility to use the contract as a

---

[1] This is outlined in a document entitled "Capital Interpretation, Synthetic Collateralized Loan Obligations" (November 15, 1999). This document is available on the Federal Reserve Web site.

hedge for any senior obligation of the reference entity (including not only loans, but also bonds, derivatives, receivables, and so on) Third, the capital treatment is favorable.

However the disadvantage of a fully funded synthetic CDO is that the loans must be funded by a high-cost funder (which is the marginal buyer in the capital markets) rather than a low-cost funder (the bank itself). Moreover, in a fully funded structure, the amount of notes issued is approximately the same as the amount of loans backing the credit default swap, hence the nomenclature. That means that there's quite a bit of funding required, and hence a high cost associated with the reduction in required regulatory capital. This is again summarized in Exhibit 8.3.

PARTIALLY FUNDED SYNTHETIC CDOS

The building blocks are the same in a partially funded structure, but the notes issued only amount to 5–15% of the notional amount of the reference portfolio. Partially funded synthetic CDOs deliver the favorable capital treatment while achieving *more favorable funding* than do fully funded CDOs. As a result, partially funded CDOs are far more common than fully funded structures.

The first partially synthetic CDO was actually the BISTRO transaction, pioneered by J.P. Morgan in December of 1997. (BISTRO stands for Broad Index Secured Trust Offering).

The structure behind partially funded synthetic CDO transactions is very similar to that on fully funded CDOs. The originating bank buys protection on a portfolio of corporate credit exposures via a credit default swap, either directly or indirectly, from an SPV. This is shown in Exhibit 8.8a. Thus, the originating bank is the protection buyer, the SPV the protection seller. As in fully funded transactions, there may or may not be an intermediary OECD bank that sells the credit protection to the originating bank and buys it back from the SPV. In the BISTRO transactions there is generally an intermediary bank, while in most other partially funded transactions, the credit default swap is directly between the bank and the SPV. The partially funded structure in which there is an OECD intermediary is shown in Exhibit 8.8b. The credit protection is usually subject to a "threshold" level of losses (equivalent of a deductible) that must be experienced on the reference portfolio before any payment is due to the origination bank under the portfolio credit swap. This accomplished by having the originating bank hold the equity issued by the SPV.

EXHIBIT 8.8   Partially Funded Synthetic CDO
a. Swap Directly Between Originating Bank and SPV

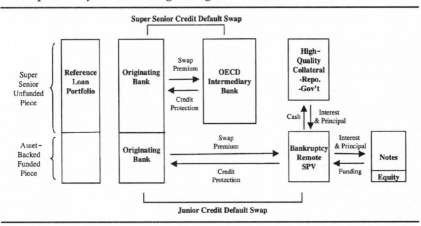

b. Partially Funded Synthetic Swap

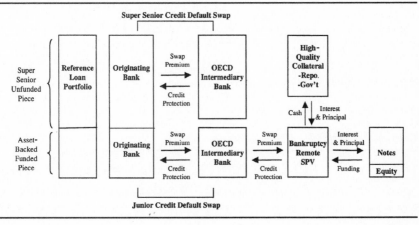

The SPV is collateralized with government securities, repurchase agreements on government securities or other high-quality collateral, and funds these through issuance of notes. Those notes are credit tranched, and sold into the capital market.

However, in a critical departure from traditional fully funded securitization, the SPV issues a substantially smaller amount of notes, and holds substantially less collateral, than the notional amount of the reference portfolio. This is clearly shown in Exhibits 8.8a and 8b. Typically, the note issuance will amount to only 5–15% of the notional amount of the reference portfolio. Thus, only the first 5–15% of losses in a particular portfolio are funded by the vehicle, which leaves the most senior risk position unfunded.

Realize that the unfunded portion—known as the "super senior piece"—is a very high quality piece of paper. Given the quality of the underlying reference portfolio, there's only a remote probability that a loss might exceed the 5–15% of the exposure that has been funded. The unfunded (super senior) piece is, in essence, better than an AAA credit risk. Another way to look at this is to realize that some of the credit support below the super senior piece is often still rated AAA. (The senior tranche issued by the SPV, which absorbs losses before they hit the super senior piece, is often rated AAA.) In bank balance sheet transactions, the risk on the super senior piece can be laid off via a second credit default swap, often referred to as the "super senior credit default swap," again shown in Exhibits 8.8a and 8b. And the swap on the funded portion of the transaction is often referred to as the "junior credit default swap."

CAPITAL TREATMENT

Investors should realize that in a partially funded structure, the super senior piece is often afforded the same capital treatment whether or not the risk is laid off on another OECD bank. If the risk is laid off via a credit default swap on another OECD bank, the bank will be afforded a 20% risk weight. If the risk is not laid off, but is retained by the originating bank, the bank may still qualify for a 20% risk weight. That is, on November 15, 1999, the Federal Reserve issued a set of capital interpretations on synthetic CLOs, which apply to U.S banks.[2] These guidelines allow the retained super senior piece to achieve a 20% risk weight, as long as a number of conditions are met including the presence of a senior class of notes that receives the highest possible rating (i.e., AAA) from a nationally recognized credit rating agency. Prior to this interpretation, if the risk on the super senior piece was not laid off there was no capital relief, and the risk weight was 100%. For European banks, the treatment will vary jurisdiction by jurisdiction.

The regulatory capital charge on the equity and on the junior credit default swap follows the same rules as on the fully funded synthetic, and are summarized in Exhibit 8.2. If the junior swap is done directly with the SPV, and the SPV is collateralized with 0% risk weight assets, then the assets backing the junior swap have a 0% risk weight. The capital charge on this would be 100% of the first loss piece (the equity portion), plus the capital charge on the super senior credit default swap. Assume, again a 1% first loss piece, and assume that the junior credit swap is for 10% of the transaction amount. Thus, the super senior portion is 90% of the notional amount. The credit charge on this portion is ([the 20% risk weight] × [the 8% capital charge] × [90% of the notional amount]) or 1.44%. Thus, the total capital charge is 2.44% (1% on equity + 1.44% on the super senior swap).

If an OECD bank serves as the protection seller to the originating bank on the junior default swap, the 20% capital charge would apply to 100% of the notional loan amount. Thus, the capital charge would be [20% of 8%] or

---

[2] The document is entitled "Capital Interpretations, Synthetic Collateralized Loan Obligations" (November 15, 1999), and can be found on the Federal Reserve Web site.

1.6%. The total capital charge on the transaction would be [the capital charge on the swaps] + [the capital charge on the equity], or 2.6%.

Under U.S. bank regulation, the capital charges would be somewhat lower. If the junior credit default swap was collateralized by Treasuries, the capital charge would be 8% on the 1% first loss position (direct credit substitute rule) plus 8% × 20% on the 90% super senior price, for a total of 1.52%. (This is obviously higher than for a dollar-for-dollar charge on the 1% piece which is retained.) If an OECD bank acts as the protection seller on the credit default swap, the direct credit substitute rule would apply on the 1% first loss piece, and a 20% risk based capital requirement would apply on 100% of the notional amount, for a total capital charge of 1.68%.

This partially funded structure has several advantages. It allows banks to reduce the risk on a large number of on-balance sheet assets. Confidentiality issues are also preserved, as is a funding advantage (since only 5–15% of the loans are funded). Finally, favorable regulatory capital treatment is achieved, as shown in Exhibit 8.4. As a result, partially funded synthetic balance sheet transactions have become the norm.

HEDGING AND ARBITRAGE TRANSACTIONS

While the overwhelming majority of synthetic CDOs has been driven by regulatory capital treatment for banks, a few came from the desire to hedge on- or off-balance sheet trading exposures. While those driven by a desire to hedge dealer exposure have thus far been very limited, we believe that this is potentially a very important growth area for the CDO market. It is also a potentially important risk management tool for dealers. For dealers, hedging credit risk is more difficult than ever, as credit spreads have been more volatile than ever historically. Moreover, default rates on high-yield securities are higher than at any point since 1991. Partially mitigating the credit risk on an inventory of trading positions (either bonds or positions in the swap book such as credit default swaps or total rate of return swaps) is very valuable for a dealer. Moreover, it is not unreasonable to think that if this method became a trusted credit risk management tool, dealers would be willing to hold larger inventories, as they would be able to lay off more of the risk than is currently the case.

While only a few hedging transactions have been done to date, many institutions are looking at these types of transactions, and quite a few are currently in the pipeline. These hedging transactions, like the bank balance sheet deals, allow an institution to delink ownership from the economic risk, and transfer economic risk on an item that is otherwise difficult to hedge.

In *arbitrage transactions*, a portfolio of bonds is purchased. The intent is that portfolio default risk will be mitigated by the credit default swap, as the bond portfolio then becomes the reference portfolio for the CDO. The arbitrage is created because the issuer believes that spreads on the underlying assets are wider than warranted by the cost of laying off the default risk.

Structural Issues—Hedging and Arbitrage Driven Transactions

Hedging and arbitrage-driven transactions are structured identically to the bank balance sheet restructuring CDOs we covered earlier in this chapter. The hedging or arbitrage-driven transactions may be fully or partly funded, with partial funding as the "norm."

The position to be hedged, or the arbitrage portfolio that has been purchased, becomes the reference portfolio for the credit default swap. In this type of structure the hedging institution is buying protection against "credit events," which is purchased from a swap counterparty. The swap counterparty, in turn, lays off the risk of the credit default swap onto the SPV. The SPV then becomes a protection seller, with the originating institution the ultimate protection buyer.

Just as in the bank balance sheet deals, the SPV issues notes, with the proceeds invested in a portfolio of high quality securities. In the aggregate, the investors receive [coupon equal to the premium on the credit default swap] + [the yield on the risk free assets].

HYBRID TRANSACTIONS

A number of traditional CDOs also had a synthetic component, at least initially, as the needed assets were either unavailable during the ramp-up period, or the assets available did not allow for appropriate diversification. For example, assume a money manager is ramping up a high-yield deal, but most of the recent issues have been telecom, so a sufficiently diversified portfolio cannot be easily purchased. The non-telecom exposure could be provided via a credit default swap. This swap could be unwound as other bonds became available. Similarly, during a short ramp-up period, there may not be enough diversification in emerging market bonds, and a money manager may want to add exposure to a given area (say Asia) via a credit default swap.

RATING CONSIDERATIONS

The rating agencies face a number of unique difficulties in rating synthetic CDO transactions. While each uses a slightly different approach, they all tend to rely on historical default and loss information. There is a considerable amount of such information on bonds and loans. However, in the credit default swap inherent in a synthetic CDO, a "credit event" need not correspond with what would have been an interruption in payment. In fact, it is not only the inclusion of restructuring into credit events that makes the rating agencies nervous, but also the acceleration of payments due to cross default/cross acceleration clauses. The definition of a "credit event" means that much of the historical work on defaults must be used very cautiously. This is a topic that has received considerable attention in both the dealer and the rating agency communities. However, it has received relatively little attention in the investor community.

The second conundrum for the rating agencies is the degree of trading that can be done in the reference portfolio. One of the largest changes in bank balance sheet synthetic CDOs through time has been the amount of trading permitted. The right of substitution was very limited in many early transactions. While it varies from deal to deal, substitutions in and out of the reference portfolio can now be made fairly freely, subject to quality considerations.

This substitution is very important in hedging and arbitrage transactions. In hedging dealer inventories, the exposures will change over time, thus so, too, must the reference portfolio. Similarly, for arbitrage transactions, the more trading that is permitted, the more flexibility the portfolio manager has. From the rating agencies' point of view, a conservative methodology is called for. Unlike market value deals, where the market enforces the discipline, in a cash flow deal with liberal substitution, the rating agency must assume the worst in their rating. This is particularly true where the equity "first loss" piece is small in relation to the total transaction.

The third issue for the rating agencies is the use of unusual asset classes as the reference portfolio. For example, there is very little historical experience on the default history of swaps, as the transactions are private. As with all new asset classes, the rating agencies tend to be very conservative.

Having said this, it is important to realize that synthetic CDOs are a new product. Furthermore, the rating process for these products is being refined, as experience accumulates and deals keep sporting new variations. Again, with new products, the rating agencies are apt to be initially conservative, which works to the advantage of investors.

SUMMARY—STRUCTURAL DIFFERENCES

There are a number of structural differences between a synthetic CDO and a CDO backed directly by bond or loan collateral. These differences all stem from the fact that ownership and economic risk of the securities or exposures have been delinked.

- *The term of the synthetic instrument is well defined.* The investor is not dependent on the cash flows of an underlying bond or loan instrument. The maturity of the instrument is governed solely by the maturity of the underlying credit default swaps.
- *On the synthetic CDO, there is no interest rate risk, either at initial investment or at liquidation.* This is because the credit default swap addresses only the credit risk on the instrument. If there is no "credit event," but the security is worth considerably less at liquidation, then that is not the problem of the rated noteholder.
- *The synthetic CDO cannot benefit (or lose) on any discretionary trading done in the portfolio.* The results of this discretionary trading would be reflected in higher (lower) market values when the security is eventually sold, but the synthetic is not dependent on changes in market values.

CONCLUSION

Synthetic CDOs have grown tremendously in a short period of time. Bank balance sheet deals have increasingly been effected in synthetic form rather than in CLO form. The debut of synthetic hedging and arbitrage deals was in 2000. These deals represent a huge growth area for the CDO business.

Rating synthetic deals presents some unique challenges to the rating agencies, and methodologies will be refined over time. Meanwhile, in early deals in newer asset categories, the rating agencies tend to err on the conservative side, which gives investors an opportunity to invest at generally favorable conditions. However, investors must understand the unique characteristics of these instruments in order to profit from this.

CHAPTER 9

Synthetic Arbitrage CDOs

Synthetic arbitrage deals are the fastest growing part of the CDO market. As explained in the previous chapter, in a synthetic CDO, the CDO entity does not actually own the pool of assets on which it bears the credit risk; credit exposure is obtained by selling credit default swaps. This structure has a number of advantages over their cash counterparts. Most importantly, the super senior piece in a synthetic CDO is generally not funded. In addition, there is only a short ramp-up period, plus credit default swaps often trade cheaper than the cash bond of the same maturity. In this chapter we explore the advantages of synthetic arbitrage deals in depth.

It is important to realize that not all synthetic CDO deals are structured identically. There are truly huge differences, depending on whether deals are static or managed (the latter increasingly frequent), and how they are structured. Yet structuring choices are rarely "good" or "bad"; rather, there are pluses and minuses to each. In this chapter we will also explore some of those structural variations within the synthetic CDO market, and the relative advantages/disadvantages.

GROWTH OF SYNTHETIC ARBITRAGE CDOs

In 2001, far more arbitrage CDO deals were issued than balance sheet CDO deals. Specifically, arbitrage deals comprised approximately 75% of the CDO universe, as measured by the dollar amount of funded CDO tranches. Within arbitrage deals, even though cash deals continued to dominate, synthetic CDOs were the fastest growing segment. In 2001, funded tranches of synthetic deals grew to 9% of total arbitrage transactions, up from 4% the prior year. Over the same period, cash flow CDOs expanded from 79% to 87% of total arbitrage CDOs, while market value deals actually dropped from 17% to 4% of the total.

Yet these measures vastly underestimate the importance of synthetic CDO structures, as they totally miss the super senior tranche that is sold in unfunded (credit default swap) form. That is, they only account for the total funded capitalization (debt plus equity) of the CDO market and omit the unfunded portion. CDOs collateralized by cash purchased assets must be fully funded; that is, the assets purchased are roughly equal to the amount of liabilities and equity issued, as the funding is used to purchase the assets. By contrast, there is conceptually no reason for synthetic CDOs to be funded at all. In fact, a synthetic CDO must go to some efforts to create a funded tranche. It must employ the cash by finding assets to purchase, which have little risk (repo or AAA ABS, for instance).

In practice, most synthetic CDO deals are partially funded; that is, they have an unfunded super senior tranche, with the rest of the capital structure funded by a combination of debt and equity. That super senior tranche is senior to the funded AAA class, and is generally eight to nine times the value of the funded tranches. For example, in one CDO deal issued in the first quarter of 2002, backed by a portfolio of credit default swaps on investment grade collateral, the super senior tranche was 89% of the deal, the funded AAA and AA classes were 6% of the pool, with the funded mezzanine and equity tranches comprising the remaining 5%. This meant that $890 million of the CDO was unfunded, and only $110 million was funded. Thus, the unfunded piece was eight times the size of the funded portion.

But point in fact, if one measured the CDO market by the amount of risk transferred from one party to another rather than by the dollar amount of funded tranches, most of those unfunded super senior tranches should be included. (Not all, because, in some cases, a part of the super senior bond is retained.) When measuring the composition of arbitrage CDOs by the amount of risk transferred, synthetic deals leaped to 44% of total arbitrage transactions in 2001 (versus only 9% when not counting unfunded super senior tranches), while cash flow deals slid to 54% of the total (from 87%), and market value deals halved, from 4% to 2%. Thus, measured by the actual amounts of risk defeased, in 2001 synthetic deals were almost as large as cash flow deals.

ADVANTAGES—SYNTHETIC STRUCTURE

The funding advantages possible through the use of synthetic collateral are so overwhelming that synthetic collateral will become, over time, the dominant method of doing CDOs. In particular, there are three economic advantages to using synthetic collateral:

1. The super senior bond does not need to be funded.
2. There is a considerably shorter ramp-up period for synthetic deals than for deals invested in cash securities (bonds or loans).
3. Credit default swaps can often be cheaper than the underlying cash bond.

Let us now look at each of these points in turn.

Super Senior Bond Does Not Need To Be Funded

Recall from the previous chapter that in a synthetic CDO structure risk on the reference portfolio gets partitioned into two parts—a senior section (generally about 90% of the reference portfolio) and a junior piece (generally about

10%). And that latter, junior section, absorbs losses up to its notional amount, before the super senior absorbs a single dollar of losses.

The junior section employs a typical CDO structure. Notes (equal to approximately 10% of the reference pool of assets, and customarily tranched by credit quality) are issued by a special purpose vehicle (SPV). Proceeds from that note issuance are generally invested in a portfolio of high quality securities, which is then used as collateral. The protection buyer (often the CDO manager, but not necessarily) then enters into a credit default swap with the SPV ("junior credit default swap"). Essentially, the CDO manager (the protection buyer) is buying default protection on the reference entities from the CDO investors (the protection seller). Thus, the CDO manager is paying a premium, this premium is used to subsidize the coupon compensation to investors, as the investors are bearing the default risk (first loss) on the entire portfolio of reference entities. Intuitively, investors receive an interest payment equal to the yield on the high-quality securities plus the credit default swap premium.

The super senior piece is then left unfunded and often sold off as a credit default swap. It is important to realize that this risk is of very high quality. Given the investment-grade quality of the underlying reference portfolio, there is only the remotest possibility that a loss might exceed the approximately 10% exposure that was funded. Thus the super senior piece of a synthetic CDO is, in essence, even better than a AAA credit risk. In fact, the most senior of the funded tranches, which is clearly below the super senior piece in the credit pecking order, is often rated AAA. And what risk there is on the super senior tranche is generally laid off via a second credit default swap, often referred to a the "super senior credit default swap."

The fact that this super senior piece really does not need to be funded at all is worth a tremendous amount. The AAA rated entity usually trades at LIBOR + 50, and the super senior swap costs 5–10 basis points. Assuming reinvestment on the high-quality portfolio of assets at LIBOR flat, then a CDO asset manager saves 40–45 basis points on each dollar it does not have to fund.

In terms of deal economics, this is huge. It is equal to the collateral trading 36–41 basis points cheaper (from 90% of the liabilities being 40–45 basis points cheaper). Another way to look at it is as follows. In mid-March 2002, the spread between BBB and BB industrials was 166 basis points.[1] Thus, BBs were trading 166 basis points wider than BBBs. To achieve the same funding efficiency as using a synthetic structure, CDO asset managers would have had to add a minimum of 22% BB securities to a BBB portfolio (166 basis points × 0.22 = 36 basis points). In fact, in CDO deals backed by nonsynthetic investment grade corporate bonds, the arbitrage was generally not attainable without the presence of a sizable BB piece.

The final way to evaluate the improvement in deal economics from the super senior bond not having to be funded is to look at the impact on the internal rate of return on equity (IRR). Assuming a 3% equity piece, a funding improvement of 36 basis points on the deal adds 12% (0.36/0.03) to the equity's IRR.

Short Ramp-Up Period

The second advantage of synthetic CDOs is that the ramp-up period is substantially shorter than in cash deals. Early CDO deals were priced with only a few bonds in position. That did not work out very well, as equity holders often received zero payments during the ramp-up period.

Assume, for example, that a deal had absolutely no bonds purchased at the time of closing, but ramped-up at an equal pace over the next six months. On average then, the

---

[1] The UBS Warburg 10-year BBB industrial index at the time was trading 172/10-year Treasury; the BB Index was 338/10-year Treasury.

deal is foregoing one quarter of a year's carry (on which we assumed investment at LIBOR flat over the ramp-up). So assuming a 200 basis point spread to LIBOR, this is equivalent to buying each bond $0.50 higher in price. Alternatively, it is like earning 10 basis points less on the underlying collateral.

In newer cash deals, these costs of ramping up a cash flow deal have been reduced, but not eliminated, by having a warehouse facility in place. This warehouse facility allows the issuer to start buying bonds well before the CDO is closed and investors' cash is in hand. In fact, rating agencies generally like to see about 75% of the bonds purchased prior to CDO settlement

Under a warehouse facility, bonds are usually financed when they are purchased, then hedged by selling Treasuries, futures, or by paying fixed on a swap. Thus the interest rate component is hedged out, but not the credit component. In any such warehouse facilities, it is generally the CDO equity holders who bear the spread risk. Thus, if spreads widen between the time the bond is purchased and the time the CDO is priced, that runs to the detriment of CDO equity holders. If spreads tighten, it is an advantage to their equity account. And if the CDO is not issued for any reason, the underwriting firm bears the brunt of the risk of spread widening, and obtains the majority of the benefit from any spread tightening; the remaining risk is absorbed by the deal manager. The underwriter, who provides the warehouse facility, generally charges a small fee for such service. (Prior to 9/11, the standard arrangement was that the underwriter bore the risk, but now risk-sharing arrangements are more common.)

In deals with bonds or loans as collateral, collateral availability can also be an issue. For example, if the CDO asset manager is striving to obtain collateral that fits in a given industry bucket, but which is unavailable, the ramp-up period may be extended.

EXHIBIT 9.1   BBB—Cash versus CDS

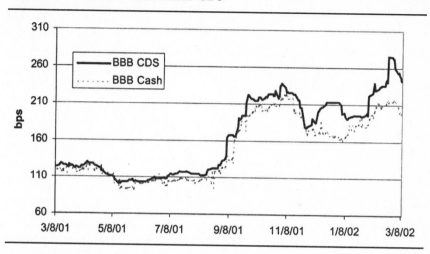

In synthetic deals, the CDO asset manager still wants to take advantage of favorable levels on credit default swaps when they appear in the market, and does not want to buy the deal in a single afternoon. As such, there are ramp-up periods on these deals, but they are generally very short.

Credit Default Swaps can be Cheaper Than Cash Bond

The final economic advantage of synthetic deals is that selling synthetic credit default protection can be cheaper than buying the underlying cash bond. In general, that difference is larger the further down the credit spectrum one goes.

To ascertain that, we looked at 5-year credit default swaps versus the 5-year spread to the LIBOR curve on the cash bond underlying a sample of 18 BBB rated credits.[2] The 18 credits were selected on the basis of credit default swap liquidity, and the ratings ranged from BBB+ to BBB–. In cases where there was no 5-year cash bond, we used the credit-specific spread calculated by the UBS Warburg Credit Delta System. We reviewed data for the 1-year period March 8, 2001, to March 8, 2002. The results of the analysis are shown in Exhibit 9.1.

---

[2] Data for the analysis were obtained from the UBS Warburg Credit Delta System.

EXHIBIT 9.2   BBB Industrial—Cash versus CDS

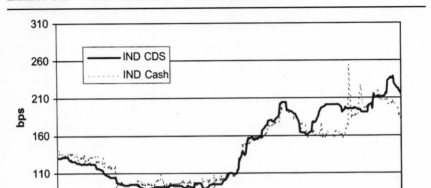

The average spread for the 1-year period examined for the 18 BBB credits was 15 basis points higher in the credit default swap market than in the cash market (for a 5-year maturity). Subsequently, that difference widened substantially. For example, on March 8, 2002, the cash spread on the 18 BBB credits was 194 basis points, while it was 243 basis points for credit default swaps—for a net difference of 49 basis points.

Just looking at the BBB industrial credits in this index over the 1-year period examined, the average spread differential between the credit default swaps and the cash securities was 3 basis points. Spread differentials shortly thereafter widened. For example, on March 8, 2002, the cash market was trading at a spread of 176 basis points, versus 215 basis points on the credit default swaps, for a difference of 38 basis points (shown in Exhibit 9.2). Similarly, looking at BBB telecom spreads in the index over the same 1-year period, the credit default swap market sold 11 basis points wider than the cash underlying. The most recent differential was 22 basis points. Results of this analysis are shown in Exhibit 9.3.

EXHIBIT 9.3   BBB Telecom—Cash versus CDS

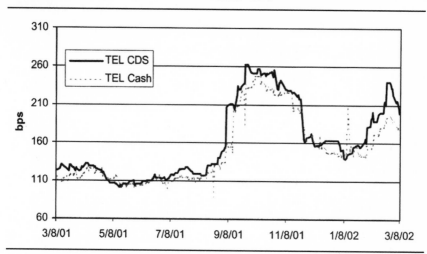

On baskets of A rated credits, the credit default and cash markets trade much more closely. Over the year investigated, A rated credits actually traded about 4 basis points wider in the cash market than in the credit default market. But credit default swaps cheapened subsequent to March 8, 2002. In early March 2002, credit default swaps were trading 7 basis points wider than the cash.

The differences between the cash and credit default swap market reflect the fact that credit default swaps are cheaper, as well as that we are, to some extent, dealing with slightly different risks. There are three major differences in risks between credit default swaps and cash bonds of the same maturity; two call for a wider spread on the credit default swaps, while one argues for tighter spreads.

First, restructuring is a credit event in both single name credit default swaps and in CDOs. That is, a restructuring of one credit triggers a cash or physical settlement on the swap. The effect of a restructuring (given that there is some flexibility in the choice of security to be delivered) is generally more severe in the credit default market than in the cash market.

Second, in the credit default market, loss is measured assuming an initial price of par. If there is a default, the investor receives the defaulted security. Consider an example in which the defaulted security trades at a price of $20. Investors would clearly rather buy a bond at an $80 price, with a spread of 500 basis points to the LIBOR curve, rather than sell a credit default swap at the same spread. The reason is that if the bond defaults, the investor can sell the $80 bond for only $20, thus losing $60. In the credit default swap case, the investor must pay the difference between par and $20, thus losing $80. Losing $60 is better than losing $80. Thus, we would expect the credit default swap market to trade wider than cash instruments, and that the difference would grow with the greater probabilities of default or restructuring, or the lower the price on the cheapest-to-deliver bond.

Third, and on the opposing side arguing for tighter spreads on credit default swaps, there is some counterparty risk in the credit default swap, as protection buyers are counting on the performance of the protection sellers. In higher rated credits, this effect is more important than the restructuring and default issues. It also explains why credit default swaps on highly rated entities can trade cheaper than cash alternatives. However, on most CDOs, the collateral used is rated BBB or lower, so this effect is less important.

In addition to the structural differences between cash and credit default swaps, there are transitory influences which are quite important in determining relative pricing at any given point in time. In particular, reinsurers can be quite active as sellers of credit protection. Since they are high-cost funders, they prefer credit default swaps to cash instruments, and, when active, push down the spread on credit default swaps versus cash. When there is a demand to buy credit protection for hedging purposes, credit default spreads will widen to the cash bond, as it is difficult to short cash instruments. Other transitory influences include the supply/demand for structured portfolio investments such as CDOs, as well as the presence of convertible bond investors looking for arbitrage opportunities around the conversion date.

STRUCTURAL ISSUES

We have now seen that synthetic structures offer a number of advantages to the cash underlying. While virtually all synthetic deals share those funding advantages we just discussed, there is still a huge variation among deals in terms of capital structures, spreads, and characteristics. We now turn our attention to the range of synthetic deals.

The best way to do this is to focus on two CDOs that represent the range of structural variations. The first we set up is a static synthetic CDO consisting of a basket of 100 investment grade names (CDO #1). The second (CDO #2) is a managed synthetic, with roughly the same credit quality on the underlying assets as those in CDO #1. Salient features of each of the two deals, as well as capital structures for both deals, and spreads for both deals are shown in Exhibit 9.4.

Static versus Managed

Synthetic deals can be done as static pools or as managed transactions. The advantage to static deals is that the investor can examine and approve credits that will enter the structure, so there are zero surprises. There are also no ongoing management fees. The disadvantage of static deals is that once a credit begins to deteriorate, there are no provisions allowing the CDO to get rid of that new problem issue; it remains inside the pool and continues to deteriorate.

Recently, there has been a pronounced trend toward managed deals. For example, out of the synthetic arbitrage transactions done in the first quarter of 2002, close to 30% of the CDO risk defeased has been done in the form of managed CDO deals, up from 20% in 2001. Static synthetics make up the remaining 70% in 2002, down from 80% in 2001.

EXHIBIT 9.4 Synthetic CDO Spectrum

	Deal #1		Deal #2	
Amount	$1 billion reference pool 100 reference entities		$1 billion reference pool 100 single name credit default swaps	
Management	Static		Managed	
Capital Structure	**Amt**	**Sprd**	**Amt**	**Sprd**
Super Senior	870	6	890	6
AAA	50	50	30	48
AA	30	90	30	85
A	5	175	14	125
BBB	15	400	20	275
Equity	30		16	
Coverage Test	None		Cash collateral ────────── >111% Class A+B+C+D	
Final maturity	5 yrs		5 yrs	
Write-down provisions	Immediately upon default		At end of life of deal	
Swap settlement	Cash		Physical	

The shift in investor preferences stemmed from the fact that, in 2001, many investment grade corporate CDO deals were done using a static structure. But sadly, all of that year, particularly the fourth quarter, was not kind to investment grade deals, and deals backed by synthetic investment grade collateral were hit especially hard. There were a number of downgrades due to pools carrying exposures to Enron, K-Mart, Crown, Cork and Seal, and/or Railtrack (a U.K. entity). And the bad news did not stop, as Global Crossing was notched down in 2002.

Capital Structure

Observe from Exhibit 9.4 that the static synthetic deal (Deal #1) has much higher equity (3% versus 1.6%) and no coverage tests. The higher equity percentage is actually a direct reflection of the absence of coverage tests. In fact, through the first quarter of 2002, all deals backed by synthetic collateral have used structures very similar to Deal #1—that is, structures without coverage tests, and no cash trapping features. Deal #1-type structures have been used for both static CDO pools and deals that involve active management. Since the first quarter of 2002, some of the cash flow CDO architectures have been applied to synthetic collateral. This has resulted in structures similar to that in Deal #2.

The key to understanding Deal #2 is the structure of the interest waterfall. The trustee fee, the senior default swap fee, and the senior advisory fee are paid out of the available interest. Next comes interest to the note holders: Classes A (rated AAA), B (rated AA), C (Rated A), and D (rated BBB), in order of seniority. The rated notes coverage test is run after the BBB noteholders are paid. If passed, remaining funds are used to pay the subordinate advisory fee, with equity holders receiving any remainders. If the rated notes coverage test is failed, then money remaining after the noteholders are paid is trapped in a collateral account. Once rated notes coverage ratios are brought back up to minimum standards, that trapped cash is released. If the deal continues to fail that coverage test, then the trapped money becomes part of the principal waterfall at maturity.

In fact, the amount of equity is actually very comparable under the two structures. The rating agencies have subjected both deals to their rating processes, and required that the deal without the rated notes coverage test carry more subordination. So we ran a test and subjected a CDO similar to Deal #2 to three scenarios:

1. uniformly distributed defaults (20% per year for 5 years);
2. front-loaded defaults (50% in Year 1, 12.5% per year for Years 2–5); and
3. back-loaded defaults (12.5% in Years 1–4, 50% in Year 5).

Assuming a 44% recovery rate, the implied subordination to the BBB class is 4.4–4.5% in the uniformly distributed and front-loaded scenarios, while it is 3.4% in the back-ended default cases. Realize that the 44% recovery rate assumed may be too high, which produces a slightly higher implied subordination than the 3% required in Deal #1. The point is that the lower amount of equity is compensated for by the cash traps created by the rated notes coverage test.

Settlement on Credit Default Swaps

Note that Deal #1 (Exhibit 9.4) has cash settlement on the reference pool of assets, while Deal #2 has physical settlement. There are advantages and disadvantages to both. Cash settlement is really clean, thus one generally sees cash settlement in static deals. With physical settlement, the CDO is not forced to sell the security at the worst possible time. The security can be held, in hope of realizing a higher market value later. Physical settlement tends to be more common than cash settlement in managed deals, although we have seen managed structures with both.

Equity Cash Flows and Timing Write-Down

In Deal #1, equity pays a fixed coupon, and has no claim on the residual cash flows of the deal. The equity holders receive interest only on the outstanding equity balance. In Deal #2, the equity holders have a claim on the residual cash flows of the deal.

The timing pattern of write-downs is very different in our two deals. In Deal #1, there is cash settlement once a credit event occurs. Thus, when a credit event occurs (1) that credit is removed from the pool; (2) the super senior piece is reduced by the cash-settled amount; and (3) the difference between the notional amount and the settlement amount gets written down. That write-down is done from the bottom of the capital structure, so it is a case of "equity first." After equity is written down all the way to zero, yet further losses occur, the lowest rated debt then gets written down. Realize that in this type of structure, with write-downs throughout the life of deal, it would be difficult to give equity a claim on the residual cash flows in the deal, as it may have already been written down.

By contrast, when a credit event occurs in Deal #2, physical settlement occurs. The security can be sold, but there is no write-down until the end of the deal. At that time, the principal cash flows go through the principal waterfall, paying off first the Class A noteholders, then the Class B, C, and D noteholders. After those are paid, remaining funds go to the equity holders.

Due to structural differences, the BBB and lower classes in Deal #1 generally sell wider than in Deal #2. In our examples in Exhibit 9.4, the BBB sells at LIBOR + 400 in Deal #1 but LIBOR + 275 in Deal #2. In Deal #1, the write-downs are immediate, and there is no way to recoup losses by better performance later in the deal's life. Moreover, if any of the classes (including the equity) begins to incur losses, the interest is reduced accordingly.

In structures like Deal #1, which experience write-downs during the life of the deal, the cost of the liabilities is actually reduced as lower rated securities experience losses. Investors are concerned that this structure provides more adverse incentive to the asset manager than structures represented by Deal #2. Let's explore this more closely.

Intuitively as Deal #1 experiences losses, the first security to be written down is the equity, which carries the highest rate of interest, followed by the mezzanine tranches, which carry interest rates higher than the senior securities. Thus, it is conceptually possible that if losses are very heavy, the sponsor/asset manager can be better off. That is because as all the higher cost liabilities are paid off (and the swap protection buyer has been paid for the defaults that have occurred), the average cost of insuring the reminder of the portfolio is lower. And the excess monies will revert to the sponsor.

While clearly a conceptual possibility, the difference in deal structures produces little practical difference in managerial incentives. In Deal #1, which is static, the investors see and approve the credits which are included; the sponsor/manager cannot alter the selection of securities after deal closing. Even if a Deal #1-type structure was used for a managed CDO, any asset manager who sought to systematically advantage themselves would never be able to come to market again. Moreover, the gain to the asset manager of pursuing this strategy is substantially diluted if the CDO asset manager owns any of the higher rated tranches. (And CDO asset managers do often retain a piece of the super senior tranche.)

CONCLUSION

Synthetic structures are rapidly gaining importance in the market. Based on the actual amount of credit risk transferred, synthetic structures were almost as important as those using real collateral.

And, given the funding advantages to synthetic structures, we can expect them to become even more popular over time. In particular, the ability to leave the super senior piece unfunded represents a huge advantage. The economics of synthetic deals are further enhanced by the ability to minimize ramp-up time, as well as the fact that credit default swaps are usually cheaper than the cash bonds.

However, not all synthetics structures are identical. Some synthetic deals are static, while others are managed. Some employ standard synthetic architecture (writing down from the bottom of the capital structure first, no cash traps, cash settlement), while others employ some aspects of the cash flow CDO architecture (no write-downs until the end of the life of the deal, less equity compensated by rated notes coverage tests, physical settlement).

CDO market participants will, of necessity, become more familiar with synthetic structures over time. We've seen in this chapter the differences within the synthetic market and compared relative features. It is very important to understand the source of those differences so as to better compare one deal to another.

CHAPTER 10

Considerations in Creating CDOs and Their Investment Implications

Both the pattern of CDO issuance—such as heavy or light volume, or which type of collateral dominates—as well as the *configuration* of completed deals—Are there AA or A rated tranches, or simply a larger AAA and BBB class?—are dictated to a large degree by CDO arbitrage. In this chapter, we first look at the CDO arbitrage and examine a "quick and dirty" analysis for benchmarking activity levels. We then focus on how the arbitrage dictates deal structure. Spread configurations and the exact collateral used are important in determining optimal deal structure. Yet when investors are looking at the merits of one deal versus another, they often look at percent subordination or percent overcollateralization as an arbiter of tranche quality. But since the arbitrage often dictates deal structure, these measures may communicate little about tranche quality per se.

BUILDING BLOCKS

In a CDO, asset purchases are financed by a combination of liabilities plus equity. The "arb" exists when those assets can be purchased and the liabilities sold with enough left over to provide a competitive return to equity holders. Mortgage market participants recognize this exercise for what it is: a kissing cousin to the collateralized mortgage obligations (CMO) arbitrage.

Like the CMO arbitrage, in any intended CDO arbitrage sample structures are always run to determine when this arb is "close." Dealers then act on those results to optimize deal structure so as to increase the likelihood that the deal can actually be executed. Let's look at some simplified examples of "arb" runs for bond and loan deals and then at how these deals can be fine-tuned to improve the arb's attractiveness.

Crude Run

The basis for the arb is the "crude run." No, that does not mean sloshing around in unrefined oil. Where we are going and what we look for is whether return-on-equity is anywhere near the actual level needed to be attractive to potential equity buyers.

To calculate the arb, dealers run the assets and liabilities through a large structuring model. These models first compute the period-by-period returns to the equity holders and then calculate the internal rate of return of the equity cash flows. These models gives the underwriting dealer, working with the CDO manager, considerable flexibility in optimizing capital structure. For example, higher quality assets can be used. In that case, overcollateralization levels are lower, and less equity is necessary to support the deal. Or BB rated notes can be used in lieu of equity capital which, in turn, increases overall leverage. Greater asset diversity can be substituted for equity capital. Spreads, prices, and coupons of the assets and liabilities also play a role in determining the required amount of capital over which the excess return must be spread.

However, to compute whether or not any arb is close, we do not need a complex CDO structuring model. Any hand calculator, plus a dose of common sense, will do.

To illustrate our point, we use a very generic collateralized bond obligation (CBO) deal (Exhibit 10.1). The assets in this representative deal consist of high-yield bonds purchased at par and with a yield equal to the yield-to-worst on the Merrill Lynch Cash pay index, which was 12.32% as of June 5, 2000. Our generic deal's $425 million of liabilities consist of $350 million senior notes paying LIBOR + 40, plus $75 million of BBB-rated mezzanine notes at LIBOR + 200. Deal structure is supported by $75 million in equity. To be realistic, we also assumed 2% in up-front expenses, and ongoing expenses of 70 basis points/year.

The CBO Arb

Now look at the CBO arbitrage as of 6/5/00 (in the last column of Exhibit 10.1). After deleting 2% in up-front expenses from our $500 million amount, $490 million ($500 million × 0.98) remains to be invested. These assets earn 12.32%, or a total of $60,368,000, per year. We also assume asset defaults of 3% and recoveries of 50%; so we subtract 1.5% per year, or $7,350,000 per year, from total asset returns. Thus the initial $500 million of assets generates a return of $53,018,000 after that 1.5% loss.

We then subtract the cost of the LIBOR-indexed liabilities. That cost would be understated, and the returns to equity overstated, if the cost of the liabilities is based on prevailing LIBOR term structure at the time. This is because LIBOR at the time of the analysis was lower than forward LIBOR, as the market was expecting LIBOR to be higher over the life of the note than is reflected in current rates.

So we sidestepped that problem by using swap rates for the appropriate maturity. In our case, we used the 7.33% fixed rate on the 7.5-year swaps plus 40 basis points as the cost of the Class A notes, which is equal to 7.73%; and the 7.32% 10-year swap rate plus 200 basis points as the cost of the Class B notes, which is equal to 9.32%. Note that with the swap curve flat, tenor assumptions are immaterial to the results. Anyway, the cost of the Class A note thus becomes [($350,000,000 of Class A notes) × (0.0773 cost)] = $27,041,525. The cost of the B Notes is [($75,000,000 of Class B notes) × (0.0932 cost)] = $6,991,275.

EXHIBIT 10.1 CBO Arbitrage, 1st Half, 2000

	($M)
Assets	500,000,000
Class A notes	350,000,000
Class B notes	75,000,000
Equity	75,000,000
Upfront expenses	2.0%
Investable assets	490,000,000
Losses	1.5%
Expenses	0.7%

Date	1/31/00	2/29/00	3/31/00	4/30/00	5/31/00	6/5/00
High-yield index	11.20%	11.31%	11.82%	12.15%	12.44%	12.32%
Class A note spread	55	50	46	45	42	40
Class B note spread	250	240	235	225	215	200
7.5-year swap yield	7.49%	7.39%	7.29%	7.42%	7.63%	7.33%
10-year swap yield	7.52%	7.43%	7.29%	7.41%	7.64%	7.32%
Class A note yield	8.04%	7.89%	7.75%	7.87%	8.05%	7.73%
Class B note yield	10.02%	9.83%	9.64%	9.66%	9.79%	9.32%

EXHIBIT 10.1 (Continued)

Arbitrage

Date	1/31/00	2/29/00	3/31/00	4/30/00	5/31/00	6/5/00
Gross return on assets	54,894,700	55,428,800	57,898,400	59,544,800	60,951,100	60,368,000
Losses	7,350,000	7,350,000	7,350,000	7,350,000	7,350,000	7,350,000
Net return assets	47,544,700	48,078,800	50,548,400	52,194,800	53,601,100	53,018,000
Cost of class A notes	28,147,525	27,599,775	27,113,100	27,557,425	28,187,600	27,041,525
Cost of class B notes	7,518,300	7,371,150	7,226,400	7,246,350	7,339,950	6,991,275
Expenses	3,430,000	3,430,000	3,430,000	3,430,000	3,430,000	3,430,000
Total cost and expenses	39,095,825	38,400,925	37,769,500	38,233,775	38,957,550	37,462,800
$ Return to equity	8,448,875	9,677,875	12,778,900	13,961,025	14,643,550	15,555,200
% Yield on equity	11.27%	12.90%	17.04%	18.61%	19.52%	20.74%

239

We added to these two costs the 70 basis points of expenses ($490,000,000 × 0.007) = $3,430,000. Thus total cost of the liabilities plus expenses equals $37,462,800. That leaves $15,555,200 as a dollar return-to-equity. Dividing that return by our example's $75,000,000 of equity delivers an equity yield of 20.74%.

Caveats

This is obviously a very basic calculation for the following reasons:

1. The bonds are usually not purchased at par. Most are at a discount.
2. Losses do not kick in immediately as assumed.
3. This is a one-period calculation, a simple simulation of returns without taking into account any asset pay-down schedule.
4. No ramp-up period (versus typical ramp-ups of 2–4 months) has been assumed.
5. We overlooked the possibility of hitting some deal triggers, even at 3% defaults that would cause automatic deleveraging.
6. Once an asset manager is selected, a deal gets fine-tuned to fit that firm's style and then-current market appetites for alternative liability structures (return-to-equity may rise or drop).
7. The calculation ignores the cost to the equity holders of deleveraging.

Consequently, approximate equity returns estimated in this fashion should be regarded as a very basic estimate of actual equity returns.

Changes Over Time

Applying the crude arbitrage calculation detailed above to the month of June 2000 suggests an equity return of 20.74%.

That is certainly quite attractive both in absolute terms as well as relative to other equity alternatives such as public or private equity. In fact, when equity return is above 15% via this simple calculation, CBO structurers know that it pays to look more closely at whether structural changes can be made to make the CBO more attractive. If the "quick and dirty" analysis indicates a return lower than 15%, then that is generally a fruitless exercise. Of course, as detailed above, this calculation is certainly not omniscient, nor perfect. But it is certainly indicative.

Now let's move back to the then-current market scenario in the first quarter of 2000. Issuance was much more limited at that point, and was mostly concentrated in CLOs. At the end of January 2000, the yield-to-worst on the high-yield index was 11.20%, which was 112 basis points lower than on 6/5/00. The cost of liabilities was also higher in January 2000, as well. Class A notes required a yield of LIBOR + 55, while the cost on the Class B notes was LIBOR + 250. On a swapped basis, the Class A notes yielded 8.04%. That is 31 basis points higher than June 2000's 7.73% level. Meanwhile, the Class B notes yielded 10.02%, 70 basis points higher than June's level of 9.32%. Thus the lower yield on the assets and a higher cost of the liabilities only delivered a dollar return to equity of $8,448,875. Dividing that gross amount by the $75 million of equity provided an equity return of only 11.27% as seen in Exhibit 10.1. That is obviously not at all attractive. It also suggests that high-yield deals were quite noneconomic in January 2000—which they were.

Issuance Patterns and CBO Arb

As can also be seen in Exhibit 10.1, the CBO arb became increasingly more attractive during the first half of 2000. Yields on high-yield bonds increased over that period, and the cost of the liabilities declined. In February, the return-on-equity was 12.90%. It then rose to 17.04% in March, 18.61% in April, 19.52% in May, reaching 20.74% in June.

Intuitively, since equity is a levered investment, an increase in asset yield or a decrease in liability costs magnifies, gears, or levers, the impact of that specific change. Equity returns benefit the most from an increased return on the assets. Each 1 basis point-rise in asset yield increases return-on-equity in our example by 6.53 times (490/75). So, the 112 basis point-rise in asset yields from January to June of 2000 increased equity yields by 732 basis points (6.53 × 112).

Correspondingly, each 1 basis point-drop in liability cost in our example increases returns on equity by 4.67 times (350/75). Therefore, the 31 basis point-drop in the cost of the liabilities added another 145 basis points to the equity return (31 × 4.67). Finally, each 1 basis point-drop in the Class B notes increases the return-on-equity by an amount equal to that drop in costs (75/75). Thus, the 70 basis points drop in the cost of the Class B notes added another 70 basis points to the equity return.

Adding it all up within our simple approximation, the arb in June 2000 should look 946 basis points (732 + 144 + 70) better than it did in January 2000 based on changes in the component parts (costs and returns). That is actually quite close to the market's real-life return-on-equity improvement of 947 basis points (20.74% − 11.27%).

Issuance Patterns on CLO Arb

The improvement in the collateralized loan obligation (CLO) arb in the first half of calendar year 2000 was less dramatic (as shown in Exhibit 10.2). We again set up a generic bank loan deal, sized at $500 million in assets. However, the capital structure differed from our earlier bond deal. In that prior deal, we had assumed $375 million Class A notes plus $75 million Class B notes plus $50 million capital. A lower capital requirement from the rating agencies stems from the fact that bank loans are often secured, and have much higher recovery rates than do high yield bonds.

EXHIBIT 10.2 CLO Arbitrage, 1st Half, 2000

	($M)
Assets	500,000,000
Class A notes	375,000,000
Class B notes	75,000,000
Equity	50,000,000
Upfront expenses	2.0%
Investable assets	490,000,000
Losses	0.75%
Expenses	0.7%

Date	1/31/00	2/29/00	3/31/00	4/30/00	5/31/00	6/5/00
Loan spread	3.25%	3.25%	3.25%	3.25%	3.25%	3.25%
Loan yield	10.77%	10.68%	10.54%	10.66%	10.89%	10.57%
Class A note spread	55	50	46	45	42	40
Class B note spread	250	240	235	225	215	200
7.5-year swap yield	7.49%	7.39%	7.29%	7.42%	7.63%	7.33%
10-year swap yield	7.52%	7.43%	7.29%	7.41%	7.64%	7.32%
Class A note yield	8.04%	7.89%	7.75%	7.87%	8.05%	7.73%
Class B note yield	10.02%	9.83%	9.64%	9.66%	9.79%	9.32%

243

EXHIBIT 10.2 (Continued)

Arbitrage

Date	1/31/00	2/29/00	3/31/00	4/30/00	5/31/00	6/5/00
Gross return on assets	52,794,560	52,323,180	51,622,480	52,242,820	53,344,340	51,801,330
Losses	3,675,000	3,675,000	3,675,000	3,675,000	3,675,000	3,675,000
Net return assets	49,119,560	48,648,180	47,947,480	48,567,820	49,669,340	48,126,330
Cost of class A notes	30,158,063	29,571,188	29,049,750	29,525,813	30,201,000	28,973,063
Cost of class B notes	7,518,300	7,371,150	7,226,400	7,246,350	7,339,950	6,991,275
Expenses	3,430,000	3,430,000	3,430,000	3,430,000	3,430,000	3,430,000
Total cost and expenses	41,106,363	40,372,338	39,706,150	40,202,163	40,970,950	39,394,338
$ Return to equity	8,013,198	8,275,842	8,241,330	8,365,657	8,698,390	8,731,992
% Yield on equity	16.03%	16.55%	16.48%	16.73%	17.40%	17.46%

Calendar year 2000 loan spreads were consistent at about LIBOR + 315 basis points. "Loan yield" converts this to a fixed rate, which is constructed by adding in the rate payable on a 10-year swap (7.32%). June's asset yield thus becomes 10.57%. We then assume defaults are the same 3% (as on high-yield assets in our CBO deal example), but that recoveries would be higher, at 75%. Thus losses become 0.75% (= 3.0% × 0.25) per annum. We assume liability costs identical to those on the CBO at LIBOR + 40 on the AAA rated notes, with a 7.73% yield; and LIBOR + 200 on the BBB-rated notes, for a 9.32% yield. We also assume identical up-front expenses of 2% and ongoing expenses of 70 basis points. Based on these levels, Exhibit 10.2 shows that as of June 5, 2000, return to the $50 million in capital would have been 17.46%.

The CLO arbitrage improved somewhat during the first half of calendar year 2000, but not nearly as dramatically as did the CBO arbitrage. The return-to-equity on our representative CBO was 16.03% in January 2000. But by June, that return had risen to 17.46%. That improvement stems from reduction in the cost of liabilities. The Class A notes tightened 15 basis points (from LIBOR + 55 to LIBOR + 40), while the BBB rated notes tightened by 50 basis points (from LIBOR + 250 to LIBOR + 200.)

It is quite interesting to compare Exhibits 10.1 and 10.2. The disparity is the difference in asset behavior—high-yield spreads widened in the first half of 2000, while spreads to LIBOR were roughly constant for loan deals. As a result, the CBO arbitrage improved dramatically, while the CLO arbitrage improved much less.

Activity levels bear this out. In January and February of 2000, it was difficult to do CBO deals (since return-on-equity was too low to be appealing). For example, the total volume of deals rated by Moody's in the first quarter of 2000 was $5.63 billion. Most of those were CLOs (backed exclusively by loans) or CDOs (backed primarily by loans). Few CBOs were involved. By contrast, in the second quarter of 2000, Moody's rated over $15 billion in deals, the majority of which were backed primarily by bond collateral. This reflected the fact that return-to-equity was higher on the high-yield bond deals than on the loan deals.

Improving the Arb

Now we know what is driving the arbitrage. And once a deal is "close," structurers can tinker and nudge it closer to the needs of equity buyers. Trade-offs can be made between leverage, the level of overcollateralization for triggering tests, asset quality, liability ratings, diversity, as well as acquisition prices and coupons. There is actually quite a basketful of structuring nuances.

Certainly, one of the ways to increase the potential equity return is to expand leverage. Greater leverage heightens yield responsiveness of the assets to default rates. To show this, we first compute yield responsiveness of our representative CBO deal (that detailed in Exhibit 10.1, a CBO with 15% equity, based on $75 million equity within a $500 million deal). We use June 2000 data for the calculations. The dotted line in Exhibit 10.3 shows the yield profile for CBO equity in our representative 15% equity deal. Note that at 3% defaults, the equity return is 20.74% (That's exactly the same number as in Exhibit 10.1.) At default rates below 3%, return-to-equity is greater; at higher default rates, equity returns are lower.

To assess the effects of higher leverage, we then decrease equity capital by $10 million (to $65 million) and introduce $10 million of BB rated notes (coupon of LIBOR + 550). The resultant structure has 13% equity plus 2% BB rated notes. We also recompute return-on-equity at different default rates. Thus, as shown by the solid line in Exhibit 10.3 (at 3% defaults) return-to-equity is 21.84% in this "high leverage" deal. By contrast, it is 33.15% at 0% defaults and 3.00% at 8% defaults.

EXHIBIT 10.3 Effect of Increasing Leverage

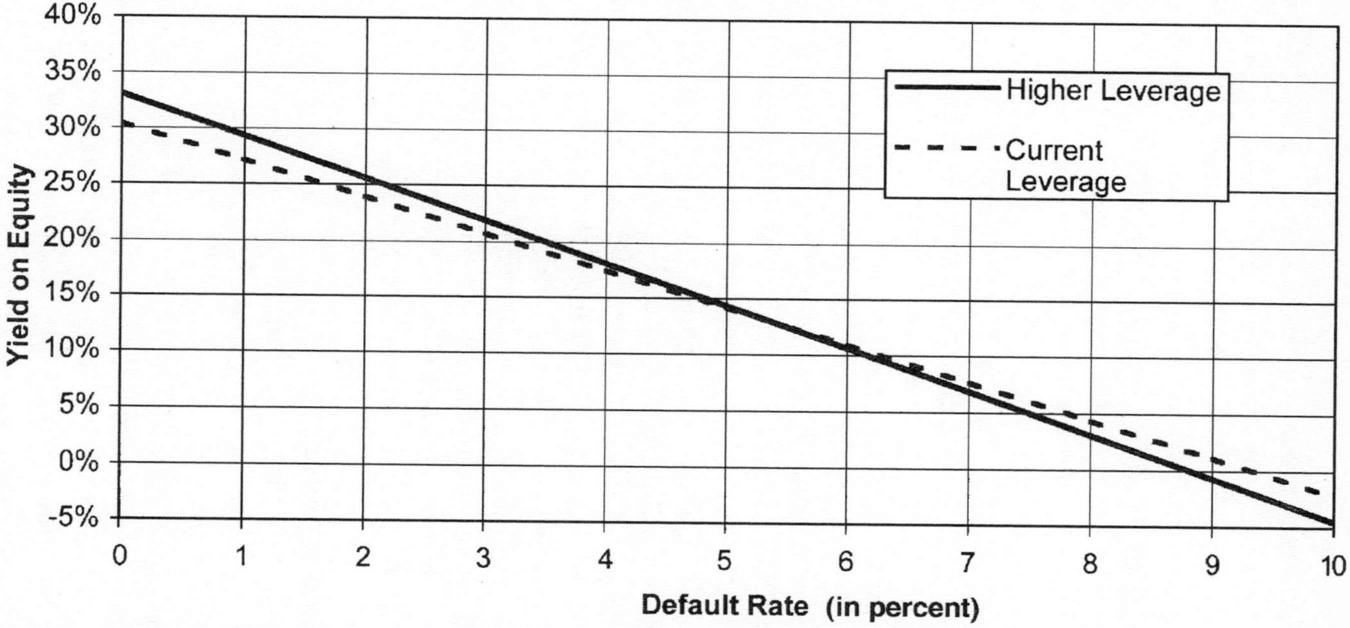

Effect of Higher Leverage

It is useful to compare results of an "average leverage" deal with what might evolve from one more highly levered. The net effect is that more highly leveraged deals have steeper return profiles. In our simple analysis, at default levels below 5–6%, the more highly levered equity piece yields more; while at default levels above 5–6%, it yields less. Specifically, at 0% defaults, a deal with "average" leverage only returns 30.44%, while that with higher leverage throws off 33.15%. At 9% defaults, the average leverage deal generates 1.04%, while the deal with high leverage yields –0.77%.

In point of fact, this analysis is too kind to the more highly geared deal. The deal with greater leverage would also have tighter overcollateralization levels, which would also hit the triggers sooner and thus delever more quickly. So overall, that would create a far more negative impact on returns than shown in Exhibit 10.3. (Remember, we used a simple one-period analysis, and ignored trigger events.)

Rating agencies ultimately dictate capital structure supportable within a deal's parameters. Any increase in leverage, all other factors constant, reduces protection for the rated classes. Therefore, any such higher leverage must be accompanied by raising the quality of assets, or by tightening overcollaterization. The latter is done by decreasing the level of overcollaterization necessary to trigger a deleveraging.

Gauging Activity Levels

To create a CDO, two conditions are necessary. First, the arbitrage must be favorable. Second, CDO assets must be available.

Our basic calculation allows rated note buyers to gauge how favorable the CDO arbitrage is. Then, one needs to consider asset availability so as to figure activity levels. In June 2000 (the time period analyzed), the current return-to-equity was very attractive, as evidenced by our sample deals, and collateral was readily available. It was no surprise that there were a dozen new deals in the market.

IMPACT OF CDO ARBITRAGE ON STRUCTURE

Many decisions made in the CDO structuring process are a function of the arb. If certain classes are more expensive than combinations of other classes, those classes more expensive are less apt to be created. The output of such structuring decisions will be bonds with different characteristics.

We make this point by looking at trade-offs inherent in deal structures. We show that greater subordination and more overcollateralization, can, at times, result in greater extension risk. It is very important for investors to examine an entire deal structure in light of their portfolio objectives.

Rules of CDO Deal Structuring

Following are two rules of CDO structuring. Rule #1 is never leave money on the table! If (all things being equal) a deal structure can support 80% AAA rated bonds, it is unlikely that any issuer will construct that deal with 78% AAA rated bonds. So if two tranches of different deals, both rated AAA by the same rating agency, are in the market simultaneously, then it is likely that both contain the maximum amount of AAA bonds supportable by their structures. If one deal carries a higher percent of AAAs, then trade-offs were made elsewhere in the structure.

Rule #2 is optimize deal structure. It is survival of the fittest out there. Issuers try various deal structures, and come up with one or two that look the "best." (Structurers' trash cans generally overflow with printouts of trials failed because they were "nonoptimal.") Optimal structure in CDOs is that for which each of the rated notes can receive a market-determined interest rate, with IRR maximized on the equity piece. If one dealer structures an equity return of 17% while another offers 18% off the same collateral at similar leverage then an investor will clearly run, not walk, to that higher return.

Interest Costs Drive Subordination

We now look at how the CDO arbitrage and current spread configuration dictates structure. Note that many investors (particularly at the AAA level) look at percent subordination as an indicator of protection. While it is certainly one such bellwether, it should not be used as the be-all and end-all. In fact, Rules #1 and #2 above are so powerful that if two tranches are created at the same time with the same rating, there is unlikely to be any strict dominance of one over the other.

Exhibit 10.4 displays five different structures, using typical combinations of structured finance collateral (ABS, MBS, CMBS, and REITs). The first three (labeled Deals "A," "B," and "C") are backed by exactly the same collateral. The cost of that collateral was assumed to be $97.88, which includes the CMBS IO that is often included in these deals. The diversity score is 17, also very typical of mortgage deals, and the weighted average rating factor is 345, which corresponds to the BBB level. The WAC on the collateral is 8.30%, which again, includes the effects of the CMBS IO.

In Deal A, liabilities were tranched into AAA, A−, and BB rated notes and equity, proportioned 86.67%, 9.0%, 1.67%, and 2.67%, respectively. Note that this structure maximized the amount of AAA rated notes permitted (shown in the middle section of Exhibit 10.4). The bottom part of the exhibit shows that after paying a liability holder the spreads shown separately in Exhibit 10.4, the return-to-equity (assuming no defaults) is 17.09%.

Deal B has essentially the same structure. The only difference is that the A− and BB amounts are collapsed into a BBB class. Equity yield then expands to 17.24%, although that is not all that much different from Deal A's 17.09%.

EXHIBIT 10.4 Structuring Tradeoffs

	Liability Spread	Deal				
		A	B	C	D	E
Principal face		300	300	300	310	310
Total cost		97.88	97.88	97.88	94.70	94.70
Rating factor		345	345	345	320	320
WAC		8.30%	8.30%	8.30%	7.45%	7.45%
AAA	L + 50	86.67%	86.67%	76.67%	70.30%	70.30%
AA	L + 90	—	—	11.67%	17.25%	17.58%
A–	L + 150	9.00%	—	7.33%	—	6.92%
BBB	L + 250	—	10.83%	—	7.89%	—
BB	T + 700	1.67%	—	1.67%	4.56%	5.21%
Equity		2.67%	2.50%	2.67%	—	—
Min. AAA I/C required		122	122	144	120	120
Min. AAA O/C required		110	110	128	130	130
Equity yield		17.09%	17.24%	15.69%	NA	NA

In Deal C we recarved the AAA and A– cash flows into AAA, AA, and A– rated notes, holding constant the amounts of BB and equity. This structure would be considered suboptimal, as return-to-equity drops to 15.69%, versus Deal A's 17.09%. No matter how gifted a salesperson is, they would *not* be able to sell equity at this level.

Anyway, the reason the arb is much less attractive in Deal C is due to the spread configuration. The deals shifted 10% of the AAA rated bonds (paying LIBOR + 50) and 1.67% of the A– bonds (paying LIBOR + 150) into the AA bucket, which pays LIBOR + 90. That raised our interest costs 25.7 basis points on 11.67% of the deal. By the way, note that there is a relative value implication here: The AA rated bonds are quite attractively priced.

Don't Look Exclusively at Subordination

Suppose an investor is considering buying AAA rated paper. The investor is trying to decide between the bond in Deal A or that in Deal C. Which should the investor want in his portfolio? At first glance, the one in Deal C looks "better" because of its 23.23% subordination, rather than the 13.67% subordination in Deal A. Furthermore, the minimum I/C and O/C levels are much higher for Deal C's AAA rated bond.

But don't forget that according to Rule #1, you should "never leave money on the table." Each of the deals has already maximized the amount of AAA bonds that can be created in that structure. Thus, rating agencies consider the bonds roughly equivalent.

Many believe Deal C could never be worse than Deal A. That is wrong. The application-of-cash waterfall typically pours collateral interest and principal cash flow into AA interest payments prior to paying any AAA principal. More precisely, rating agencies will not allow a AA rated class to defer interest payments. However, if defaults are very high, cash flows in the deal will be lower. Thus, Deal C's AAA rated notes are more likely to extend than are Deal A's. Intuitively, an additional 40 basis points of interest on 10% of the deal plus the entire interest payment on 1.67% of the deal are "earmarked" to pay the AA rated noteholders who are ahead in line of the AAA rated notes in getting principal back.

Collateral is an Important Determinant of Structure

Besides the rate configuration, type of collateral is another important determinant of the deal arbitrage and the resulting structure. We assume Deals D and E in Exhibit 10.4 are backed by low dollar price collateral (with a lower WAC). This enabled more overcollateralization and less interest coverage. Thus for the same investment as in Deal A, we could buy $310 million of collateral, rather than $300 million. In Deal A we had $300 million par of collateral, at a price of $97.88, for a total investment of $293.64 million. In Deals D and E, for the same $293.64 million investment, we bought $310 million of collateral at an average price of $94.7.

This cash flow structure which utilizes collateral selling at a large discount to par, lends itself to a different liability structure. Given the level of overcollaterization on the deal, no equity tranche was necessary. That is because the deal can take $10 million in losses (3%) and still pay par to the bottom (BB) tranches.[1] Assuming recoveries at 45%, then 3% losses translate into defaults of 5.5% (3/0.55). That is an incredibly high number for BBB rated collateral.

Investors should be aware that the BB rating addresses the return of principal and a stated rate of interest. This stated rate of interest (the coupon) will generally be less than the market rate of interest in the tranche. For example, in Deals D and E, we used an 8% coupon on the BB tranche, and the bond was rated with respect to the return of principal and the 8% coupon. The coupon on this tranche is low because the BB bond serves as the equity in the deal. Like a traditional equity tranche, the BB tranche has some upside, which is not

---

[1] Losses = defaults × (1 – the recovery rate).

taken into account in the rating. If the deal does exceptionally well, the BB tranche captures that upside.

Moreover, both Deal D and Deal E have a relatively low percentage of AAAs (70.30%). Deal D has AAs, BBBs, and BBs, while Deal E has AAs, A–s, and BBs. The choice between the two depends on where each of the bonds can be sold.

The reason there are so few AAAs in Deals D and E is that the interest cash flow is very limited, as the WAC on the deal is 7.45%. Thus, interest cash flows in Deals D and E are roughly 90% of what they were in Deal A.

Now remember that collateral cannot be liquidated to pay AAA interest. But if the deal cannot pay the AAAs on time, those AAA holders can vote to sell deal assets to protect their interest. Thus, to protect other noteholders, the amount of AAAs is very limited.

Are all AAAs Equal?

In deciphering which AAA is better, it is clear that Deals D and E have substantially greater overcollateralization. So most investors would automatically assert that either deal's AAA is "better" than the AAA rated note in Deal A. But in reality, this is not all that clear.

Deal A has a substantial amount of excess cash flow from interest payments, which could be applied to the AAA principal. By contrast, rising defaults in Deals D and E might absorb excess interest entirely. Deals D and E would then turn to principal redemption to delever the transaction.

Let's look at some numbers. Deal A begins life with 115% overcollateralization at the AAA level. For the first year, there's $25 million total interest inflow, and $19.5 million AAA interest outflow. Thus after paying the AAAs, net interest cash flow is $5.5 million. For Deal E, with 143% initial O/C, total interest inflow is $23.1 million and the AAA and AA interest outflow is $20.6 million. Thus net interest cash flow, after paying the AAAs and AAs, is only $2.5 million. (Recall that the waterfall requires that the AA rated bonds must receive all their interest in each period before the AAA rated bonds receive any principal return.) That makes for an interest cushion difference of $3.0 ($5.5 − $2.5) million. And that $3 million excess cash flow can be applied to pay down AAA principal, giving the AAA tranche in Deal A much less potential for extension risk.

CONCLUSION

In this chapter we have seen that the CDO arbitrage is the key to CDO transactions. And the arbitrage calculations also shown in this chapter allow investors to gauge activity levels. Those activity levels are especially crucial to equity buyers and to CBO managers.

Equity buyers need to check the equity returns pitched by an investment bank. If that return is materially different from what you figure on your hand calculator—investors should find out what assumptions are being made about the structure, and be very sure that they are comfortable with those.

Additionally, these arbitrage calculations allow potential CBO managers to determine when they really want to press to get a deal done. Marginal arbitrage may portend that it is better to sit tight and wait for better timing. Deal performance is certainly important to any deal manager. It impacts future deals, and a manager's own pocket is directly impacted in that he or she typically retains a large chunk of the equity.

The CDO arbitrage is also a major determinant of deal structure. We have seen how different spread configurations and different collateral can make for very different deal structures. That is, deals are generally optimized to maximize returns to equity holders, while making sure to pay rated note holders their appropriate market levels. Yet with very dissimilar deal structures, investors are unable to figure relative value simply by looking exclusively at subordination in a deal, or exclusively at the amount of overcollateralization. That is because the benefits of higher subordination can be offset, depending on the waterfall rules. And the benefits of higher overcollaterization can be offset by lower interest coverage ratios.

The bottom line is that since deal structures have been optimized, there are always trade-offs. Investors need to be fully aware of those choices they implicitly make.

CHAPTER 11

Participating Coupon Notes

One of the most interesting trends in the CDO market has been the increasing use of *participating coupon structures*. These structures are combinations of traditional debt securities plus an equity interest in the same deal. Participating coupon notes give investors the benefit of a rated instrument for regulatory and financial purposes, coupled with a higher base case yield than that on comparably rated CDO debt.

While these structures have been used on and off since 1996, their increased use stems from pressures on both investors and issuers. From the investor's viewpoint, participating coupon notes offer a higher yield than that available in straight debt instruments of a similar rating due to the presence of an "equity kicker." From dealers' and issuers' perspective CDO equity has become harder to sell, as many of the original investors in CDO equity have their full allocation. Packaging equity with rated debt, and selling the notes to traditional debt investors, opens up a broader equity investor base.

In this chapter, we first take a look at why participating coupon structures have grown in importance. Then a number of variations of the basic participating coupon structure will be discussed, emphasizing how these structures can be tailored to investor preferences.

EXHIBIT 11.1   Principal-Protected Trust Structure

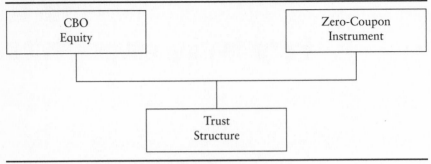

THE PRINCIPAL-PROTECTED TRUST STRUCTURE

Early attempts to combine CBO equity with debt instruments used principal-protected trust structures. In these, a zero-coupon note, which can be a Treasury zero, a note issued by a dealer, or a guaranteed investment contract (GIC) issued by a highly rated insurance company, was combined with equity, and a trust was created to house the instruments. The trust was then "rated" as to return of principal. The presence of the zero-coupon note virtually "guaranteed" investors return of principal at the end of a specified period. An example of this structure is shown in Exhibit 11.1.

However, questions arose regarding regulatory treatment of such trust structures. In particular, it is unclear if they are "qualifying" instruments for banks and thrifts. Moreover, if the trust is rated with respect to return of principal, then historically these structures have been NAIC 1 for insurance regulatory purposes.[1]

The National Association of Insurance Commissioners (NAIC) has begun to discuss the possibility that it will look through the trust to the underlying securities and require bifurcation (separating the security into two parts). If that occurs,

---

[1] Securities with an A rating or better qualify for NAIC 1, which is the highest rating given by the National Association of Insurance Commissioners; BBB rated securities warrant an NAIC 2 rating. Favorable NAIC ratings qualify an asset for a lower capital charge.

only the portion of the security attributable to the zero-coupon note would be considered NAIC 1. Extra capital would be required for the portion not considered NAIC 1. Finally, many money managers have funds that, as required by prospectus or investment guidelines, can hold only "debt" instruments. And it is not clear if principal-protected trust structures qualify as "debt" instruments for prospectus purposes.

In all cases, the regulatory issue is the same—since the trust is a combination of two securities, should regulators bifurcate the trust and look to the underlying securities? In fact, that is how it is usually treated for tax purposes.

PARTICIPATING SECURITIES—THE BASICS

Participating coupon structures combine rated notes and unrated equity (both from the same deal) into a single security in the initial structuring. Generally the principal, and in some cases a below-market coupon, is designed to be rated at an investment grade level. Investors in the security are also entitled to receive additional unrated cash flow. This structure contains a credit and yield floor, compliments of its rated debt portion, while also providing upside potential through the equity kicker.

Investors should realize that the amount of debt and equity in the security as well as the desired rating on the debt tranche can be customized to fit investors' risk parameters. The larger the rated component (the more rated debt) and the lower the unrated component (less equity), the lower the risk, but also the lower the expected total return on the participating coupon note.

The ability to tailor the risk allows many investors to participate who would not have even considered previous trust structures. For example, an investor seeking A rated paper and needing a coupon rated to a minimum equal to that on Treasuries, but amenable to the idea of purchasing a small amount of equity, can now invest in this market. It would have been far more cumbersome to create the desired cash flow stream under the former principal-protected trust structures. An investor would have had to include a strip of zeroes as well as the equity piece.

Initial Structuring

Participating coupon notes are created at the time of initially structuring a CDO. This often allows for a higher return than could be paid if pieces were combined after the fact. Let's look at an example. Assume an A rated participating coupon structure is created, and rated to a 5.4% coupon. Because the coupon on this security is significantly below market there will be more excess cash flows each period. This, in turn, gives the deal more of a cushion against defaults, and allows for lower subordination levels. This structure would also be consistent with less stringent interest coverage (I/C) tests due to increased excess spread and more stringent overcollateralization (O/C) tests due to the reduced subordination.

Support for Single Security Treatment

The fact that the participating coupon note is combined in the initial structuring makes a very strong case from a regulatory perspective that this is a single security. Bifurcating a participating coupon note into two securities is economically difficult, as the participating coupon security really represents two claims on the same stream of cash flows, each with different priorities in the waterfall. Moreover, the deal is different than it would have been in the absence of a participating coupon note. Finally, as a practical matter, bifurcation is much harder than with previous trust structures, as there is only one CUSIP for the participating coupon note, not separate CUSIPs for each component piece.[2]

From a tax viewpoint, participating coupon notes are taxed as a single security; and the instrument is usually con-

---

[2] In the old trust structures, there was one CUSIP for the trust, but each of component piece also had its own CUSIP.

sidered "contingent debt." The fact the notes are taxed as one vehicle gives additional regulatory weight to support that they are just one vehicle.

Together, these factors suggest it would be very difficult for regulators to argue that a participating coupon note should be bifurcated. So from a regulatory perspective, that makes these securities far more appealing than the old Trust structure.

VARIATIONS ON A THEME

Even though all participating coupon structures are combinations of equity and rated notes, the amount of debt versus the amount of equity can vary widely between structures. Some structures are rated as to [principal only], while others are rated to [principal + a submarket coupon].[3] The largest determinant of the amount of debt versus equity will be how much coupon an investor wants rated.

For example, if an investor requests a security rated A2 with a respect to [principal + a 5.4% coupon], then of a par amount, $85.41 would be invested in the debt instrument, with the remaining $14.59 going into equity.[4] A 5.4% coupon is used for this example, as that is the yield on the 10-year Treasury. For a security rated A with respect to principal only, the amount invested in the debt instrument drops to $45.64, with the other $54.36 going into the equity.[5]

Risk-Return Tradeoffs

We now look at the risk/return tradeoff on the debt and equity securities, highlighting that:

---

[3] The brackets ([ ]) denote the structure.
[4] We calculate this by assuming the securities have a 10-year average life and would trade at the 10-year Treasury rate plus 210 basis points (or equivalently, on a swapped basis, LIBOR plus 130 basis points). With 10-year Treasuries at 5.40% at the time this illustration was developed (May 2001), this places the discount rate at 7.50%.

1. The first security (larger debt component) has a lower risk/ lower potential return than the second security.
2. Both cases above have a substantially higher risk/return profile than bonds which lack a participating coupon component.

[Principal + Submarket Interest] Rated

Most investors in participating coupon structures want at least some of their coupon rated. They often want to know that, within an acceptable risk range, they are likely to receive a minimum return. Common requests include (1) rating a fixed coupon in the context of the Treasury curve (for example, to a level equal to Treasuries flat, or Treasuries plus or minus a bit); or (2) rating a floating coupon in the context of the LIBOR curve. (A common request is to rate the coupon to a level equivalent to the institution's cost of funding; LIBOR + 25, for example.)

We refer to structures rated with [principal + a submarket coupon] drawn from one spot on the waterfall, combined with equity drawn from another spot on the waterfall, as *contingent payment notes* or CPNs. The best way to understand the risk/return tradeoff on a CPN is to look at a representative example. We assumed that a deal is backed by high yield collateral, and rated A2 with respect to [principal + a 5.4% coupon]. We set the coupon rate to equal the yield on the 10-year Treasury. From the numbers provided above, we know 85.4% of the market value of the security is derived from the rated note, and 14.6% from the equity.

---

[5] We calculate this by assuming the securities have a 10-year average life and would trade at the 10-year Treasury rate plus 260 basis points (or equivalently, on a swapped basis, LIBOR plus 180 basis points). With 10-year Treasuries at 5.40% at the time this illustration was developed, this places the discount rate at 8.00%. This discount rate is higher than that on the coupon bearing security, as the 10-year zero rate was considerably above the 10-year coupon rate, courtesy of a steep yield curve. Moreover, the CBO credit curve was also upward sloping.

EXHIBIT 11.2   Yield on CPN versus A2-Rated Fixed-Rate Note

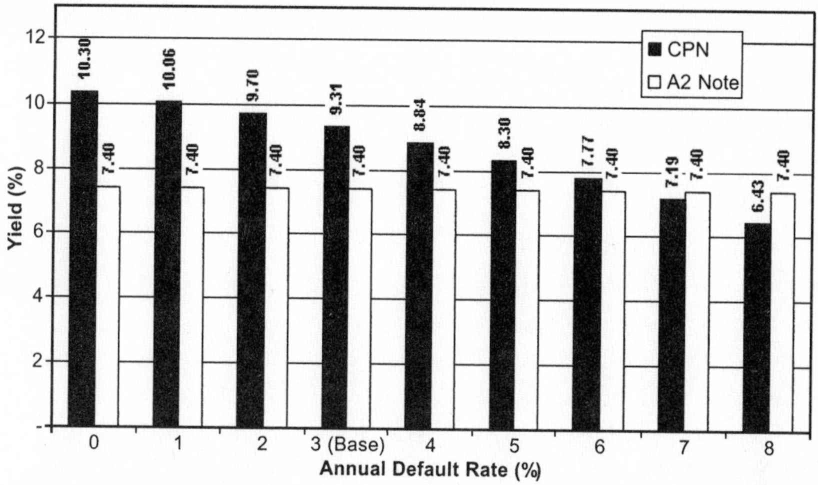

The risk-return profile for this security is shown in Exhibit 11.2. As can be seen from this analysis, the base case yield on this security is 9.31%. We assumed base case default rates of 3.00%. The average default rate computed by Moody's using data from the prior 30 years of data was roughly 3.25%. CDO asset managers must have above average track records. Moreover, Moody's default rates are based on the number of defaulting issuers. To the extent that the bonds that are more likely to default are initially purchased at a discount, portfolio default rates will be lower than the average. Thus, we use 3% as the base case return. We also assume a 45% recovery rate.

The intuition behind these numbers is quite simple: the yield on the combination can be approximated by the yield on each bond, weighted by (1) its cost and (2) its duration. This is provided by the following equation:

$$Y_{cpn} = Y_b\left[\frac{MV_b \times D_b}{(MV_b \times D_b) + (MV_e \times D_e)}\right] + Y_e\left[\frac{MV_e \times D_e}{(MV_b \times D_b) + (MV_e \times D_e)}\right]$$

where

Y_{cpn}, Y_b, Y_e = Yield on coupon, bond, and equity, respectively
MV_b, MV_e = Market value of bond and equity, respectively
D_b, D_e = Duration on bond and equity, respectively

Since our representative security has $85.41 invested in the debt (which has a duration of 6.8) and 14.59 invested in the equity (duration of 4.0), then roughly 91% of the contribution to yield is coming from the debt, and only 9% from the equity component. Since the base case debt yield is 7.5% and the base case equity return is 27.3%, then the combination yield will be 9.31% [(0.91 × 7.5) + (0.09 × 27.3)].

Exhibit 11.2 also shows the returns on a note which is fully rated with respect to [principal + interest]. We assume that this note pays 7.4% in the base case (10-year Treasury plus 200 basis points or LIBOR plus 120 basis points), which is very typical for an A2 rated CBO instrument. Note that in the base case (3% defaults), the return on the CPN is 191 basis points (9.31% minus 7.40%) higher than a traditional A2 rated CBO. If default rates are *lower* than the base case, then the CPN *outperforms* the straight rated note by a higher margin. But if default rates are *higher* than the base case, the CPN will outperform by less than 190 basis points. But interestingly, the CPN does not underperform the straight debt issue until default rates are close to 7%.

[Principal Only] Rated

Structures rated as to principal only require a much lower investment in the debt securities. In our example, we showed that an investor can purchase a hypothetical A2 rated zero-coupon note at a yield (accretion rate) equal to [the 10-year Treasury plus 260 basis points]. At the time of this analysis, this corresponds to a yield of 8.0% and to a dollar price of $45.64 on the debt. Thus, the remaining $54.36 [$100 – $45.64] can be invested in the equity.

EXHIBIT 11.3 Yield Profile on VIP

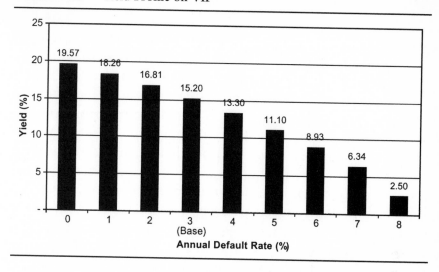

We refer to bonds rated only with respect to principal as *variable interest participating securities* or VIPs. The yield profile on this security is shown in Exhibit 11.3. Note that the base case return is 15.20%. This compares to the 7.40% yield on the fully rated debt of the same rating, and the 9.31% yield on the CPNs (see Exhibit 11.2). Thus, in the base case, the VIP has a considerably higher yield than either of the alternatives.

Since in a VIP a higher percentage of the cash flows come from the equity, it makes sense that this structure should have much higher return potential, but also much more risk than either of the alternatives. At a 1% default rate, the yield on the VIP security is 19.57%, versus 10.06% on the CPN and 7.4% on the straight A2 CBO debt. At a very high 8.0% default rate, the VIP yields 2.50%, versus 6.43% for the CPN and 7.4% for the rated debt. Note that even at a 6% default rate, which we definitely can consider a stress case, the VIP return of 8.93% is higher than that of either the CPN or the ordinary fixed rate bond.

Structural Issues with [Principal Only] Rated

We discussed earlier that when the CDO debt is rated, a lower coupon on the rated note means more excess cash flow each period. That can be used to absorb defaults, which in turn means less subordination is needed.

From the structurer's perspective, there is a slight advantage to a zero-coupon structure. The principal obligation to the investor at each point in time is the accreted value, which is the initial value, compounded by the accretion rate over the holding period. Thus, if the VIPs are retired by special redemption prior to the target repayment rate, the holders of these participating coupon structures will receive rated cash flow equal to the initial investment plus the cumulative accreted amount as of that date. For the purpose of overcollateralization tests, it is the accreted value, *not* the full par amount, which is used in the calculations. That allows for still greater leverage (less equity). This, in turn, gives the participating coupon noteholder a higher yield than otherwise possible from the same mix of debt and equity if the combination had been created after the fact.

Although this bond is rated as to principal and investors may get less than full principal back if the bond gets redeemed early, investors must realize that they are receiving these cash flows early, so they can be reinvested at the discretion of investors. If interest rates have fallen, this works to the detriment of investors; if rates have risen, it works to their benefit. Clearly this structure contains an additional element of risk, but the investor is getting compensated for that by a substantially higher base case yield.

While our simple examples focused on A2 rated notes, the rated component can actually be rated anywhere from AAA to BB. Obviously, the lower the desired rating on the principal component, the more yield to participating coupon noteholders.

EXHIBIT 11.4 Advantage of CPNs at Different Ratings

Rating	Fixed CPN Return	Fixed Return on Fully Rated Security	Difference
AAA	190	136	54
AA	240	160	80
A	380	220	160
BBB	500	315	185

Thus an investor can get securities highly customized to fit their risk preferences. In Exhibit 11.4 we assumed that [principal + submarket coupon] is rated, with the level on the CPN at Treasuries flat. We show approximate base case returns for each rating category compared with what could have been achieved in a straight fixed rate note. (In Exhibit 11.4, the fixed returns on the fully rated security are 10 basis points higher than representative new issue floating rates swapped back into fixed. This adjusts for the fact that a balance guaranteed swap is necessary.) Note that resultant differences are larger the lower the rating on the debt tranche. Intuitively this makes sense; for a lower rated bond, the Treasuries flat coupon is more below market than it would be on a higher rated security. Thus, for a given coupon rate, the lower the rating on the debt portion, the lower the market value of the participating coupon note invested in debt and the higher the market value initially riding on equity. Moreover, the differences will be even larger if an investor is willing to have a coupon rated to a level lower than Treasuries flat.

Realize also that the coupon to be rated can be stated in either fixed or floating terms. This gives investors the flexibility to receive a floating coupon equal to their funding costs.

Dealers are generally quite eager to accommodate investor needs. Equity is the most difficult part of a deal to sell, even though in a typical high-yield deal it is only 10–12% of the total market value of the deal, with the asset manager often taking a significant piece. (It is a lower percentage of the deal in structured finance backed and investment grade corporate deals.) Straight equity, however, does not interest traditional debt investors, nor does the traditional equity investor customarily look at this market. That leaves a very small "natural" buyer base. By offering participating coupon notes, the dealer community expands its buyer base for equity in their deals.

Participation Share—Capped versus Uncapped

The participation share may be *capped* or *uncapped*. In the examples provided in this article, we assumed that the participation share is *uncapped*. That is, an investor in the participating coupon note is essentially paid *pari passu* with the equity holders. However, if the participation share is *capped*, it means the investor can never receive more than a preset yield on the equity. Normally, when the participation return is capped, the unrated cash flows are senior to those on the equity.

Combination Notes

Thus far we focused on participating coupon structures both structured and rated as to [principal only] or with respect to [principal + a submarket coupon]. *Combination notes* or *combo notes* are closely related instruments. Combo notes are combinations of two or more classes in the same deal. The rating on the combination notes is usually done after structuring, but before closing. For example, some of the AA note and some of the equity can be combined into a single security. The investor may choose to have the combination bond rated at the BBB2 level with a submarket coupon.

Ratings on combination notes are basically done in a very similar manner to that on any CDO. The cash flows of relevant tranches are combined, and all calculations are based on those combined cash flows. The expected present value of losses in each scenario is calculated; these losses are summed across scenarios (each weighted by the probability of occurrence). This is then compared to a benchmark bond to determine the rating.

Obviously, when combining bonds after structuring, structural flexibility is more limited. For example, a capped participation note in which the cash flows are senior to the equity itself cannot be created, as an unrated tranche senior to the equity does not exist. Similarly, zero-coupon structures cannot be duplicated as such, although the rating agency can rate as to return of principal. Furthermore, when done in the initial structuring, yield can be optimized, often allowing investors to eke out a few extra basis points. However, most CPN structures can be replicated very closely in combination form. Moreover, combo notes give the investor more time to decide exactly what they want. They can decide immediately prior to closing what bonds they wish to buy in what proportions.

Furthermore, if the combination cash flows are rated prior to the deal closing, they can be combined into a single security, with a single CUSIP, which then also advantages them for regulatory purposes.

CONCLUSION

The use of participating interest structures benefits both issuers and investors. From an issuer's perspective, it aids placement of the equity class, which is the hardest cash flow in the deal to sell. Often the problem with placing equity is really only that there has been a limited audience, rather than any relative value imbalance or a structural issue or problem. However, many debt investors cannot buy equity, and traditional equity investors do not focus on this relatively small segment of the market. Thus, the equity buyer base is limited, and the participating coupon structure provides a way to expand the existing group of equity buyers.

From the investor's viewpoint, participating coupon structures enable the purchase of a rated debt instrument for regulatory and financial purposes, which delivers higher yield potential than comparably rated investments.

For these reasons, the participating coupon structure will gain in popularity over time, and investors can be well rewarded for looking carefully at this product.

CHAPTER 12

Relative Value Methodology for Analyzing Mezzanine Tranches

The mezzanine tranches of collateralized debt obligation deals appeal to many different types of investors. The fixed-rate cash flows of the mezzanine tranches are an ideal fit for insurance companies, which seek to manage portfolio assets against their long-term, fixed-rate liabilities. The floating-rate coupons of mezzanine tranches fit quite well into LIBOR-plus portfolios. As with any asset, investors need to evaluate whether or not mezzanine tranches offer sufficient compensation for the risk accepted. Part of that process entails developing a comfort level about investing in mezzanine tranches via relative value comparison to other products. However, the risk-return profile of mezzanine tranches is very different from that on a typical corporate bond. Moreover, the collateral for a CDO deal, and therefore the mezzanine tranches, is often different from a corporate bond of the same rating.

This chapter provides a methodology to determine value in the mezzanine tranches. We discuss the risk-return profile on the mezzanine tranches and focus on comparing the mezzanine tranche to corporate alternatives. We begin our demonstration of the relative analysis methodology for mezzanine tranches by looking at risk-return profiles of a BBB rated

This chapter was coauthored with Jeffrey Ho of UBS Warburg.

CDO mezzanine tranche backed primarily by high-yield bank loans versus a BBB rated corporate bond. For a hypothetical CDO deal described in the next section and based on the spread configuration typical of 1999, we compare yields on representative bonds as a function of defaults. Based on the spread configuration, we show the difference in the yield profiles between the two types of bonds. The methodology then involves determining the better yielding bond at the same level of risk by calculating breakeven default rates necessary to produce the same yield on the two bonds. These default rates are then evaluated relative to historical experience. For the hypothetical CDO deal and the spread configuration assumed in the analysis, the BBB rated mezzanine tranche did yield considerably more than typical corporate bonds, even at the highest default levels the underlying collateral ever experienced over the period 1970–1999. This indicates that there was definitely relative value within CDOs for the time period analyzed. While this conclusion of relative investment value is dependent on the spread configuration for the time period analyzed, the methodology is more general.

There is no question that part of any incremental yield on a mezzanine tranche of a CDO is a function of liquidity. CDO tranches are smaller and clearly less liquid than equivalently rated corporate bonds. Consequently, this liquidity difference must be recognized by an investor performing relative value analysis. The incremental yield is also a function of the fact that the CDO market is relatively new, and investors are usually compensated well for entering a market at the early stages. Indeed, as the CDO market matures, liquidity will improve, and the new product yield premium should erode.

HYPOTHETICAL CDO DEAL ANALYZED

To illustrate the methodology for assessing the relative value in mezzanine tranches, we will use a hypothetical CDO deal. There is no standard, generic, or "plain vanilla" CDO deal.

Each has slightly different collateral and a slightly different structure. The representative CDO we use for this comparison is a cash flow structure deal. For pricing purposes, we assume that the deal is backed by collateral consisting of 80% bank loans and 20% high-yield bonds. Funding has been divided into three classes:

- 74% AAA rated senior floating-rate notes
- 16% BBB+ rated subordinated floating-rate notes
- 10% unrated equity tranche

Our hypothetical CDO deal has a 7.25-year expected maturity and a 12-year legal maturity. In this chapter, we focus on the BBB+ tranche, which is commonly called the "mezzanine" tranche, and compare it to 10-year BBB corporate securities. We assumed the CDO deal was issued in December 1999 and use price and spread information at that time.

We also assumed a coupon on our representative Baa1/BBB+ rated CDO of LIBOR + 225. The bond was also issued at a slight discount, which produced a yield of roughly LIBOR + 230. To compare yield on the CDO mezzanine tranche to yield on an equivalently rated, fixed-rate corporate bond, we used the swap curve in December 1999 to convert the floating-rate LIBOR-based yield into a fixed-rate security. With 10-year swap yields at the time at 6.78%, the equivalent fixed-rate yield on the CDO mezzanine tranche was 9.08% (6.78% plus 2.30%).

As a proxy for a fixed-rate BBB security, we used the Merrill Lynch BBB rated corporate index (C0A4). We assumed that our representative corporate bond has the same coupon as the weighted average coupon of the index—7.356%—and same yield as the index—7.76%. This corresponds to a spread of 180 basis points over the 10-year Treasury note. (The then-prevailing 10-year Treasury note was 5.96%, which equates to the 10-year swap yield of 6.78%, less the 82 basis points swap spread.) Assuming a 10-year average life, then the dollar price of the representative corporate bond is $97.32.

COMPARING DEFAULTS

It is a challenge to compare defaults on CDO collateral to those on a BBB corporate bond, as the underlying assets are so different. The CDO consists of both high-yield and bank loan collateral, while our straw dog is a portfolio of BBB corporate bonds. We set up two alternative scenarios, which represent the upper and lower default bounds. We first assumed that the BBB corporate never defaults, while the collateral for the BBB CDO defaulted at rates assumed in the box in Exhibits 12.1 and 12.2. In our second iteration, we assumed that the two securities defaulted at the same rate. Both of these are obviously wrong. We know that BBB corporate bonds do default, although at a much lower rate than high-yield bonds, and they are usually downgraded first. Still, our assumptions provide bounds, albeit very wide bounds, for our analysis.

Exhibits 12.1 and 12.2 compare the yield profile on our representative BBB rated CDO mezzanine tranche to that on a BBB rated corporate bond. We assume zero defaults for the first six months and then the annual default rate depicted on the horizontal axis of the two exhibits for the remainder of the term. Note that recovery rates on bank loans have typically been much higher than on unsecured bonds because of the built-in, risk-mitigating features of many bank credit facilities. For instance, bank lenders often require collateral before a loan is extended, which makes most bank loans senior to unsecured bonds and therefore likely to have a higher recovery. Accordingly, a lower recovery rate is used for both the high-yield bonds and the BBB corporate issue.

In Exhibit 12.1 we assume 82% recovery on the loans, and 45% recovery on the unsecured corporate debt. In the exhibit, the yield profile on the CDO mezzanine tranches is denoted by a solid line. The yield profile on the BBB rated corporate bond is presented as a dotted line. These levels correspond to historical evidence of recovery rates discussed later in this chapter. In Exhibit 12.2 we assumed 60% recovery on the loans and 36% recovery on the high-yield bonds. This is in line with the rating agencies' stress scenarios for recoveries.

EXHIBIT 12.1 BBB CDO Mezzanine Tranche versus BBB Corporate with Base Case Recoveries

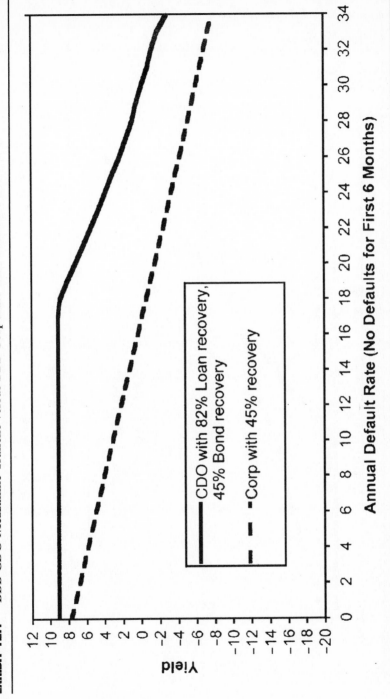

275

EXHIBIT 12.2 BBB CDO Mezzanine Tranche versus BBB Corporate with Stressed Recoveries

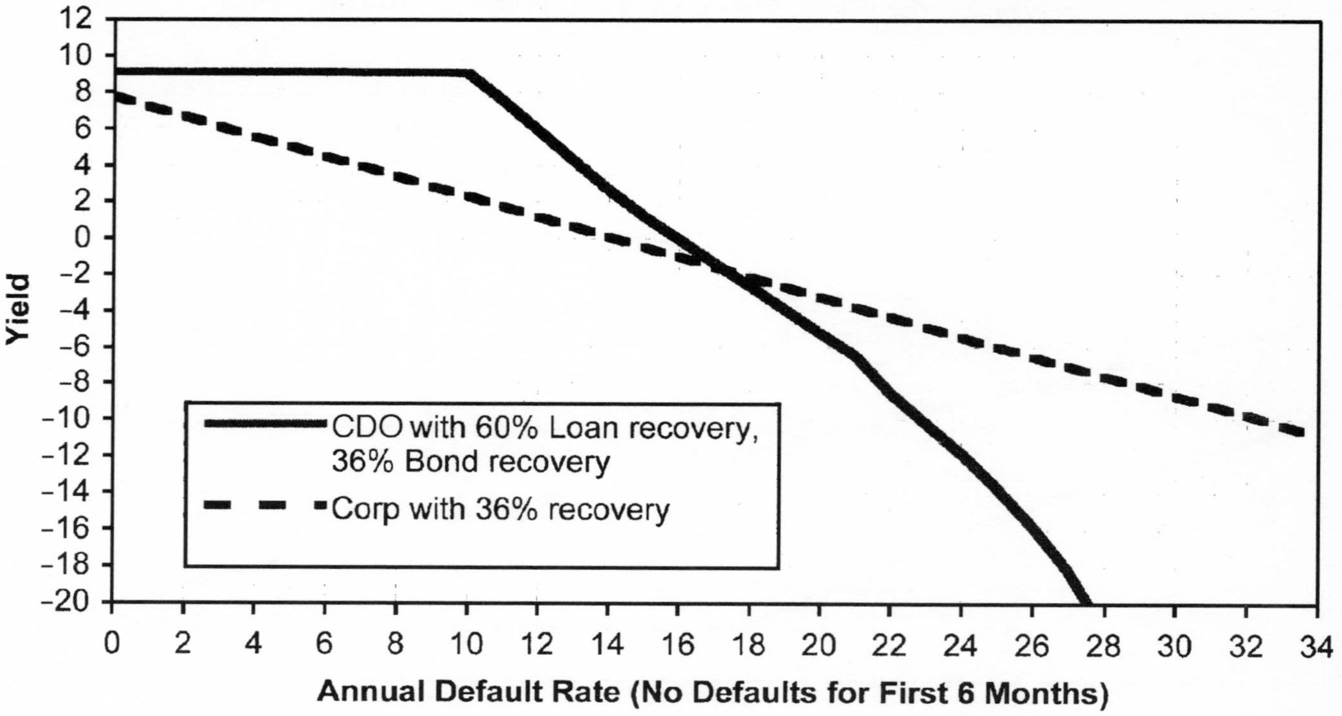

Legend:
— CDO with 60% Loan recovery, 36% Bond recovery
- - Corp with 36% recovery

Y-axis: Yield (12 to -20)

X-axis: Annual Default Rate (No Defaults for First 6 Months) (0 to 34)

Exhibits 12.1 and 12.2 demonstrate that the yield profile on the CDO mezzanine tranche is much more leveraged than that for the corporate bond. This conveys how the CDO mezzanine tranche maintains its spread for a much longer period of time, but then deteriorates far more quickly.

RISK-REWARD PROFILES

Look at risk-return profiles using the historical recovery rates in Exhibit 12.1. If we assume that the BBB corporate bond never defaults, and that all the collateral backing the CDO defaults at the annual rates shown on the horizontal axis of Exhibit 12.1, then the "breakeven default rate" is 19.4%. That is, at a 19.4% default rate on the CDO collateral, the postdefault CDO mezzanine tranche yields the same 7.76% as does the zero-default corporate bond.[1] In fact, as will be shown in the next section, this 19.4% default figure is nearly double the highest level of high-yield default rates ever experienced over the last three decades. If we assume that annual default rates on the CDO and the BBB corporate bond are the same, then the CDO outperforms the corporate bond in all default scenarios. The exhibit shows results as high as a 34% annual default rate, which is the highest we tested.

We repeat the same analysis in Exhibit 12.2, using a rating agency stress scenario for recoveries. Assuming zero defaults for the BBB rated corporate bond, the collateral on the CDO can default at close to 11% and the CDO mezzanine tranche will still outperform on a yield basis. This is higher than the highest default rates experienced by high yield bonds in the early 1990s. Assuming the BBB corporate defaults at the same rate as does the high-yield bonds, then the breakeven default rate is even higher—17%. We now

---

[1] To replicate this, find the point on the CDO curve in Exhibit 12.1 where the yield is 7.76%, and observe the corresponding default rate.

see that this number is well outside the range of historical experience.[2]

HISTORICAL DEFAULT RATES

In Chapter 3, we discuss default rates and how to select the relevant rates when analyzing CDOs. Here we look at the default rates for high-yield bonds from 1971 through 1999 since our hypothetical CDO deal was analyzed as of December 1999. Exhibit 12.3 shows Moody's compilation of historical default rates for the high-yield market since 1971. These are trailing 12-month default rates, and are expressed as the percentage of defaults per annum. The statistics are tallied both by the number of issuers and by outstanding balance. The latter understandably tilts the average towards the results of larger issuers, while the former gives equal weighting to all issuers.

As measured by percent of balance, the average default rate over the 1971–1999 period was just 3.24% (with a standard deviation of 2.49%). As a percent of the total number of issuers, the historical default rate was 3.37% (standard deviation of 2.22%).

However, it's readily observable from Exhibit 12.3 that the "average" is heavily skewed by several very high-default years during 1989–1991. Peak bond defaults typically occur two to three years after issuance. During the leveraged buyout mania of 1987–1989, quite a few marginal deals were brought to market. Fallout from that was reflected in the high-default rates during the 1989–1991 period.

---

[2] Clearly, these results are dependent on assumptions. We have assumed equal annual default rates after the first six months. Changing the default timing will make a difference. In particular, defaults early in the life of the CDO have a larger negative impact. Changing the recovery assumptions will also have an impact. In addition, we have assumed a stable interest rate environment. Changing this assumption will alter reinvestment rates and could trigger call provisions on the corporate bond, the collateral underlying the CDO structure.

EXHIBIT 12.3   Historical Annual Default Rates

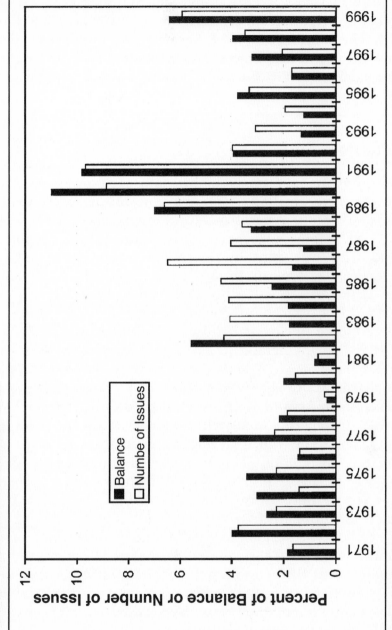

Source: Moody's Investor Service.

This skewness is also easily seen by looking at the frequency distribution of defaults, which is shown in Exhibit 12.4. The data in Exhibit 12.3 are regrouped into buckets to show the distribution more easily. Measured by outstanding loan balance, in fewer than 15% of the years were defaults greater than 4%.

BOTTOM LINE

Even though "average" numbers are skewed by the high default years of 1989–1991, we can still use these actual results to compare performance of our representative BBB+ CDO mezzanine tranche to a traditional BBB corporate bond. This was done by interpolating data from Exhibit 12.1. (We can look up the yield for each of the two securities that corresponded to the average default rate of 3.24%.) It is clear that the CDO mezzanine tranche delivers its promised yield of 9.08%, while the BBB index is impacted by any defaults that occur. Assuming the BBB corporate bond never defaults, its base case yield is 7.76%, which the CDO mezzanine tranche outperforms by 132 basis points. Assuming the bonds both default at the 3.24% annual average for high-yield bonds, then the yield on the CDO mezzanine tranche is 9.08% versus the 6.25% for the BBB corporate bond. This is a 283 basis point difference. Using this market pricing, the CDO mezzanine tranche is expected to outperform by 132–283 basis points, and is hence, the more attractive opportunity.

For the time period analyzed, the case for the mezzanine tranche is even stronger than indicated above. Even gilding the lily of the BBB corporate by assuming it never defaults, the mezzanine tranche could still have sustained default rates higher than ever been experienced over the period 1971–1999 and still outperform.

EXHIBIT 12.4 The Distribution of Annual Defaults

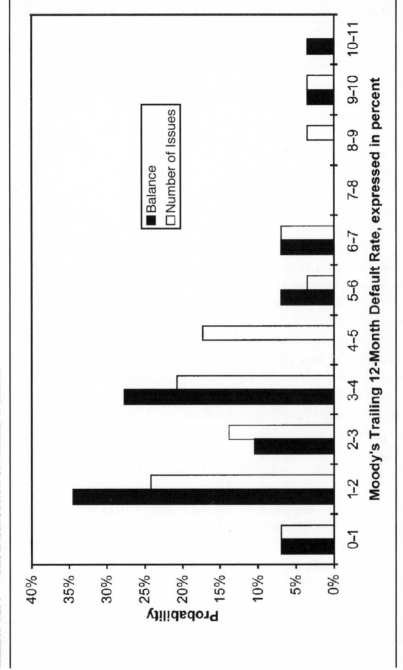

STRESS TESTING

In performing any analyses, results are only as robust as the assumptions upon which they stand. The two we have made are that

1. recovery rates are higher on bank loans than on bonds; and
2. the BBB corporate bond either doesn't default at all, or defaults at the same rate as high-yield bonds.

While we believe that our first assumption is fair, and our second assumption provides fair bounds, it is certainly prudent to stress the assumptions.

Historically, recovery rates have been far higher on bank loans than on bonds. Nonetheless, we can test the comparison by assuming identical recovery rates and look at the results. Exhibit 12.5 shows the results of a single 36% recovery rate on both the loans and the bonds. Remember, this is the stress scenario. As can be seen, the breakeven default rate—the default rate at which the two securities have the same yield— is 7%, assuming no defaults on the BBB corporate. That breakeven default rate is 10% if we assume equal defaults on the BBB corporate and the high-yield debt. These numbers are at the very higher end of historical experience (those high-default years following LBO issuance mania). Thus, even in the stressed scenario, the CDO mezzanine tranche holds up very well relative to the BBB corporate bond.

Defaults on BBB securities are certainly lower than defaults on a portfolio of high-yield securities, but it is not clear how best to make the comparison. Annual default numbers are unfair, as the BBB bond will need much more time to default than a high-yield bond. It is even more difficult to compare BBB rated bonds to a portfolio of 80% bank loans, 20% high-yield bonds, as the default patterns on bank loans are not that widely studied. Thus, it really is not crystal clear how to best set up and make a comparison between the BBB corporate and the BBB+ rated CDO mezzanine tranche.

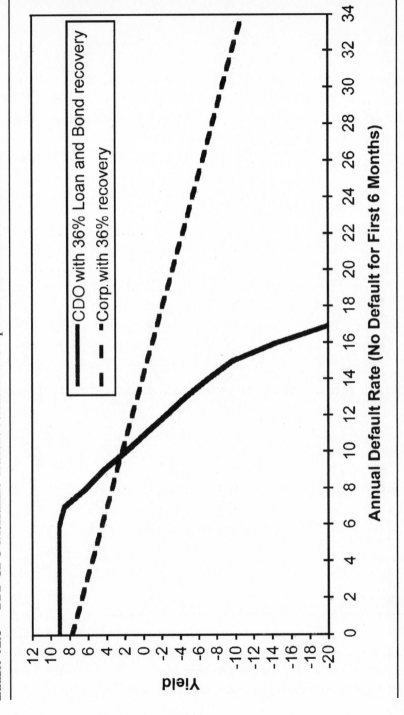

EXHIBIT 12.5 BBB CDO Mezzanine Tranche versus BBB Corporate with Extreme Recoveries

Upper and lower bounds were essentially set on the breakeven default rates by assuming that the BBB corporates either (1) do not default at all or (2) default at the same rate as high-yield bonds. We can try to place a more reasonable number on the breakeven, by juxtaposing actual cumulative default rates over a 10- to 12-year period. Moody's data indicate that the cumulative losses on Baa securities are 4.39% after 10 years, 5.04% after 11 years, and 5.71% after 12 years.

By contrast, high-yield bonds (all speculative grades combined) have a cumulative default rate of 28.32%, 30.16%, and 31.96%. Therefore it seems reasonable to assume that default rates on the BBB corporate bond are approximately one-sixth as high as those on the CDO mezzanine tranche. Thus, a 12% default rate on the CDO mezzanine tranche corresponds to a 2% default rate on the BBBs. The results of this analysis are shown in Exhibit 12.6. At close to a 21% default rate on the BBB rated CDO mezzanine tranche and a 3.5% default rate on the BBB rated corporate bond, the yields on the two securities are nearly identical. Column 1 shows the default rates on the CDO mezzanine tranche; Column 4 shows the default rates on the BBB rated security and the horizontal line denotes the approximate crossover point. At default rates above the crossover (lower default rates), the CDO mezzanine tranche represents the higher-yielding alternative. Clearly, for all default rates over the past three decades, even assuming that the default rate on the CDO is six times as high as on a BBB rated corporate bond, the CDO mezzanine tranche represents the better relative value.

CONCLUSION

The risk-return profile on the mezzanine tranche of a CDO is much more leveraged than that on the corporate bond. Moreover, the collateral behind a CDO will often be different than on a corporate bond of the same credit rating.

EXHIBIT 12.6   BBB CDO Mezzanine Tranche versus BBB Corporate Yields

High-Yield Default Rate*	CDO Yield with 82% Loan Recovery and 45% Bond Recovery	Corp. Yield with 45% Recovery	BBB Corp. Default*	Which Yields More?
0	9.08	7.76	0.00	CDO
1	9.08	7.68	0.17	CDO
2	9.08	7.60	0.33	CDO
3	9.08	7.53	0.50	CDO
4	9.08	7.45	0.67	CDO
5	9.08	7.37	0.83	CDO
6	9.07	7.29	1.00	CDO
7	9.07	7.21	1.17	CDO
8	9.07	7.14	1.33	CDO
9	9.07	7.06	1.50	CDO
10	9.07	6.98	1.67	CDO
11	9.07	6.90	1.83	CDO
12	9.07	6.83	2.00	CDO
13	9.07	6.75	2.17	CDO
14	9.07	6.67	2.33	CDO
15	9.07	6.59	2.50	CDO
16	9.07	6.51	2.67	CDO
17	9.07	6.44	2.83	CDO
18	8.88	6.36	3.00	CDO
19	8.11	6.28	3.17	CDO
20	7.23	6.20	3.33	CDO
21	6.33	6.12	3.50	CDO
22	5.50	6.05	3.67	Corp
23	4.65	5.97	3.83	Corp
24	3.82	5.89	4.00	Corp
25	3.06	5.81	4.17	Corp
26	2.25	5.73	4.33	Corp
27	1.55	5.66	4.50	Corp
28	0.88	5.58	4.67	Corp
29	0.41	5.50	4.83	Corp
30	−0.20	5.42	5.00	Corp
31	−0.83	5.34	5.17	Corp
32	−1.27	5.27	5.33	Corp
33	−1.87	5.19	5.50	Corp

* Annual default rate expressed as a percent.

In this chapter, we saw how to make relative value comparisons between a mezzanine tranche of a CDO and corporate bonds. The correct approach is to compare "breakeven" default rates on mezzanine tranches versus corporate alternatives under a range of assumptions. This allows an investor to gauge under what scenarios the mezzanine tranche will outperform, and determine if those scenarios are likely, particularly given the range of historical experience.

CHAPTER 13

Analyzing CDO Equity Tranches

In Chapter 1, we explained the key role of the CDO equity in an arbitrage transaction. Many investors in CDO debt tranches tend to look at the equity tranche of a CDO solely as a part of their subordination, rather than as an independent investment in its own right.

In this chapter we look at how to analyze CDO equity tranches. In the first part, we see where CDO equity cash flows come from and how to evaluate them. The discussion also provides a brief review of how to assess the relative attractiveness of equity cash flows backed by different collateral. In the second part of this chapter, the factors that affect CDO equity returns are discussed.

EQUITY CASH FLOWS

Equity cash flows, sometimes called "preferred shares" or "preference shares," are not bonds at all. They are equity investments in a trust in which the assets are actively managed. Strict rules are in place to preserve credit quality. Moreover, as we will demonstrate, the cash flows themselves are far more front-loaded than is the case with most bonds. Actually, equity cash flows often fall somewhere between those of a bond and those on an interest-only (IO) security. This also means that CDO equity tranches that have been outstanding for awhile, even if performing well, will sell in the secondary market at a lower dollar price than they did at inception of their respective deals. This reflects the fact that equity holders have already received a disproportionate amount of their equity cash flows. Therefore, the value of this security like any IO deteriorates over time. So in evaluating CDO equity tranches, the extent to which the cash flows are front-loaded is quite important.

Both cash flow and market value CDOs use equity tranches as first loss pieces for the senior and subordinates tranches of the deal. While the equity tranche has the highest risk, it offers the highest potential return. To see how cash flows are allocated to the equity tranche, we need to review the entire deal. We can use the Duke Funding 1 deal that was priced in November 2000. The deal, described in Chapter 2, has three bond tranches—Classes A, B, and C—and equity, and is backed primarily by structured finance collateral.

The cash flow waterfall and coverage tests for this CDO deal were reviewed in Chapter 2. Exhibits 2.1 and 2.2 of Chapter 2 show the cash flow waterfall. The coverage tests are clearly intended to protect bondholders, not the equity holders who are subordinated to bondholders. However, these tests are really of interest to equity holders, and should be watched, as test violations can lead to consequences that seriously erode equity returns. This is because the equity tranche is clearly last in line to receive interest and principal cash flows (see Exhibits 2.1 and 2.2 of Chapter 2). For this reason, the equity tranche receives excess interest from the collateral only after the expenses are paid, and all senior and mezzanine bonds have been paid in full. And principal is paid to the equity tranche only after every more senior tranche is satisfied.

Note the important role in the waterfall played by the coverage tests. Before any payments are made on Class B or Class C bonds, interest coverage tests are run to assure the deal is performing within guidelines. If that is not the case, consequences to the equity holders are severe. Note from Exhibit 2.1 in Chapter 2, if either of the Class A coverage tests is violated, then excess interest on the portfolio goes to pay down principal on the Class A bonds, and cash flows will be diverted from all other classes to do so. If the portfolio violates the Class B coverage tests, then interest will be diverted from Class C plus the equity tranche to pay down first principal on Class A and then class B principal.

As can be seen in Exhibit 2.2 of Chapter 2, which shows the simple principal cash flows for this deal, principal is paid down purely in class order. Any remaining collateral principal from overcollateralization gets passed onto the equity tranche.

Incentives Keep Equity Flowing

Cutting off cash flows to the equity tranche due to violation of coverage tests generally cuts seriously into equity holders' return. Once the equity holders lose the cash flows it is difficult to get them back later, as the deal also begins to delever. This means that the portfolio will be smaller going forward, and that some of the lower cost funding (i.e., the Class A bonds) will have been paid down. Effectively, tripping the overcollateralization or interest coverage tests also means that equity returns are apt to be lower.

However, it should be realized that in many deals, the asset manager is also a substantial equity holder. The most common arrangement is for the asset manager to own 49% or 49.5% of the equity.[1] In addition, in some deals such as in the Duke Funding 1 deal, incentive management fees are subordinated to the equity return. Thus, an asset manager has every incentive to assure that the tests are not violated.

Realize also that the asset manager is generally able to forestall violation of coverage ratios by judicious portfolio trading. If there are high defaults and the overcollateraliza-

---

[1] If 50% or greater is owned, all assets of the deal must be consolidated on the issuer's balance sheet.

tion test is close to activation, an asset manager can sell higher priced bonds with higher coupons and buy lower priced bonds with lower coupons (consistent with portfolio eligibility criteria) to bring the overcollateralization test back into line.[2] Similarly, if the interest coverage test is close to activation, the asset manager may elect to sell lower coupon assets and buy higher coupon ones. In the final analysis, these actions work to benefit the asset manager but not the bondholders. However, the interests of equity holders are aligned with those of the asset manager. This helps to ensure that the impact of these tests on equity holders will be minimized as much as possible.

What Do Cash Flows Look Like?

Exhibit 13.1 shows equity cash flows on the Duke deal at three different default rates: 0%, 0.3%, and 0.5%, all assuming a 30% recovery rate. Note that the cash flows are based on the collateral already purchased as well as that which has not yet been included. Moreover, to some extent the bonds in the deal can also be traded on a discretionary basis, as well as because of changes in credit status. Thus, the cash flows on which a deal's numbers are calculated may be a rough guide to the ultimate, actual cash flows.

In our example, the initial cost of the equity was $8 million. Note that receiving close to $1 million per semiannual period for the first few years constitutes extremely front-loaded cash flows (assuming 0.3% defaults and 30% recoveries, the initial investment has a payback period of only 4 to 4.5 years). So the entire initial investment is recouped before the end of 4.5 years. The more front-loaded the cash flows on a deal, the more desirable, as there is less time for uncertain events to happen which can cause deterioration in deal assets.

---

[2] Although in this case, selling higher priced bonds to buy lower priced ones keeps the overcollateralization tests in compliance, it is likely to hurt the interest coverage ratio.

EXHIBIT 13.1 Cash Flow of Equity of Duke Funding 1 Deal (30% Recovery)

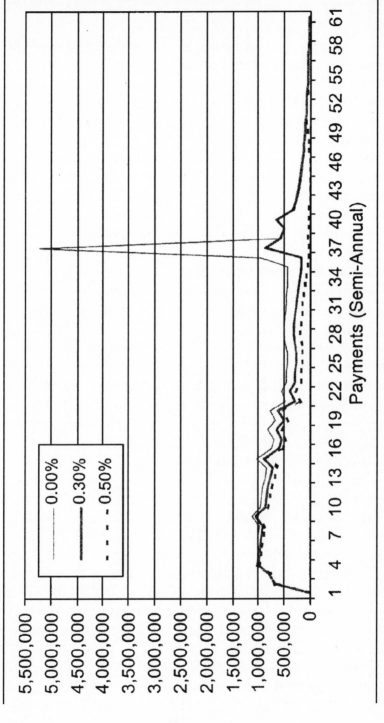

The best way to measure the front loading of cash flows is to look at the weighted-average time to receipt of the cash flows, a measure referred to as "Macaulay duration." Weighting is based on the contribution to the present value. Thus, if 50% of the market value of the deal will be received in 1 year, and the other 50% will be received in 10 years, the average life of the deal is 5.5 years. In the case of the Duke funding deal, assuming 0.3% defaults and 30% recoveries, the Macaulay duration is 4.1 years. This will generally be shorter than the payback period, as it accounts for the present value (the time value) of the cash flows.

Techniques for Evaluating CDO Equity

There are two techniques used to evaluate CDO equity: internal rate of return (IRR) analysis and Monte Carlo simulation model.

IRR Analysis

The most common way to compare deals is via the internal rate of return (IRR) under different default and recovery scenarios. An example is shown in Exhibit 13.2. Defaults are measured in terms of a conditional default rate (CDR). Thus at a constant 0.3% CDR per annum and 30% recovery, the equity cash flows in our Duke deal have an IRR of 19.01%. At 1.0% defaults they yield 6.24%. The Duke deal equity cash flows have an IRR of 0% only if annual default rates rise to between 1.2% and 1.3%; higher default rates will generate negative IRRs.

Obviously, the equity looks considerably better with higher recovery assumptions, especially if defaults are higher. For example, at 50% recovery and a constant 1% CDR per annum, the equity yields 12.72% at inception, versus only 6.24% at 30% recovery.

While IRR analysis is a very useful way to look at equity in any given deal, it is a difficult tool for making comparisons across deals for a number of reasons. First, it is not clear how to compare two different IRR profiles with different leverage. Two deals with identical collateral and different amounts of leverage will have different IRRs (see Exhibit 13.3). The bond with greater leverage will generally have a higher IRR at pricing speed, and a steeper profile. That is, deals with higher leverage have both greater upside and greater downside. The problem that one then encounters is how to measure the tradeoff.

EXHIBIT 13.2 IRR at Different Recovery Rates for Duke Funding 1

Default Rates	Recovery Rates (%)		
	30%	40%	50%
0.0	22.22	22.22	22.22
0.1	21.23	21.38	21.53
0.2	20.17	20.49	20.81
0.3	19.01	19.54	20.04
0.4	17.71	18.49	19.23
0.5	16.23	17.34	18.35
0.6	14.78	16.05	17.40
0.7	12.72	14.85	16.35
0.8	11.12	13.16	15.33
0.9	8.69	11.70	14.19
1.0	6.24	9.93	12.72
1.1	4.74	7.85	11.63
1.2	1.71	5.76	10.13
1.3	−3.28	4.82	8.38
1.4	−7.98	2.27	6.61
1.5	−15.10	−1.94	5.78
1.6	−21.40	−6.11	4.88
1.7	−37.61	−11.51	2.35
1.8	−76.08	−16.57	−0.84
1.9	−75.20	−22.73	−4.56

EXHIBIT 13.3 Effect of Increasing Leverage in Duke Funding 1

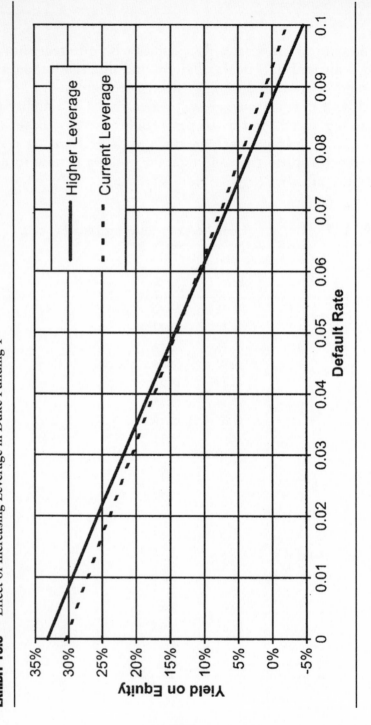

Second, constant default scenarios (i.e., constant CDR assumptions) do not consider whipsaws, which would cause different equity tranches to behave very differently. For example, if defaults are front- or back-loaded, what are the implications? That depends, in turn, on how binding are the overcollateralization and interest coverage tests. The less binding, the better for equity holders, as cash flows to the equity tranches are less likely to be cut off. Realize that only by whipsawing the CDO deal do these consequences become clear. In fact, if investors ask to see the IRR of the equity under different timing scenarios, dealers can usually run this analysis. However, further complicating the analysis is the fact that there is some interaction between leverage and the overcollateralization and interest coverage tests. If leverage is higher to achieve a given rating, the rating agencies require that coverage tests be more binding.

Finally, comparisons across different types of collateral are extremely problematic. As hard as it is to compare equity on two different deals backed by the same type of collateral, it is even tougher to compare deals backed by different types of collateral. For example, if comparing equity in structured finance CDO deals to equity in high-yield CDO deals, what are reasonable assumptions for defaults and recoveries? With similar collateral, at least similar assumptions can be made. Later in this chapter we suggest that comparison of current equity yields to historical ones starts addressing this issue.

Monte Carlo Simulation

Several dealers realize equity holders' frustration in evaluating different IRR profiles. There does not seem to be a good way to aggregate default and recovery rates across different scenarios so as to compare the equity in two different deals. The obvious solution is a more sophisticated Monte Carlo simulation analysis, where the default and recovery rates are themselves random variables. In each Monte Carlo simulation, a random variable is drawn from the default and recovery distribution. The approach allows an investor to look at distributions of returns. Thus, the investor can assess the probability of receiving a return below $X\%$. The investor is also able to determine applicable confidence intervals. This will tell an investor that with an 80% probability, the range of returns will be between $Y\%$ and $Z\%$

Monte Carlo simulation when applied uniformly and consistently across deals (with broad agreement on parameters) is really a great tool. However, only a subset of dealers have developed this analytical technique, and there is no uniformity in the application of assumptions. Even so, it is an extremely useful form of analysis. Equity investors should certainly seek Monte Carlo simulation analysis if available from a dealer. However, an investor should ask about the inputs before accepting the results of an analysis. Such inputs include the mean and standard deviation used for the default and recovery variables. The analysis should be used only after an investor is comfortable with the assumptions used.

Impact of Time on Cash Flows as Time Goes by

One implication of the front-loading of cash flows is that the equity tranche, like an IO, pays down over time. Thus, even absent any credit deterioration in the deal, the price of the equity tranche drops as time passes. Take, for example, Duke Funding 1. We know from Exhibit 13.2 that at 0.3% defaults and 30% recovery, the par priced equity cash flows have an IRR just over 19%. Three years later, assuming that same 19% IRR, the price of the cash flows would be $86 per $100 par. That is, the total value of the equity would be $6.9 million rather than $8 million. Thus, an investor attempting to re-sell that equity, even if performing well, should not expect to receive par. Some of the principal cash flows have essentially already been returned as interest in the prior years. Thus, the equity tranche is essentially an amortizing asset, with a net present value that declines with time.

EXHIBIT 13.4   Summary of Representative Deal ($Million)

	High Yield		Structured Finance		Investment Grade	
	Amt	%	Amt	%	Amt	%
Assets	$500,000,000		$500,000,000		$500,000,000	
Class A notes	385,000,000	77	400,000,000	80	420,000,000	84
Class B notes	70,000,000	14	75,000,000	15	60,000,000	12
Equity	45,000,000	9	25,000,000	5	20,000,000	4
Upfront expenses	1.25%		1.25%		1.25%	
Investable assets	493,750,000		$493,750,000		$493,750,000	
Losses	2.40%		0.18%		0.18%	
Expenses	0.6%		0.3%		0.3%	

What Type of Collateral is Best?

While the choice of a deal is important, we believe that CDO equity is most importantly a portfolio allocation decision. Which is: Do you want to take a leveraged position in that collateral at this point in time?

To answer, it is important to know historic equity returns on various types of collateral. We create a simple spread sheet as a crude measure of relative attractiveness of equity backed by different collateral. We set up sample high-yield, structured finance, and investment-grade corporate deals. Deal descriptions are provided in Exhibit 13.4. Our "straw dog" $500 million high-yield deal consists of three tranches: 77% AAA rated notes, 14% BBB rated notes, and 9% equity. The ABS deal has 80% AAA rated notes, 15% BBB rated notes, and 5% equity. The investment-grade corporate holds 84% AAA rated notes, 12% BBB rated notes, and 4% equity.

The high-yield collateral is assumed to have a fixed rate equaling the UBS Warburg High Yield Index. The investment-grade corporate debt is set to a fixed yield equaling the UBS Warburg BBB Index. Yield on the ABS/MBS collateral is assumed to be the yield on BBB home equity paper. And the liability spreads are provided monthly by the UBS Warburg desk.

A sample equity calculation is shown in Exhibit 13.5 for the high-yield deal. As of the time this analysis was performed,

4/20/2001, the yield on UBS Warburg's high-yield index was 11.28%. We assumed the AAA rated liabilities had a 7.5-year average life and paid LIBOR + 50. The BBB rated liabilities are floating rate, paying LIBOR + 225 for 10 years. Both floating-rate liabilities were swapped into fixed for the entire period.

EXHIBIT 13.5　　Sample Calculation of Equity Yield: High-Yield Deal

	Amount
Assets.	$500,000,000
Class A notes	385,000,000
Class B notes	70,000,000
Equity	45,000,000
Upfront expenses	1.25%
Investable assets	$493,750,000
Losses	2.40%
Expenses	0.6%

Date	4/20/01
B corp. index	11.28%
Class A note spread	50
Class B note spread	225
7.5-yr swap yield	5.87%
10-yr swap yield	6.10%
Class A note yield	6.37%
Class B note yield	8.35%

Arbitrage

Date	4/20/01
Gross return on assets	$55,714,750
Losses	11,850,000
Net return assets	43,864,750
Cost of class A notes	24,539,900
Cost of class B notes	5,844,300
Expenses	2,962,500
Total cost & expenses	33,346,700
$ Return to equity	10,518,050
% Yield on equity	23.37%

Equity yield calculation is then straightforward. First, calculate interest cash flow, then subtract losses. We assume defaults of 4%, and recoveries at 40%. Thus, losses equal 2.4% (4% defaults × 60% losses). We also need to subtract payments to the noteholders plus payment of trustee and deal manager expenses. The remainder is cash flow directed to equity holders. We divide these cash flows by the size of the equity tranche ($45 million), which results in the equity yield. Thus, as shown in Exhibit 13.5, the equity yield on our high-yield deal is 23.37%.

This actually overstates the equity yield that will be quoted to investors. In our spreadsheet we implicitly assume the deal is fully operational at all times—which ignores any ramp-up period, as well as any period during which the deal is paying down.[3] Nonetheless it is a useful guide, as we have the same overstatement at all points in time and across all of our sample deals.

A summary of this analysis is shown in Exhibit 13.6. Notice that high-yield CDO deals, which looked extremely unattractive in early 2000, looks quite attractive at the time of the analysis, one year later. And structured finance CDO deals, while less attractive than in early 2000, still look quite attractive on an equity return basis at the time of the analysis. Equity returns on the investment-grade deal typically look unappealing (and, in fact, only looked attractive in late November 2000 through early January 2001).

This analysis clearly indicates that as of April 2001 the most favorable collateral—relative to historical levels—is the high-yield class. While structured finance equity still looks good, investment-grade corporate spreads at the time of the analysis were too tight to make investment-grade equity yields appealing to equity holders. While the relative atractiveness of different types of collateral will change over time, the methodology is a very valuable tool for evaluating equity.

---

[3] It also ignores any trading gains, calls, and tenders. These are positive events that may influence equity returns, but they are unlikely to offset the upward bias to our return calculation.

EXHIBIT 13.6 Historical Relative Equity Yields for Three Sample CDO Deals: High-Yield, ABS/MBS, and Investment-Grade Corporates

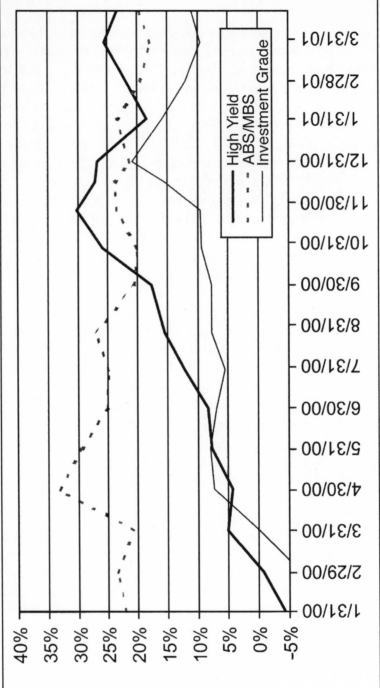

FACTORS THAT DRIVE CDO EQUITY RETURNS[4]

In the remainder of this chapter, we review the factors that drive CDO equity returns. These factors include:

- nonrecourse term leverage
- option on collateral tightening to LIBOR
- exposure to default timing
- front-loaded cash flows
- option on after-default cash flows
- option on declining interest rates.

Nonrecourse Term Leverage

The most obvious feature of CDO equity is that it achieves nonrecourse term financing of the CDO's underlying assets. From this perspective, CDO equity is basically a leveraged position in the assets of a CDO, with the CDO's debt tranches being the financing for the equity position. Equity sustains the risk of payment delays and credit losses, but also receives the upside if CDO assets generate cash flow in excess of debt tranche requirements. Meanwhile, noteholders only have recourse to the CDO's assets, and cannot make any additional claims against equity holders.

A CDO's financing is in place for up to 12, or even 15, years. The financing rate is locked in, either fixed or as a spread above a designated floating reference rate (usually LIBOR). CDO debt is subject to early amortization only if asset quality deteriorates according to objective measures (such as overcollateralization and interest coverage tests). In that case, principal repayment is due only to the extent the asset portfolio provides cash flow, and asset sales are never required.

This is in contrast to financing obtained in the repurchase agreement (or repo) market or other short-term secured financing arrangements. In those financing arrangements, financing rates can fluctuate and higher levels of security

---

[4] We thank Douglas Lucas for his contribution to this section of the chapter.

(larger collateral haircuts) can be demanded. Similarly, collateral assets can be subject to sale by the creditor. Moreover, there is recourse to the borrower if collateral is insufficient to extinguish the debt. Again, by contrast, the CDO leveraged investor (also known as the *equity tranche owner*) avoids all such funding risks with CDO financing.

Potential return to CDO equity is often measured by the funding gap which is measured by the difference between the yield on CDO assets and the average cost of CDO debt tranche financing. But what an investor really needs to know in order to assess potential CDO equity returns is the after-default funding gap. That is the difference between after-default collateral yields and debt tranche financing costs.

But even in the presence of high credit spreads and favorable funding costs, an investor needs to know more. For example, in December 2001, the "gap" between speculative grade bond yields and financing costs for debt tranches was just about the highest it had been since January 1999 (and one could argue since 1991). Specifically, an investor needs to know whether high credit spreads that may prevail in the market will result in high after-default collateral spreads over the next few years. Or will high defaults negate high credit spreads that exist in the market and create low, or even negative, after-default spreads?

For clues, we turn to the past behavior of credit spreads and default rates. Exhibit 13.7, compares speculative-grade spreads and after-default spreads. To compute after-default spreads, we take historic five-year default rates, annualize them, and then subtract that result from the high-yield bond spread that had been in effect at the beginning of each relevant five-year period. From Exhibit 13.7 we can see a loose positive relationship between wide spreads and wide after-default spreads. So wide spread are likely to be indicative of wide after-default spreads in futures years. If so, this would bode very well for CDO equity, which is, after all, a leveraged bet on collateral default performance.

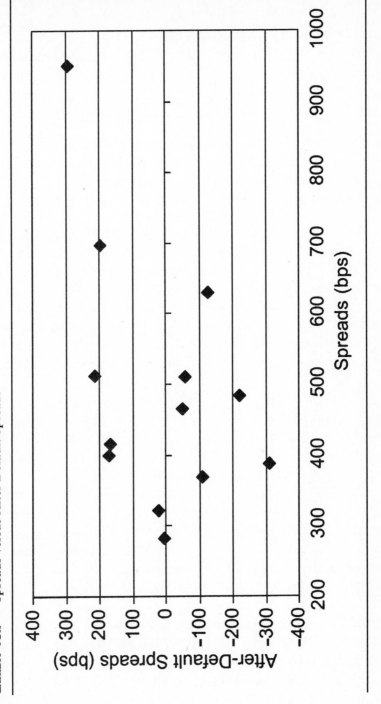

EXHIBIT 13.7 Spreads versus After-Default Spreads

Benefit From Collateral Tightening to LIBOR

The typical high-yield bond-backed CDO uses interest rate deriv-atives to hedge payments of LIBOR-based coupons. One way is via interest rate swaps, as explained in Chapter 1 and flow-charted in Exhibit 1.1 of that chapter. In that case, the CDO:

- receives fixed coupons from the bond collateral
- pays a fixed rate to its swap counterparty
- receives LIBOR from its swap counterparty
- pays LIBOR plus a spread to CDO debt tranches

This particular arrangement gives CDO equity a position in bond collateral tightening to LIBOR (actually to the fixed swap rate that equates to the expected LIBOR forward curve). Such tightening increases the value of the CDO asset portfo-lio, but does not change the value of the LIBOR-based interest rate swap or debt tranches. So for bond-backed CDOs, the bond portfolio value can rise, while the value of the swap does not go any further out-of-the-money against CDO equity holders.

For CDOs backed by LIBOR-based loans, there is typi-cally no interest rate swap and the impact of loan collateral tightening to LIBOR is more straightforward. When loans tighten to LIBOR, their value simply increases relative to the value of the LIBOR-based debt tranches.

For both the bond- or loan-backed cases, collateral tighten-ing to LIBOR presents opportunities for the CDO to sell assets, pay down debt tranches, unwind any interest rate swap, and thereby capture the collateral's appreciation to LIBOR. Of course, that is subject to any constraints such as non-call peri-ods, or early-call penalties on CDO debt tranches.

Market Value Exposure to Appreciated Assets or Default Loss Exposure to Credit-Deteriorated Assets

CDO equity enjoys a favorable asymmetrical position in the CDO collateral. As mentioned before, in the context of the CDO's term financing of assets, a CDO is never forced to sell collateral before that collateral's maturity. Thus, deterioration in the market value of CDO collateral does not force its sale or the unwinding of a cash flow CDO. In fact, distribution of cash flows to the equity tranche is indifferent to the market value of CDO assets. Likewise, deterioration in collateral rating or credit quality, except in the extreme case of default, rarely impacts CDO equity cash flows. The asset manager can hold market-impaired or credit-deteriorated assets to maturity, betting against a default and hoping to realize scheduled cash flows.

But as mentioned in the context of CDO collateral tightening to LIBOR, the asset manager, acting for the benefit of CDO equity holders, can sell collateral to reap collateral price appreciation. The asset manager can also selectively sell or retain individual assets for the benefit of CDO equity holders. Gains from selling specific appreciated assets can either be passed on to the equity tranche immediately or reinvested in additional assets. Similarly, the asset manager can selectively retain individual assets and wait out any market or credit impairment.

Exposure to Default Timing

CDO equity returns are sensitive to the timing of any defaults. If a default occurs—the later in the life of a CDO it does—the less of a drag on equity IRR. The is because previous excess asset coupons paid before that collateral defaulted were collected by equity holders. So the longer equity investors go on collecting their spread over financing, the better off they are.

For a specific example, we can use a 7-year CDO based on certain assumptions about collateral and debt tranche spreads. In Exhibit 13.8 we see equity cash flow in this representative CDO, first assuming 14% portfolio defaults at Year 2 of the CDO; then 14% defaults at Year 6. Although the overall gross amount of cash flow to equity is quite similar, the timing of cash flows shifts significantly. That shift really drops the IRR of the cash flows: in this example, from 24.2% IRR if defaults occur in Year 6 to 17.9% if defaults hit in Year 2.

EXHIBIT 13.8 CDO Equity Cash Flows 14% Defaults at Year 2 and Year 6

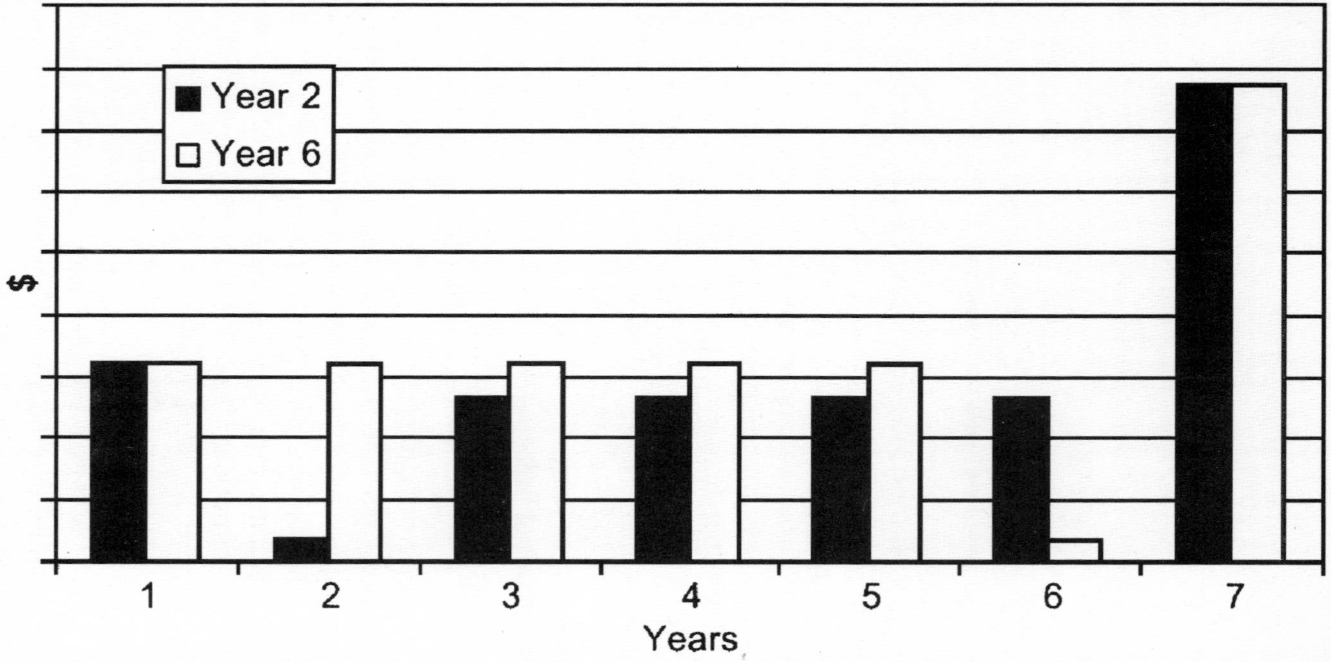

EXHIBIT 13.9   Effect of Default Timing

Defaults Occur at Year	CDO Equity IRR
1	16.0%
2	17.9%
3	19.8%
4	21.5%
5	23.0%
6	24.2%
7	25.2%

In Exhibit 13.9 we see the effect on equity IRR of this one-time default of 14% of the CDO's portfolio (with a 50% recovery), staged at varying times in the CDO's life. The clear trend is that the later any defaults occur in CDO collateral, the higher that particular CDO's equity IRR. Absolute levels of IRR, which are going to vary by collateral and tranche spreads, are not important in making our point. It is instructive to note that by moving the default date from Year 1 to Year 7, IRR increased by 50%.

Front-Loaded Cash Flows

An environment in which investors expect continued high defaults before historic norms return would not be the best environment for CDO equity. But partially offsetting this in higher than normal expected default rates is the fact that CDO equity cash flows are usually highly front-loaded, and are even more so in a high spread environment. As discussed, CDO equity owns a residual interest in all cash flows generated by the underlying CDO asset portfolio. However, a distinction is made between the distribution of coupon cash flow versus principal cash flow.

- With respect to coupon, normally equity tranche holders periodically receive the excess of asset coupons over whatever is required to service debt tranches.
- Regarding principal, however, in the majority of CDOs, equity must wait until all debt tranches have been retired to receive excess asset principal.

In toto, despite the delay in receiving asset principal, the relative size of excess asset coupons front-loads the cash flow pattern to equity, even in "normal" spread environments. And that front-loading is really speeded up in a high-spread environment.

To reinforce this point, we can go back to the sample CDO from Exhibit 13.8 and assumed 2% annual defaults and 50% recoveries. As shown in Exhibit 13.10, equity's cash flow in the first year of that CDO's life (when excess asset principal is finally paid to equity) is only 2–3 times annual cash flow to equity in previous years. In this CDO, equity achieves a 0% IRR after four years of cash flows. Subsequent cash flow over Years 5 through 7 builds equity IRR to 22.0%.

Equity's receipt of periodic excess asset coupons is interrupted if the CDO asset portfolio deteriorates such that the coverage tests are violated, resulting in equity payments that may be reduced or suspended until the CDO returns to compliance with the tests.

Partially mitigating the effect of early timing of defaults is the front-loading of equity cash flows. While payments to equity from excess asset coupon are diminished by collateral defaults, so too are payments to equity from excess asset principal. The pattern of equity cash flow remains front-loaded. In Exhibit 13.11, we can compare cash flows of our sample CDO under 2% and 4% annual default assumptions. While the higher default scenario obviously reduces equity IRR (to 8.3%, as compared to 21.0%), the duration of equity is also reduced from 4.0 to 3.5.

CDO Equity Is Long Volatility

A CDO equity holder's position is analogous to owning a call option on the CDO's assets. We already discussed that option in market value terms and the tightening of collateral spreads to LIBOR. After a noncall period, CDO assets can be liquidated and the proceeds used to pay down CDO debt tranches and unwind any interest rate swaps. To the extent proceeds from liquidation of CDO assets exceed the cost of repaying debt and unwinding the swap, then equity holders benefit dollar-for-dollar. Certainly, if the market value of the CDO assets is less than the cost of unwinding a CDO, then equity holders will not liquidate assets. A CDO portfolio under water will still throw off some cash, some of which might reach equity (provided that coverage tests are not violated).

CDO equity holders also have a call option in the after-default cash flows of a CDO's asset portfolio. If CDO asset cash flow exceeds debt tranche requirements, the equity tranche also gains dollar-for-dollar. And if after-default cash flow is insufficient to satisfy debt tranches, it "loses" the same amount of return, whether the debt service shortfall is $1 million or if it is only $1. So CDO equity holders actually have two similar options:

1. on the market value of the assets of the CDO asset portfolio that is exercised by liquidating and unwinding the CDO; or
2. on the after-default cash flow of the CDO asset portfolio that is reaped by simply waiting to see how actual defaults and coverage tests interact to produce equity cash flow.

Like all option holders, CDO equity tranche holders are long volatility. They benefit if the underlying has greater market risk and if the underlying has greater after-default cash flow risk. This is because all underlying outcomes below the strike price have the same outcome for the option holder—that is, the option is worthless. But volatility on the upside creates greater and greater returns for the option holder.

To illustrate the benefit of the volatility of after-default cash flows in the environment that existed in December 2001—a wide-spread high-default environment—we assumed that asset spreads over Treasuries are indicative of the asset's risk of credit losses. That is, a spread of Treasuries + 100 indicates expected credit losses of 100 basis points. We then compared the one-year after-default cash flow distributions of two CDO portfolios, each consisting of $90.25 of collateral. One has a 100 basis point spread over Treasuries (and therefore expected losses of 100 basis points according to our assumption), while the other has a 500 basis point spread over Treasuries (and therefore expected losses of 500 basis points).

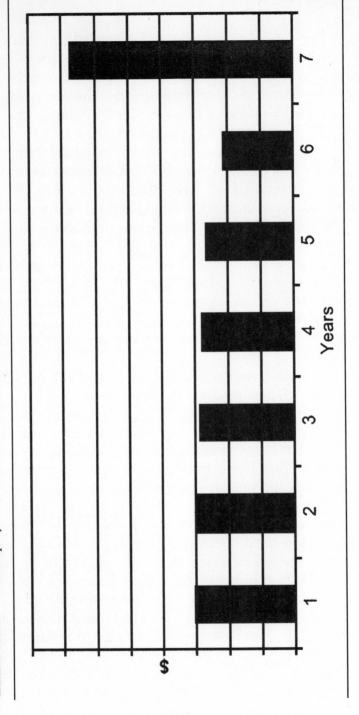

EXHIBIT 13.10 CDO Equity Cash Flows 2% Default/50% Recovery Per Annum

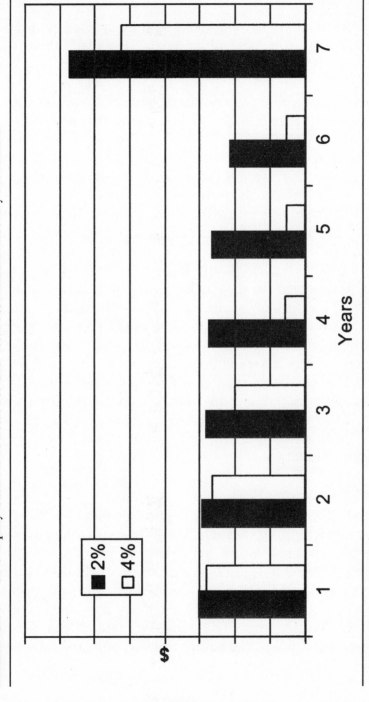

Note that for both portfolios, the expected return is the Treasury return, which we set at 5%. For the 100 basis point spread portfolio, the highest return it can attain (if it experiences zero defaults) is Treasuries + 100 basis points or 6%, which is about $96 with return of principal. For the 500 basis point spread portfolio, the highest return it can attain (if zero defaults) is Treasuries + 500 basis points or 10%, about $99 with return of principal.

Exhibit 13.12 shows the distribution of after-default cash flow of the 100 basis point spread assets in solid bars and the 500 basis point spread assets in white bars. Note the wider distribution of after-default cash flows of the more credit-risky assets (higher probability of large default losses and of higher cash flow). If debt service on CDO debt tranches (which is the strike price of equity's cash flow option) is arbitrarily set at, say, $96 on the scale above, then the equity associated with the low credit risk asset portfolio is worthless. That is because there is zero possibility that the low-credit risk assets will generate more than $96 of cash flow. But the 500 basis point spread assets have a 26% chance of generating more than $96 of cash flow—in which case, CDO equity receive the overage, as much as $3 ($99 − $96). In this example, equity's expected cash flow is approximately $0.26.

Benefit From Declining LIBOR

As explained in Chapter 1, a high-yield bond-backed CDO's most efficient interest rate hedging strategy is the purchase of interest rate caps rather than entering into an interest rate swap (see Exhibit 1.1 in Chapter 1). In a LIBOR-based interest rate cap, if LIBOR rises, the CDO receives the difference between its bond collateral's fixed coupon and LIBOR. If LIBOR declines, the CDO's bond collateral's fixed coupon exceeds LIBOR and the equity tranche gains the difference.

EXHIBIT 13.12 Impact of Credit Quality on After-Default Cash Flows

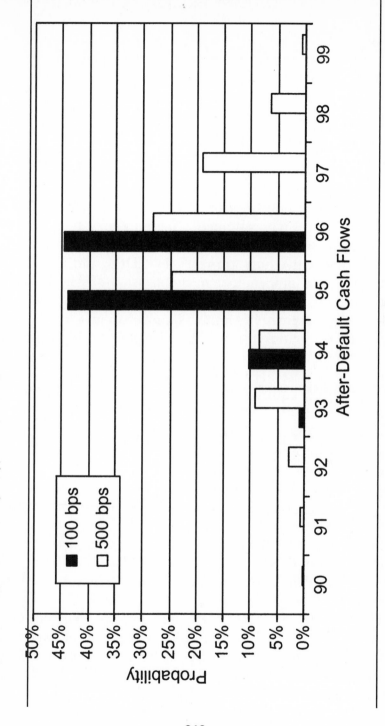

CONCLUSION

In this chapter we explained where cash flows for the CDO equity come from and how to analyze CDO equity cash flows. Despite its limitations and the superiority of Monte Carlo simulation, the most common method of cash flow analysis is the internal rate of return method. What is important to remember is that buying CDO equity is really an asset allocation decision. That is, the investor will want to ask: Is this the time to buy a leveraged position in this particular underlying collateral? Here, we examined a methodology that can provide some preliminary insight in answering this question.

So in buying equity tranches in CDOs, individual deal selection is less important than the decision of what assets to take a leveraged position in. While there will be differences between deals, sensitivity analysis allows an investor to ferret out if one is obviously better than another. So if an investor believes deals are largely equivalent, the behavior of the underlying collateral will prove far more important than whether to buy equity in Deal A or in Deal B backed by the same collateral.

In this chapter we also examined CDO equity's unique exposures and options. One favorable investment attribute is the CDO equity's nonrecourse term leverage of CDO assets. Another important favorable attribute is the CDO equity's option on collateral tightening to LIBOR. This is accentuated by a high-collateral-spread environment, such as that seen in recent years, as it suggests a greater likelihood of spreads tightening from these levels, rather than widening. In an environment of high volatility, CDO equity's option on after-default cash flow is valuable.

Historically, at least, high spreads have helped CDO equity from both a buy-and-hold perspective as well as a total return perspective. However, an environment of high defaults partially offsets the benefits of current high collateral yields. These are especially unfortunate at the beginning of a CDO's life, if there is an early cut-off of excess collateral coupon cash flow to CDO equity. Slightly ameliorating that factor is the front-loading of cash flows to CDO equity, plus the fact that it will take some time before coverage tests deteriorate to the point where cash flows are diverted from equity tranches.

CHAPTER 14

Payment-in-Kind CDO Tranches

High-default rates can cause some CDO tranches to stop paying current interest or to then "pay-in-kind." The tranches are referred to as *payment-in-kind* or PIK tranches. And when modeling CDO returns, it is not unusual for investors to request default scenarios severe enough to also cause tranches to become PIK-able.

In this chapter, we define what is meant by a PIK feature. We then focus on structural issues behind PIKs within CDOs and discuss rating agency approaches to PIK tranches. Finally, we show the relationship between CDO PIK tranches and loss of internal rate of return among CDO tranches.

PIK BONDS

Payment-in-kind is a clearly disclosed, structural feature within some bonds whereby an issuer can—instead of paying a current coupon—increase the par value of the bond by paying the bond's then-due coupon with more of the same bonds, thus "paying-in-kind." So if a $5 coupon is missed, the par value increases, say, from $100 to $105. The next coupon is calculated based on the larger $105 par amount.

This chapter was coauthored with Douglas J. Lucas of UBS Warburg. A version of this chapter appeared as an article in the *Journal of Fixed Income*.

PIK securities are generally issued by corporations with a speculative grade rating whose future cash flows are uncertain. The option to pay-in-kind helps these issuers conserve scarce cash or even to avoid default. Traditional high-yield corporate PIK bonds differ from zero-coupon bonds in that in PIKs, the issuer decides at each coupon date whether to pay the current coupon, increase the principal amount of the debt, or even to repay previously unpaid but accrued coupons. Zero-coupon bonds have a completely built-in, 100%, accrual of coupon into principal.

PIK PLUS CDOS

In a CDO, a tranche can be denied coupon even though the CDO has adequate cash flow to make the payment. Withheld cash flow is instead used to pay principal on the CDO's most senior tranche. This occurs through the operation of overcollateralization and interest coverage tests applied to more senior tranches. These two particular tests measure, respectively, the amount of collateral par as a percent of tranche par, and the amount of collateral coupon as a percent of tranche coupon. If these ratios fall too low, then available cash flow is used to pay down the seniormost tranche in the CDO until that ratio (or both ratios) returns to conformity.

WHEN DOES A CDO PIK?

After the coupon on the seniormost (say Class A) CDO tranche is paid, the two coverage tests are then calculated:

$$\frac{\text{Collateral par}}{\text{Class A par}} \quad \text{and} \quad \frac{\text{Collateral coupon}}{\text{Class A coupon}}$$

If these ratios are too low in relation to their triggers, Class A par must be paid down until the ratios meet their target trigger levels. Only then is any remaining cash flow available for servicing coupon on Class Bs. Thus, even though there is sufficient collateral cash flow to satisfy the Class B coupon, that cash flow is instead directed to pay down Class A principal. It is the presence of overcollateralization and interest coverage tests on a Class A tranche that causes a Class B tranche to be PIK-able. In practice, par overcollateralization tests are more important because they typically become binding before interest coverage tests.

There are also Class B coverage tests that come into effect after Class B interest is paid. Such ratios test collateral par and collateral coupon in relation to the sum of Class A + B par and the sum of Class A + B coupon, respectively:

$$\frac{\text{Collateral par}}{\text{Class A + B par}} \quad \text{and} \quad \frac{\text{Collateral coupon}}{\text{Class A + B coupon}}$$

If these tests are violated, then cash flow is denied Class C until those particular two ratios meet their trigger levels. Class C and tranches further subordinate might also have coverage tests that divert cash flow away from still-lower tranches.

However, throughout this decision tree or cash flow waterfall, diverted cash flow is still applied against Class A par until it is retired (and then to subsequent classes in declining order of seniority). All coverage tests, at each tranche level, delever the CDO from its seniormost tranche on downward.

REASONS FOR PIK-ABLE CDO TRANCHES AND THEIR EFFECT

The PIK-ability of subordinate tranches and the diversion of cash flows to cause early amortization of the Class A tranche naturally strengthen the Class A tranche. The Class A tranche can therefore either achieve a higher rating, or its size can be increased while still maintaining its original rating. CDO equity holders benefit from an overall lower cost of funds: They either have a lower coupon on the Class A tranche; or the Class A tranche, which enjoys the CDO's lowest funding cost, is larger. Either case lowers interest costs to the CDO and thus increases return to equity holders.

The effectiveness of PIK-ing in bolstering the credit quality of the Class A tranche depends upon the amount of collateral cash flow that exists in excess of Class A coupon. The higher the coupon on collateral, and the longer the tenor of collateral, then the more cash flow potentially available for diversion to pay down Class A principal. The effectiveness of PIK-ing (in bolstering the Class A tranche) also depends upon the looseness or tightness of the overcollateralization and interest coverage tests. The tighter the coverage tests are to the CDO's original par and coupon ratios, the sooner a deterioration in those ratios will cause cash flow to be diverted to repay Class A principal.

The effect of cash diversion to the Class A tranche in a high-yield backed CDO can be dramatic. It is not unusual for subordinate tranches of a CDO to have been downgraded (and to be PIK-ing without any chance of ultimate payment) while the CDO's Aaa tranche maintains its credit quality and rating. That's due to the outlook for Class A receiving all cash due, because of the diversion of cash to Class A principal.

In determining optional capital structure, CDO equity must weigh reduction in the overall cost of CDO debt against the potential for equity to receive less cash flow in severe default scenarios. Distribution of collateral cash flow amongst tranches in a CDO is a zero-sum game. And since equity receives residual cash flow after debt tranches are satisfied, PIK-ing and the diversion of cash flows to Class A principal affects it the most. First, the CDO's average cost of funds increases. Second, the CDO becomes more delevered. Finally, less cash reaches the equity tranche, and that which does is delayed.

RATING AGENCIES' VIEW

Rating agencies have been wary of PIK CDO bonds. With the exception of one rating agency, they have been concerned that above a certain rating, investors do not expect their CDO to PIK; thus PIK-ing is viewed as a form of default. PIK-ing (under this interpretation) is only conventional and acceptable below a certain rating or with a qualification on the rating. Note that with corporate debt, PIK bonds are rarely issued by companies carrying better than a speculative grade rating.

S&P will not grant any CDO tranche a rating of A or higher if it has a PIK feature, unless it is clearly disclosed in the title of the security that interest is deferrable. For tranches seeking a rating of A−, S&P treats PIK-ing for more than a year under their stress testing as a default. For tranches seeking a rating of BBB+ or below, the length of any PIK-ing under their stress testing is irrelevant, as long as the tranche eventually makes up accrued interest, interest on interest, and principal. In the distant past, a PIK-able CDO tranche would have been qualified with a subscripted "r" to indicate the presence of usual risk characteristics. Now, it's inherent within the rating.

Up until the summer of 2002, Moody's also refused to grant any PIK-able CDO tranche a rating of A2 or higher. Now, however, Moody's will issue ratings on a PIK-able CDO tranche up to and including the Aaa level. This is in accord with that agency's "expected loss" rating approach, which takes into account both the probability of default and also the potential severity of default. Thus, on an expected loss basis, a bond that PIKs but subsequently repays accrued interest (with interest on interest) has no loss. Thus, there would be no rating agency penalty, as documentation of a CDO certainly envisions and allows PIK-ing. Moody's conversion to this policy in the summer of 2002 reflects its overcoming previous reluctance to treat interest accruals as they do current payment of interest.

Fitch neatly makes a distinction between a CDO bond that passes its default and recovery scenarios while paying current coupon all along, versus one that accrues coupon and eventually pays it off. Fitch will rate the former for timely payment of interest and principal; the latter only for ultimate payment of interest and principal. This rating agency makes this distinction evident in both its rating letter and in the rating report on the CDO.

For investors focused on internal rate of return (IRR) and indifferent to timeliness, the S&P approach to PIK-able CDO tranches rated A– is overly conservative (relative to S&P's ratings of non-PIK-able tranches), in that some scenarios which S&P considers a default actually do not cause any loss of IRR. For investors focused on the timely payment of cash flows—Moody's approach to PIK-able CDO tranches is generous (relative to Moody's ratings on non-PIK-able tranches) in that timeliness is not factored into the expected loss methodology. Note that our comments compare PIK and non-PIK-able ratings intraagency. They do not address whether one rating agency's standards and net rating results are generally harder or easier than another's.

It is interesting to consider how, given their approaches to rating new CDOs, each rating agency might update their rating on a CDO bond that is PIK-ing. For Fitch (where Fitch is addressing timely payment), a PIK-ing CDO tranche is in default. Therefore, a D rating would seem appropriate even if it looked like the bond would ultimately make up accrued interest. Moody's and Fitch (where Fitch is addressing ultimate payment) would look either at the severity of IRR loss or the probability of ultimate payment, respectively, and could therefore rate a PIK-ing CDO tranche much higher than a D rating.

MODELING DEFAULTS AND PIK CDO TRANCHES

Investor should be interested in better understanding the relationship between PIK-ing and loss of IRR. Specifically, if a bond PIKs, does that mean it is definitely going to lose IRR? Worded differently, what are the chances of a bond PIK-ing but eventually catching up on accrued interest and making holders whole? Also investors are interested in how the relationship between PIK-ing and IRR loss are affected by the pattern of defaults, whether they are evenly distributed through time or are front-loaded or back-loaded.

Furthermore, since Moody's is newly open to more highly rated PIK-able tranches, an investor would be interested in knowing what the effect of having overcollateralization and interest coverage triggers on the first tranche (therefore making the second tranche PIK-able) and how much does this improves the credit quality of the first tranche, yet harm that of the second or lower tranches.

To answer these question about the effects of PIK-ing on CDO tranches, we modeled a CDO with $102.1 million of high-yield collateral, a WAC of 10.11%, and a life of seven years, all supporting tranches as described in Exhibit 14.1.

Constant Default Rate Scenario

The constant default rate (CDR) scenario assumes that the same default percentage rate is applied annually to the then-current amount of collateral. Note that after previous defaults and recoveries, an ever-decreasing amount of collateral is subject to the same annual default rate. Thus, a decreasing amount of collateral defaults each year. The effect is analogous, but opposite, to the effect of compound interest (where interest increases each period).

EXHIBIT 14.1   CDO Modeling Assumptions

Class	Rating	Principal	Coupon (%)	Over-Collateralization Trigger (%)	Interest Coverage Trigger (%)
A	Aaa	$70	5.31	121	145
B	A3	10	6.45	116	135
C	Baa2	5	7.65	110	124
D	Ba2	5	12.10	105	119
Equity	NR	10	Residual CF		

EXHIBIT 14.2 Constant Default Rates

Tranche	PIK-ing Begins (%)	IRR Loss Begins (%)
A3	13.50	11.50
Baa2	9.00	9.50
Ba2	7.00	7.00

EXHIBIT 14.3 Front Loaded Defaults

	CDR at which	
Tranche	PIK-ing Begins (%)	IRR Loss Begins (%)
A3	25.00	26.50
Baa2	12.00	21.50
Ba2	10.50	14.50

As shown in Exhibit 14.2, we find that as the CDR increases, the relationship between PIK-ing and the loss of IRR is tranche-specific. For the A3 tranche, a loss of IRR occurs at 11.5% CDR, while PIK-ing occurs at 13.5% CDR. The tranche loses IRR before it PIKs because of the lack of principal repayment in the tranche's last period. For the Baa2 tranche, IRR losses begin at 9.5% CDR and PIK-ing at 9.0% CDR. For the Ba2 tranche, losses and PIK-ing both begin at 7.0% CDR. Note that for each tranche, PIK-ing and IRR loss occurs close together.

Front-Loaded Default Scenario

The front-loaded default scenario assumes high defaults in the first two years of the CDO's life, followed by 4% default rates thereafter. This default scenario more closely captures current economic conditions and default patterns that could result.

As shown in Exhibit 14.3, this scenario shifted the onset of tranche PIK-ing to before any loss of IRR. In other words, there were more and greater examples of tranches PIK-ing, but later making up accrued but unpaid interest and thus making investors whole. For the A3 tranche, PIK-ing began at 25.0% CDR while IRR loss began at 26.5% CDR; while for the Baa tranche, PIK-ing began at 12.0% CDR and IRR losses at 21.5% CDR. For the Ba tranche, PIK-ing began at 10.5% CDR while IRR loss began at 14.5% CDR.

In Exhibit 14.4 we show the unusual shape of Baa2 cash flows under a 20% annual default rate in a CDO's first two years, right before the tranche begins to lose IRR. Note that in the middle of the tranche's life, it receives no interest for 1.5 years, then a partial interest payment, and then full payment of current and accrued interest. Given high defaults the market is likely to see a fair number of Baa tranches PIK-ing. But if this is followed by defaults returning to reasonable levels before too much damage is done, investors would come out whole.

Baa Tranche

We look closer at the Baa tranche, because the difference between the timing of IRR loss and PIK-ing were greatest in our analysis. We examine this tranche under variations of both the constant default rate front-loaded default scenarios above, plus under back-loaded default assumptions.

EXHIBIT 14.4   Baa2 Cash Flow in 20% CDR

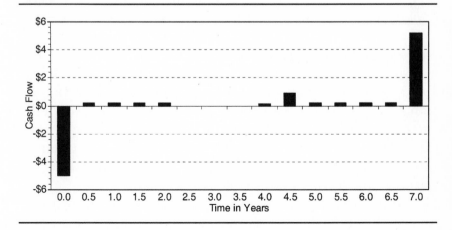

EXHIBIT 14.5   Baa2 Tranche Scenarios

Default Scenario	PIK-ing Begins (%)	IRR Loss Begins (%)	Difference (%)
Two-year initial defaults, 40% recovery	12.00	21.50	9.50
Two-year initial defaults, 30% recovery	10.50	18.00	7.50
Three-year initial defaults, 40% recovery	10.50	15.50	5.00
Three-year initial defaults, 30% recovery	9.00	13.00	4.00
Constant defaults, 30% recovery	7.50	8.50	1.00
Constant defaults, 40% recovery	9.00	9.50	0.50
Three-year final defaults, 30% recovery	10.50	11.50	1.00
Three-year final defaults, 40% recovery	12.00	13.50	1.50
Two-year final defaults, 30% recovery	19.50	16.50	−3.00
Two-year final defaults, 40% recovery	23.00	19.00	−4.00

Under the constant default scenario, and in the front- and back-loaded default scenarios, we see the Baa tranche with 30% and 40% recovery assumptions. In the front-loaded default scenario, we used high defaults in the CDO's first two years, followed by 4% annual defaults; as well as high defaults in the CDO's first three years and then 4% annual defaults. In the back-end default scenario, we used high defaults in two versions: for the CDO's final two years and its final three years. Before the high final defaults, the CDO experiences 4% annual defaults.

In Exhibit 14.5, we see the default rate for each scenario in which the tranche first begins to lose IRR, and the default rate at which it begins to PIK. If the tranche PIKs at a lower collateral default rate than when it begins to lose IRR, the tranche PIKs between the two default rates but eventually catches up on accrued interest and pays the tranche holder in full. Alternatively, if the tranche loses IRR at a lower default rate than when it begins to PIK, it receives current interest, but does not receive full principal repayment.

Exhibit 14.5 shows that the incidence of PIK-ing without loss of IRR is highest in the severe front-end loss scenarios.

Put differently, the probability of PIK-ing seems far greater than the probability of losing IRR in front-end scenarios. Conversely, the probability of PIK-ing without losing IRR is non-existent in the extreme back-end scenarios.

Class A OC and IC Tests

We are also interested in the effect of having (or not having) Class A overcollateralization and interest coverage tests. The presence of these tests on the CDO's top-most tranche can potentially cause the Class B tranche to PIK and divert cash flow to pay down Class A principal. In the past, rating agencies were reluctant to award high ratings to PIK-able tranches. Now that Moody's has relaxed its standard toward CDO PIK-ing, there may be more A2 and higher rated PIK-able Class B tranches. It seems appropriate to quantify the difference that Class A coverage tests and Class B PIK-ing have on the credit quality of various CDO tranches.

Class A Tranche

From the point of view of the Class A tranche, the maximum it can gain from its own coverage tests is diversion of Class B interest to pay down its own principal. As show in Exhibit 14.6, this helps the Class A tranche avoid IRR loss in the extreme range of 15.5% and 16.5% CDR. In more severe scenarios, the advantage of having Class A coverage tests is 16 to 184 basis points of IRR (as also shown in Exhibit 14.6). The boost, or assistance provided to the Class A tranche, is similar in front-loaded default scenarios.

Class B Tranche

The impact of Class A coverage tests on the Class B tranche is more complicated. The diversion of cash flow from Class B coupon to Class A principal repayment is not good for Class Bs; but paying down the Class A tranche does decrease the CDO's leverage and move the Class B tranche up in priority. In Exhibit 14.7, we see that over the range of 11.5% to

15.5% CDR, Class A coverage tests actually helps Class B's IRR. However, in more severe CDRs, the Class A coverage tests severely impair the Class B tranche. The advantage and disadvantage of Class A coverage tests, to the Class B tranche, is similar in front-loaded default scenarios also.

EXHIBIT 14.6 Class A Tranche IRR

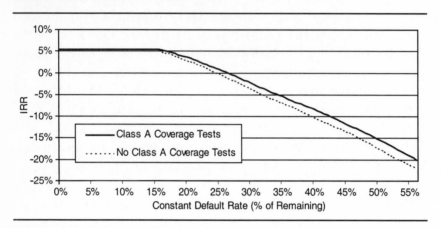

EXHIBIT 14.7 Class B Tranche IRR

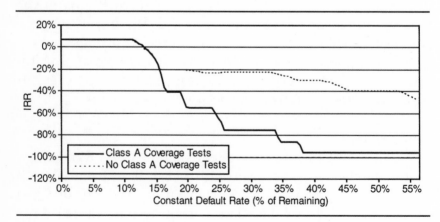

Class C and D Tranches

Finally, for Classes C and D, the presence of Class A coverage tests makes little difference. That is because if Class A coverage tests do not divert cash from the Class C and D tranches, then Class B, or Class B and Class C coverage tests will. This result holds true as long as the coverage tests are fairly "in sync" as to when they take effect. If Class A coverage tests are tight relative to Class B and Class C coverage tests, then the introduction of a Class A coverage test will adversely affect Class C and D cash flows.

Conclusions of Modeling Default Analysis

In the most likely default scenario (of high immediate defaults followed by a return to historic averages), PIK-ing without the ultimate loss of IRR is more likely than loss of IRR. In our modeling that was particularly true of the Baa tranche, less true for the Ba tranche and still less true for the A tranche.

In a high-default-rate environment such as in 2001 and early 2002, the market is likely to see a fair number of Baa tranches PIK-ing over subsequent years. But as long as defaults return to reasonable levels, they will not cause loss in the long run.

Additional overcollateralization and interest coverage tests on the Class A tranche modestly help that tranche by denying coupon to the Class B tranche in severe default scenarios. However, that diversion also helps the Class B in the lower range of such severe defaults. Class A coverage tests make little difference to Class C and D tranches.

CHAPTER 15

Secondary Market Trading Opportunities and Managing a Portfolio of CDOs

In this final chapter, we focus on two topics. In the first section we focus on trading opportunities in the secondary market and look at specific examples of relative value analysis. In the second section, we take a more macro look and go over rules that should apply in managing a CDO portfolio.

SECONDARY MARKET TRADING OPPORTUNIES

With the increase in the volume of CDOs outstandings, evolution of a secondary market was inevitable. And that fledgling secondary CDO market now presents a great relative value opportunity for money managers. As a new market, CDOs also tend to be quite price inefficient. Although participation is growing, there are still relatively few buyers and sellers. Adding to that, there's often a lack of information in usable form. For example, there is no source of information on deal cash flows. The dealer which underwrote a particular CDO already has it modeled, and will generally work an order when asked. But other dealers must invest quite a bit of effort up front before they can bid, or even work an order, on any security. Absent any centralized source of information, each deal must first be reverse-engineered before it can be bought or sold in secondary by any other than the originating dealer. And that is done via remittance reports, which is a painstaking process. While there are several vendors which have some deals modeled, dealers are generally unable to access deals which are not their own. Furthermore, modeling issues and limited clientele are even more significant issues for the more unusual CDO structures. The net effect is that CDOs often trade very cheap in the secondary market.

Consequently, the acquisition of CDOs in the secondary market offers opportunities for diligent investors to acquire CDOs at very attractive spreads to primary issues, taking advantage of a significant liquidity premium, and, on occasion, strong seller motivation. Furthermore, despite the lack of certain information noted above, the secondary market has an information advantage over the primary market: The contents of the underlying portfolio are known, and performance history is available.

Secondary supply has grown as the CDO market has matured. Natural sources of supply include investors selling to realize gains, make portfolio adjustments, or change allocations among security types. Moreover, secondary supply continues to trickle out of mergers and acquisitions among institutional investors.

DUE DILIGENCE IS EASIER IN THE SECONDARY MARKET

Let's focus on the information advantage for investors. They are in a better position buying a CDO in the secondary than in the new issue market because instead of assumed portfolio parameters and guidelines, investors have access to the actual collateral. Given the current holdings, investors can form a much more detailed picture of the manager's performance to date as well as the portfolio's projected performance under different economic, interest rate, and credit scenarios than if they bought an otherwise comparable CDO at issue.

When evaluating a secondary CDO, investors' fundamental tools are the offering memo and the most recent trustee's report. The offering memo will detail the structure, investment guidelines, trading requirements and restrictions, and other terms of the original issue. The trustee's report lists portfolio holdings, highlights rating actions on holdings, provides current average rating, overcollateralization and interest coverage ratios, as well as the deal's standing in relation to its covenants.

The rating agencies can be sources of additional published information about transactions. This material is available either by mail, website or both and is a normal outgrowth of the surveillance function. More importantly, the agency surveillance analysts themselves can provide considerable insight into the CDO's structure. The CDO asset managers are also excellent sources of information about the portfolio holdings, their anticipated strategies, and other issues relevant to projecting collateral performance and generally prove to be willing to talk to investors.

Indeed, in this regard, investors contemplating secondary CDO trades who are willing to do some digging are at a distinct advantage to dealers because both rating agency analysts and the CDO asset managers tend to be far more forthcoming with investors than with Wall Street traders (as reflects their direct fiduciary responsibility to investors). Questions and answers that might never find their way into print are far more likely to be addressed in phone conversations with these "hands-on" sources.

Moreover, with respect to the manager track record, the uncertainty regarding manager performance that exists for buyers of new CDO transactions is largely absent in a secondary market trade. Instead, investors have real evidence in the form of the actual holdings.

EXHIBIT 15.1 Example: CDO-1

Coupon: LIBOR + 40 bp
Offer spread: LIBOR + 200 bp
Price: 93:00
Original rating: Aa2
Current rating: Aa2 on watch for possible downgrade
Collateral: 30% Emerging Market, 70% high-yield bonds
Issue date: May 1997
Reinvestment period: 3 years
Noncall period: 3 years
Original WARF: 2720
Current WARF: 3000
Original senior OC ratio: 145%
Minimum senior OC ratio: 136%
Current OC ratio: 139%
Original interest coverage ratio: 185%
Minimum interest coverage ratio: 153%
Current interest coverage ratio: 176%
Current weighted-average fixed coupon: 9.8%
Minimum weighted-average fixed coupon: 9.5%
Maximum CCC concentration: 5%
Current CCC concentration: 9%

Illustration

Here we will see the important characteristics for both buyers and sellers evaluating secondary CDO trades. We use an example that is actually a composite of a few bonds that were traded by the UBS Warburg CDO desk around the time of the analysis. A composite is used in order to cover as many characteristics as realistically as possible in a single example.

We label the deal CDO-1. It is a senior tranche in a bond deal backed by 30% emerging market obligations and 70% high-yield bonds. Initially rated Aa2, the bond is on watch for possible downgrade. Signs of deterioration include slippage of the overcollateralization ratio and weighted-average rating factor and expansion of the triple-C bucket. The characteristics of the tranche are detailed in Exhibit 15.1. Note that the example is a cash flow structure. We use a cash flow structure rather than a market value structure because the latter represent a small fraction of outstanding issues. As a result, market value structures trade much less frequently in the secondary market. Also note that, although this example is a bond deal, many of the issues that we discuss have application to loan deals as well.

Average Rating

As explained in previous chapters, a critical indicator of a CDO's value is its average rating. Changes in this deal characteristic roughly reflect the upgrade/downgrade experience of the underlying collateral. In general the average rating is calculated by converting the rating to a numerical value and weighting it by the dollar amounts in each rating category. This numerical value also reflects an expected frequency of default for a given rating category (based on cumulative corporate default rates observed by the rating agencies), and, accordingly, the rating factors are skewed exponentially upward as bonds move down the rating spectrum. As we would expect, the "factors" vary slightly among agencies (that is, between Moody's and Fitch; S&P does not explicitly calculate this parameter in applying its rating methodology). Moody's uses the rating factors listed in Exhibit 15.2 (and already discussed in Chapter 2 on cash flow CDOs) to calculate the weighted-average rating factor (WARF). Should a deal fail the test, the bond indenture prohibits the bond manager from engaging in any trade (including a reinvestment of principal) that would further lower the average rating.

In our example, CDO-1, at the inception of the CDO, the minimum WARF specified was 2,720. At the time of the secondary market sale, the WARF was 3,000. In other words, the bond was failing its average rating test by 280 rating points. To fail by a margin of 200 to 300 ratings points is not disastrous. On the scale indicated in Exhibit 15.2, failing by 200 or 300 rating points is more of a near miss—it would not necessarily change the average rating in terms of a letter category. On the other hand, failing the test by margin of 500 to 600 rating points is a red flag, indicating the rapid growth of the triple-C bucket.

Triple-C Concentration

The rapid pace of downgrades in emerging and high-yield markets since 1997 helped to swell triple-C buckets in a number of CDO transactions. Normally, triple-C concentrations are required to be held to 5% or less of principal amount. As the concentration rises, raising the risk of default or sale at a loss to avoid rating agency action, the likelihood that the overcollateralization cushion will be depleted increases. A triple-C concentration at 9% or higher should be considered a serious warning signal. The example, CDO-1, is just touching that level.

EXHIBIT 15.2   Rating Factors

Rating Categories	Rating Factors
Aaa	1
Aa1	10
Aa2	20
Aa3	40
A1	70
A2	120
A3	180
Baa1	260
Baa2	360
Baa3	610
Ba1	940
Ba2	1,350
Ba3	1,780
B1	2,220
B2	2,720
B3	3,490
Caa1	4,760
Caa2	6,500
Caa3	8,060
Ca	10,000

Diversity Is a Secondary Consideration

Interestingly, diversity is less of a consideration for an off-the-run CDO. The diversity score is more important during the initial investment period, when the manager is building the portfolio. Once fully invested, transactions generally do not fail their diversity score test.

Overcollateralization Cushion

Overcollateralization is a chief means of providing structural credit enhancement. At the deal level, overcollateralization is equal to the difference between the aggregate principal amount of rated liability tranches and the aggregate principal amount of the collateral. (Alternatively, it can be expressed as a ratio, the overcollateralization ratio, of the aggregate principal amount of the collateral to the aggregate principal amount of the rated liability tranches.) The amount of overcollateralization cushion under an individual tranche is equal to the difference between the principal amount of the tranche plus any tranches senior to it and the aggregate principal amount of the collateral. As explained in Chapter 2, if the overcollateralization ratio test is violated, cash flows are redirected to pay down the most senior tranche until the test is once again met.

A comparison of current and closing overcollateralization levels will indicate the degree to which defaults and sales of distressed assets have eroded the "par" cushion. How par is lost can indicate manager style. Some managers, for instance, will sell bonds at a loss to avoid raising a flag to the rating agencies by failing the average rating or hitting a concentration limit. Indeed, sales out of the triple-C bucket typically account for most of the loss of par in a transaction. Nonetheless, the important issue is not how the overcollateralization was reduced, but the amounts that were lost and still remain. In our example, CDO-1 lost a portion of its overcollateralization cushion, but it still has an overcollateralization ratio of 139%, 3% more than its test level of 136%. Attention should be paid to the overcollateralization ratio for the most junior-rated tranche, which generally will have a lower test as well as less of an initial cushion than senior classes and is most vulnerable to failure.

Interest Coverage

Interest coverage, in the sense of excess spread, provides a second form of credit support, after overcollateralization, to senior tranches in a CDO. (In the event that either test fails, interest payments to lower priority tranches and equity interests are diverted to pay down principal on the seniormost tranches.) An interest coverage minimum or test is mandated for a deal, along with the requirement, if failed, to pay down seniormost bonds until the test is again satisfied. However, in practice, the test is rarely failed. Instead, investors should focus on current interest coverage levels in relation to overcollateralization levels as a measure of combined structural credit support. A fat interest coverage cushion in a deal can compensate for some erosion of the par cushion. In the example, the current interest coverage ratio is 176%, down slightly from 185% at closing, but it is still comfortably above the test level of 153%.

Interest coverage can also provide clues regarding the managers' trading activity. Normally, interest coverage declines with overcollateralization. First, defaults and sales of distressed bonds typically erode coupon as well as the par amount of assets. In addition, managers can attempt to recoup par by buying low coupon assets at discounted prices. By comparing changes over time in the overcollateralization cushion to those in the interest coverage cushion, investors can gain some insight into manager style. Likewise, investors should also look at average coupon (in the case of fixed-rate assets) and average margin (in the case of floating-rate assets). When evaluating average coupon or margin, investors should bear in mind that the required level will reflect the market in which the transaction was structured rather than current market conditions and should be evaluated versus initial and test levels for the particular transaction.

Manager Trade-Offs

Investors evaluating secondary CDO purchases should bear in mind that the overcollateralization and interest rate coverage ratios, as well as the WARF and other parameters established for a deal, should be considered together rather than separately. That is, managers can chose to allow one parameter to weaken in order to stabilize another during difficult economic/credit environments.[1] For instance, managers can bolster par value by selling assets priced close to par and replace them with bonds priced at a discount. The effect would be to lower average coupon or margin and interest coverage.

Managers holding equity positions in a deal may have an added incentive to do this in order to keep cash flowing to the equity. Tradeoffs can also be made between the average rating and triple-C concentration, on the one hand, and overcollateralization levels, on the other. For example, rather than sell an asset at a loss, lowering the par value, the manager might chose to hold it as it tumbles down the credit ladder. The point is that investors looking at the whole picture have a better gauge of the CDO's relative value and are in a better position to discern where managers have made tradeoffs in the past and how they may perform in the future.

Call/Prepayment Upside

The possibility of early repayment is a further enticement to many secondary CDO trades. The possibility of early repayment typically arises from three sources:

- The average life convention that the market follows to price CDOs
- Early retirement of senior bonds in the event a coverage test fails
- The possibility of optional redemption of a transaction by the equity holders.

---

[1] Investors should also bear in mind that managers are subject to trading limits and may not be able to trade out of a problem.

To the extent that CDOs are purchased at a discount, repayment earlier than anticipated at pricing can significantly enhance yield.

In order to price a CDO tranche in the secondary market, traders normally take the initial weighted-average life of the bond as stated on Bloomberg (deal details are usually provided by the underwriter) and subtract from that number the amount of time that has elapsed since the transaction's closing date. It is important to note that the initial average life established for a tranche on Bloomberg is generally derived from assumptions that extend the bond to its maximum average life. That is, the underwriter typically assumes that the average life of the assets at closing is at the maximum allowed average life mandated for the transaction (negotiated by the manager and underwriter along with other structural details and incorporated in the indenture and set forth in the offering circular). In turn, the average life of the assets implies a principal repayment schedule and average lives for the tranches by rating priority.

The divergence between convention and fact creates opportunities for investors. In practice, the average life of the actual assets bought in as collateral is often much shorter than the mandated maximum average life. This means that the actual average life of the CDO tranche can be much shorter than the average life on Bloomberg would imply. This "hidden" foreshortening is realized in a higher yield-to-maturity than anticipated in the price paid and is pure gravy for the buyer.

Failure of a coverage test can also shorten the average life of CDOs. (Again, if failed, interest is diverted to pay down seniormost tranches until the test is cured. Such an event is not assumed when tranche average lives are determined.) For investors buying at a discount, this event would provide a yield pickup as well.

Finally, most transactions are structured so that they can be called at the option of a majority of equity holders after a defined period of time has elapsed (three to five years is common). We described this option feature in Chapter 2. At the time of the analysis, a large number of CDOs issued to date have now been outstanding for two or three years, placing them much closer to their call dates. In our example, the call period was three years at issue and is now nearly expired. With access to the actual holdings, a prospective buyer should be able to market the collateral to market and evaluate directly the likelihood the deal could be called.

Relative Value

Our example also captures the relative advantage investors often enjoy in the secondary CDO market. The trades on which our example is based suggest that a bond with these characteristics might trade at LIBOR + 200 basis points. This level conservatively assumes that CDO-1, already on credit watch, will be downgraded from Aa2 to a single-A. This level reflects a sizable secondary, liquidity premium as well—a new issue rated A1 with 35% emerging market bonds would come at LIBOR + 160 to + 170 basis points at the time of the analysis. (A generic high-yield or loan-backed A1 would come at LIBOR + 125 to + 140 basis points.)

In other words, in the worst case, that CDO-1 is downgraded to the next rating category, the buyer picks up 30 to 40 basis points over a comparable new issue. As a matter of fact, investors who look closely at the underlying collateral and speak directly to the rating agency analysts who follow the issue may come to the conclusion that this is too severe a rating assumption. For instance, they would note that the deal had lost par but still had a good interest coverage ratio and not an overly large triple-C basket. In fact, one of the trades on which we based our example faced the same rating scenario (Aa2 on watch for potential downgrade), but it was only downgraded to Aa3—and removed from the watch list. That made it a very good buy at LIBOR + 200 basis points.

Beyond the rating "risk," there is additional upside in the trade. Priced to the maximum remaining average life at a dollar price of 93:00 and close to the end of the reinvestment and noncall periods, our example has considerable upside potential in event of early repayment or call as well. The likelihood of either outcome can be estimated by examining the underlying collateral, in the first case to form a more accurate estimate of its average life and in the second, by marking the underlying collateral to market, to determine the likelihood that the transaction will be called.

Assessment of the Proposed Trade

Obviously not all secondary trades are as attractive as the one analyzed above. In fact, there is no such thing as a generic new issue deal, and hence there are no generic secondary trades. In addition, while secondary activity is building, price discovery is extremely difficult in this environment (for instance, investors may see similar bonds at different prices from different sellers). Nonetheless, there are many opportunities for savvy buyers in the secondary CDO market. The key is doing the homework—the tools and data are already available, in greater detail than in the primary market.

CLOSER LOOK AT WHY TRADING OPPORTUNITIES ARISE IN CDO SECTORS

In this section we look at why trading opportunities arise. The best way to do this is with actual opportunities that have appeared in the CDO market. Specifically, three sectors of the secondary CDO market are highlighted that have exhibited real value: fixed rate AAAs, participating interest structures, and equity trusts. Each sector has offered a very cheap way to buy the cash flows, packaged in a nontraditional structure. These sectors may not be available, nor a good buy, at any given in point in time. However, diligent analysis using the framework provided below and in other chapters we believe can aid an investor to identify relative value opportunities in these and other sectors with readily available supply.

Fixed-Rate AAAs

Floating-rate AAAs have become the norm in the CDO market. By contrast, fixed-rate AAA bonds are less common, and without a broad investor base, tend to trade very cheap in the secondary market—at times more than 70 basis points cheap to where the fixed-rate structure should theoretically swap out! Better yet, there are times, such as in late 2000, when a number of secondary bonds became available, due to relatively low fixed rates that gave investors the opportunity to sell bonds at levels higher than any point over the prior two years.

An example should help clarify this point. PAC 1998-1A Tranche A2A is a AAA rated fixed-rate tranche of a CDO deal. The $247.5 million deal, managed by Pacific Life CDO Ltd and settled on January 15, 1998, is backed by a mix of debt and term bank loans rated below-investment grade. This AAA rated fixed-rate CDO tranche (PAC 1998-1 A2A) pays a fixed coupon of 6.56% and was offered at 96.30, corresponding to a 7.32% yield. The fixed-rate CDO tranche PAC 1998-1 A2A is sized at $90 million. This tranche does not start amortizing until February 2004. After that, principal on this AAA tranche and another, which is *pari passu*, is paid off before any of the lower rated bonds or equity receives any principal paydowns. Thus, it is reasonable to think that the amortization window will stretch from February 2004 until February 2008 or so. Consequently, assuming equal amortization over the window, average life on these securities is five years. Final legal maturity on the bonds is February 2010.

If PAC 1998-1 A2A is to be looked at as a spread over LIBOR, we would use the five-year swap rate as our LIBOR proxy. In that case, the bond would be quoted at the time as

LIBOR + 150 basis points. However, that is a bit of an over-statement. In reality, this is an amortizing swap with some optionality. However, the fact that the cash flows are amortizing, rather than received as a single bullet, is only worth 4 basis points. More significantly, there is optionality.

How Much Optionality?

The optionality in this structure comes from uncertainty about the amortization schedule as well as the risk of early amortization. After the reinvestment period that runs until February 2004, the asset manager must start paying down the AAA bonds. The amortization schedule for the AAA rated CDO tranche will depend on whether or not call provisions on the underlying bonds are exercised. If there are a substantial amount of early calls on the bonds, the average life of the CDO tranche will be shorter, if not, then it will be longer. While this is not strictly an economic option, if rates are lower then it is more likely that calls (on the bonds and loans) will be exercised early. This is usually undesirable from the point of view of the investor in the AAA rated CDO tranche, as the investor is losing a fixed coupon that is higher than current reinvestment alternatives.

It is very difficult to estimate how large an effect call options can have. However, for more than 95% of the high-yield portfolios, the effect of call options will not shorten a AAA rated CDO tranche by more than 0.75 year, nor lengthen it by more than 0.5 year. The AAA tranche is such a large percentage of the structure that it is hard to shorten or lengthen its average life considerably.

Now we turn to the risk of early amortization. The bottom line is that this has at most a very modest impact on the average life of a deal. In a weak economy, the underlying high-yield loans and bonds are apt to perform worse (defaults will be higher). In that case it is more likely that overcollateralization or interest coverage tests will be tripped. The first set of tests to be triggered are those measuring the overcollateralization and interest coverage for the mezzanine tranches. If these tests are triggered, then cash flows to the equity tranche are cut off. When this occurs, the deal structure requires that excess interest cash flows (otherwise payable to the equity tranche) should be directed to start paying off the AAAs. Assume that AAA bonds are 75% of this deal and that excess interest cash flows are 2%. (Equity tranches are commonly 10% of an overall capital structure and a current return of 20% is typical.) This implies that 2.667% of the deal is paid down each year until the amortization period is finished. That will shorten the average life by 0.25 year, at most.

We can now bracket the optionality. Our expected average life on the bonds is five years. We assume that the bonds could reasonably be as short as four years (0.25 year less from the early amortization + 0.75 year less from the call risk). The average life of the bonds could reasonably be as long as 5.5 years. To determine the value of optionality, we suppose some option pricing model can be used. Instead, one can obtain the information from a derivative trading desk and that is what we did. The UBS Warburg Derivative Desk told us this amount of optionality is worth 25 basis points.

We are now in a position to estimate what this bond would be worth on a swapped basis. We know its optionality is worth 25 basis points. In addition, we deduct another 4 basis points because the AAA rated CDO tranche (PAC 1998-1 A2A) is an amortizing structure rather than a bullet structure. Thus, after netting out the optionality and the amortization window, this deal is really selling at LIBOR + 121 [(LIBOR + 150) – (25 basis points for optionality) – (4 basis points for the amortization window)]. And that is 71 basis points more than a new high-yield deal. Exhibit 15.3 summarizes this information.

EXHIBIT 15.3   Relative Value—Secondary Fixed Rate AAA CDOs

Yield	7.32
5-yr swap rate	5.82
Bond with bullet swap	LIBOR + 150
Value of amortization	<4 bp>
Value of optionality	<25 bp>
Theoretical value of CDO + swap	LIBOR + 121
Yield on new AAA CDO floater	LIBOR + 50
Difference	71

Relative Value

The question that the investor must ask is: Can I swap into a floating rate bond that exactly matches the amortization on this CDO? The answer is yes, but not at a level equal to its economic value of LIBOR + 121. The swap counterparty has to model the deal and get comfortable with the cash flows. Moreover, there is no way for the counterparty to exactly hedge those cash flows. Thus, bid-ask spreads on this type of customized swap would be large. However, the bond purchaser can enter into an amortizing swap, with a small amount of swaption protection (4-year average life minimum, extending to 5.5 years) and end up with cash flows of LIBOR + 121.

Consequently, this is a good relative value trade, and a wide variety of investors can take advantage of it. AAA buyers often think that there are no secondary opportunities for them, and are reluctant to take a look. In fact, there are often attractive secondary opportunities for AAA investors as we have just demonstrated.

Participating Coupon Bonds

The more off-beat the structure, the cheaper the secondary market paper. Take participating coupon bonds, for instance. They are a relatively rare structure, only brought by two primary market dealers as of this writing (Credit Suisse First Boston and Bear Stearns). However, in late 2000 and early 2001 there happened to be a great deal of supply in the market, as a disproportionate number of deals which involved participating coupon tranches had been downgraded or were on watch for downgrade. When a CDO tranche is on watch for downgrade, or a downgrade is expected, investors often choose to sell rather than "explain" why the bond remains in their portfolio.

As explained in Chapter 11, participating coupon CDO tranches pay a low coupon, but then allow investors to share in upside on the bonds by participating in the equity cash flows. The participating interest structure was created because they offer advantages from the point of view of both the deal manager and investors. From a manager's point of view, participating coupons are a terrific "plus," as they reduce the amount of straight equity that must be sold. That is the case because a participating coupon lowers the coupon cash flows committed to the debt tranches, hence the rating agencies require less subordination at any given rating. Overall, it often allows more profitable execution on the deal, because debt holders are essentially buying part of the equity, and are often willing to do so at lower internal rates of return than would pure equity buyers. This gives the actual equity holders more upside.

A disproportionate number of these deals were at risk by January 2001 for downgrade because they are quite leveraged, due to their smaller equity tranches. Thus, there was less time to get a deal back on track before some of the tranches were at risk to be downgraded. Moreover, there was also a selection bias among the managers. While not always the case, participating coupon structures tended to be used more often by money managers with a shorter track record who consequently anticipated more trouble placing the equity in their CDOs, and so chose a structure with a small amount of equity to place.

Real World Illustration

Let's take a live example of a participating interest structure—Shyppo Finance Company Ltd (CUSIP 825703AE1). This $311.5 million deal is backed mostly by high-yield debt, with a smattering of investment-grade pieces. There are $233 million senior bonds in Classes A-1 and A-2, for a very typical 75% of the deal. The participating interest bond (Class A-3, originally rated A3, now rated Baa1/BBB+) consists of $62 million, couponed at 5.58%. Equity totals $16.5 million. Note that the equity share, at 5.3%, is lower than the 10–12% equity traditionally found on a CDO backed by high-yield debt. Furthermore, the Class A-3 notes, at 19.9% of the deal, are larger than the 12–15% mezzanine notes typical in a high-yield CDO structure. These shifts reflect the fact that the Class A-3 notes have a participating interest structure, and hence, implicitly contain some equity.

The price of the now Baa1 rated Class A3 as of mid-January 2001 was $45.00 in the secondary market. The internal rate-of-return profile of this bond is shown in Exhibit 15.4. Note that the bond has a very high yield at low default rates, and a minimum yield of 2.1% at very high-default rates. The minimum yield is due to the fact that even if the investor does not get a single dollar of principal back, the 5.58% coupon carries merrily on, as this piece and the pieces senior to it have low coupons. Thus, this 2.1% return (at annual default rates greater than 8%) reflected the value of the coupon-only payments at the current, initial low price of 45 cents on the dollar. Realize furthermore that this analysis was conservative in the sense that it was assumed recoveries at only 20 cents on the dollar. Just for the record, high-yield default rates have historically been in the 3–4% area; and at those historical default rates, the Class A-3 notes yield 16–17%.

The return profile of the Shyppco Class A-3 note can be compared to that of a generic new Baa1 rated structured bond, priced at LIBOR + 220, as is shown in Exhibit 15.4. We assume the same conservative 20% recoveries on both deals. Note that the generic deal delivers less than its promised yield at default rates higher than 6%. The yield on the generic new Baa rated bond turns negative at a 8.5% annual default rate. (The profile for the generic deal is slightly less favorable than that typically shown to investors since we are assuming 20% recoveries, much lower than is typical.) The participating coupon bond has a significantly better return than does the generic new structure, except in a small range of between 6% and 8% annual default rates. At low default rates, the participating coupon structure has more than double the return of the generic new offering. At high default rates, the internal rate of return floor is very valuable. Even in the range in which the participating coupon bond underperforms, it does not underperform by much.

The bottom line is that an analytical framework such as the one used above identified participating coupon CDO tranches that offer value to investors willing to look at a slightly unusual structure.

Trust Structures

In a typical trust structure, the equity piece and other subordinated pieces of a CDO are bundled with zero-coupon bonds in a grantor trust structure. This is often done to "flatten" the return profile of the equity or subordinated notes. An investor may find the equity attractively priced, but the risk profile is more volatile than he wishes to commit to. Pairing the equity with a zero-coupon note limits the downside (as the zero returns par at maturity), in exchange for less of the upside. It also gives insurance companies an NAIC rating.

EXHIBIT 15.4   Return on Shyppco Participating Interest Structure versus Generic Baa1 Alternative
(On Shyppco: Px = $45, 20% recovery assumed)
(On Generic Baa1: Yield = LIBOR + 220, 20% recovery assumed)

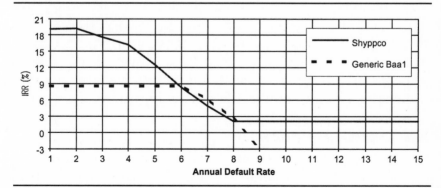

EXHIBIT 15.5   Trust ABC

	Initial	1-year Later
Assume:		
Zero-coupon note maturity	11 yrs	10 yrs
Rate	7%	6%
Face amount of zero	$40M	$40M
NAV on zero	18.77	22.15
Price	46.92%	55.36%
Equity investment	$20M	$14.63M*
Percent of original	100%	73.40%
Value of unit	$38.77M	$36.78M
	(18.77 + 20)	(95% of original)

* Derived value.

A number of trust structures retraded in the secondary market in late 2000. In some cases, they traded intact. But at times the trust has been collapsed and the zero sold apart from the equity. The only prerequisite for collapsing a trust is that a single entity owns or controls all the pieces.

The supply of these trust structures at the time came from investors who needed to sell and are finally able to get the best bids they have seen in quite a while. The reason was the bond market rally, a substantial one at that, resulted in a large gain on zero-coupon notes. As a result, prices on the trust (equity + subordinated notes + zero-coupon note) can be still high enough to appeal to those desiring to sell, while allowing the equity and subordinated notes to implicitly trade very cheap. Secondary equity usually trades very cheap to new equity. Thus, if a trust unwinds just after issue, the equity suffers a steep loss. However, the higher value of today's zeros offsets that ding to the equity portion, and enables a non-painful sale of trust positions.

Trust Valuation—Hypothetical

Now look at how a trust can be valued. We first use a simple hypothetical case, illustrated in Exhibit 15.5. Assume that

Trust ABC, issued one year ago, consisted of $40 million face of an 11-year zero-coupon note and $20 million face of CDO equity. At issuance, the rate on the zero-coupon note was 7.0%, which corresponds to a price of $46.92. The NAV on the zero-coupon note at that same time was $18.77 million [($40 million face) × (price of 0.4692)]. This makes the issuance value of the unit $38.77 million based on [($18.77 million NAV of zero-coupon notes) + ($20 million equity investment at a price of par)].

One year later, market rates on the then-10-year zero-coupon note are 6.0%, for a price of $55.36. So at that point, NAV on the $40 million face of zeros becomes $22.15 million ($40 million × 0.5536). Now assume that the trust owner is willing to sell at 95% of original value, or $38.83 million ($38.77 × 0.95). This means that with the increase in the zero's value, the equity investment is implicitly valued at $14.63 million [($36.83 million sale price) − ($22.15 million NAV on zero)]. This corresponds to 73.4% of the original equity value—which is quite a markdown. At this level, investors might take a look at this trust, regarding it as a source of cheap cash flows.

Trust Valuation—Real World

Most trusts are a tad more complicated than our simple example above. They tend to combine equity pieces from different deals, or may contain several tranches (equity and subordinated notes) from the same deal. To be compellingly convincing that this is very cheap equity—we delve into a real deal, whose name we are reluctant to divulge. We will refer to it as Real Deal CDO Ltd.

This CDO is backed by a combination of high-yield and emerging market debt. The trust contains $54 million face of passthrough certificates, with $4 million aggregate principal amount of third priority senior secured fixed-rate notes (Class C Notes, rated B3); $23 million of senior subordinated floating-rate notes (Class D Notes, senior equity tranche); $5 million junior subordinated notes (Class E notes, otherwise known as equity); and $54 million face amount zero-coupon senior notes ("the zero-coupon securities"). The zeros are issued by NationsBank, an Aa3 rated entity. At the time of the analysis, the package of securities sells for 57 cents on the dollar in the secondary market.

The B3 rated notes pay a coupon of 12%; the senior equity tranche carries a coupon of LIBOR + 1300; and the equity receives all excess cash flows. When the overcollateralization and interest coverage ratios are tripped for the B3 class, that cuts off cash flows simultaneously to both the nonrated debt tranche and the equity tranche. There are no separate overcollateralization and interest coverage ratios that apply to the senior equity tranche.

This trust would sell at a price of approximately $57. Each of the units in this trust consist of $100 of zeros, $4/54 of the Class C Notes, $23/54 of the Class D Notes, and $5/54 of the Class E Notes, with prices broken down as follows:

- dollar price of the zero-coupon bonds = $39.75
- price of the Class C Notes (B3 rated debt) = $47.00
- price of the Class D Notes (senior equity) = $27.30
- price of the Class E notes (the equity) = $23.00

Real deal CDO trust valuation
= $(4/54 \times \$47) + (23/54 \times \$27.3) + (5/54 \times \$23) + \$39.75 = \$57$

Exhibit 15.6 shows internal rates-of-return on each of the equity and subordinated note pieces at different default rates. Note that this analysis is quite conservative, in that we assumed 20% recoveries. In fact, as explained in Chapter 3, high-yield bond recovery rates are generally much higher. Moreover, at 7% defaults (more than double the historic average) this trust still yields 6.50%. (And the zeros yield 7.49%, explaining why internal rates-of-return on the other pieces can be so low, yet the combination yield still respectable.)

Bottom line is that CDO trust structures provide a very cheap opportunity to buy secondary equity.

EXHIBIT 15.6   Internal Rate-of-Return on Real Deal Trust (Annual Default %)

Class	0	1	2	3	4	5	6	7	8
C	28.02	24.21	23.20	21.80	19.15	14.95	1.73	−21.99	−59.45
D	73.30	73.00	67.50	49.90	11.50	−2.70	−11.10	−18.10	−45.60
E	102.20	93.80	75.20	58.10	43.90	26.30	23.90	−2.60	−3.60
Trust	20.90	18.10	14.23	10.12	7.78	7.30	6.87	6.50	6.15

MANAGING A CDO PORTFOLIO

Portfolio managers accumulate positions in a number of CDOs. Some even have quite an extensive collection, with positions in more than 100 different CDO deals. Yet most portfolio managers tend to look at buying each additional CDO as if they were buying their first. In doing that, they spend a disproportionate amount of time trying to evaluate the manager and often end up trying to differentiate on the basis of track records.

Although one should look at individual asset managers, it is crucial to look at the incentive structure in a CDO. Performance of existing CDOs provides much more information than do general track records of asset managers. Moreover, it is of utmost import to manage a portfolio of CDOs within general portfolio framework and parameters.

The key to diversification in CDOs comes from holding different types of collateral. A CDO with a low-diversity score may actually increase the diversity of a portfolio, depending on its contents. Style (or asset class) is the most important factor in explaining investment returns.

General Rules For CDO Portfolio Management

Here are four general rules for CDO portfolio management:

Rule 1. In picking managers, track records cannot be taken at face value. Common sense goes a long way.

Rule 2. Look at the incentive structure for a manager. If possible, see how strong an impact that has had in outstanding deals.

Rule 3. Collect CDOs backed by different types of collateral. Asset class is a far more important determinant of returns than is choice of specific managers. Buy a certain type of CDO when you believe the underlying collateral is cheap.

Rule 4. Look at diversity on a portfolio basis. Buying a number of CDOs, backed by different types of collateral, creates your own diversification. So don't necessarily avoid CDOs with low diversity scores.

We discuss the reasoning behind each of these rules below.

Track Records

When marketing a CDO deal, the first words spoken to the investor are often "The most important aspect of picking a CDO is selecting a manager; so look at the track record of this manager." But it is very difficult for investors to assess a manager on track records alone, as they do not necessarily allow easy comparison. The best one can hope to establish is that a manager has been managing that particular asset class for a long period of time, their investment approach can be articulated clearly, and risk management parameters are strictly adhered to.

There is good reason to be very skeptical about track records. They contain three biases—"creation bias," "survivorship bias," and "size bias." A discussion of these biases is beyond the scope of this chapter. It should be noted, however, there is a good deal of academic literature on these biases as they pertain to the equity mutual fund arena. The same biases apply to fixed income funds, as well.

Common Sense

Rule 1 states that the key to evaluating manager performance is to use common sense. Don't be duped by performance numbers. Here is what to look for:

- Make sure the firm has a track record with every asset class it is including, and that the money manager is not stretching into asset classes in which they have not historically been active.

- Make sure the firm has a disciplined, consistent approach to investing, which is followed in good times and bad.

- Look at the stability of both the firm and the manager. A management team that has been at a firm for a long period of time, with significant equity, is less likely to leave. (Ideally, CDO investors would like to handcuff managers to the firm for the life of their deal. One obviously can't do that, but bigger manager stakes mean there is less likelihood of leaving.) Moreover, the longer a group of people has been working together, the less chance of a sudden shift in strategy.

There is an assumption on the part of investors that Wall Street dealers who underwrite CDOs act as gatekeepers, allowing only the top-notch performing managers to pass through their pearly gates. That blind trust, however, is to some extent misplaced. More money management firms wish to manage CDOs than there is dealer pipeline capacity. Thus, a dealer wants to underwrite CDOs (from managers) they believe will sell quickly.

However there are often other considerations, including overall quality of the relationship between the dealer and a money manager, as well as help the asset manager can provide in marketing the deal and taking some of the equity. Consider two money managers; one has a very good track record, the other only an average one. The manager with the average track record will take all the equity in the CDOs, plus some of the subordinate securities. The manager with the better track record wants the dealer to market all the equity. Who will the underwriters pick? It's a no brainer—the manager with the average track record who is willing to provide more help in underwriting the deal.

Realize that the Wall Street dealer community does require at least a minimum performance threshold. The manager's investment philosophy and track record do have to be good enough to market the deal. Moreover, since dealers are looking at the overall quality of the relationship between the dealer and asset manager, as well as an asset manager's willingness to take down some of the equity, it is natural that larger, better established money management firms are likely to have an edge. This is a good thing for investors, per our common sense tests above.

Checking Out the Incentive Structures in Existing CDO Deals

One of the most important pieces of analysis in evaluating a new CDO deal is to look at how managers have responded to incentive structures on their outstanding deals. In most deals, the deal manager owns between 25% to 49.5% of the equity. (If they owned 50% or more, the entire deal would get consolidated onto their balance sheet.). We believe that in a CDO structure, a deal manager usually has a powerful incentive to keep cash flow going to the equity tranche, even if that works to the detriment of bondholders and net asset value of the deal.

Recall that cutting off cash flows to the equity tranche due to violation of coverage tests generally cuts seriously into equity holders' return. Once equity holders lose the cash flows, it is difficult to get them back later on, since the deal begins to delever. Thus, when the manager is also the equity holder, he has every incentive to avoid tripping the overcollateralization and interest coverage ratios. Let's look at how this can be done.

Portfolio managers are often able to forestall violation of coverage ratios by judicious portfolio trading. If the overcollateralization test is close to being tripped, selling a bond trading at par, and buying two bonds priced at 50, can temporarily boost the overcollateralization test. Additionally, sometimes if a bond is priced at 75 on the way to 40, it might also be kept in the pool. Moody's acknowledged this problem in a *Special Report* where it stated:

> We have noted some managers that are lax in righting a deteriorating portfolio, while concurrently distributing excess interest out of the structure. These collateral managers do not actively utilize the O/C test at a possible corrective lever that can efficiently be used to remedy a deteriorating deal. Some common examples include cases where a collateral manager is tardy at treating a security as defaulted securities, buying deep discounted securities, or holding on to severely impaired securities.[2]

It is very difficult for an equity holder to manage a deal and totally ignore their own incentive interests. However, some managers can be egregiously self-serving. This can usually be spotted by looking for a huge deterioration in WARF scores or a big growth in the allocation to assets that fall into the CCC rated bucket.

Realize that poor performance on previous deals is not necessarily indicative of abusive management. Often, market conditions have deteriorated, and most CDOs of that asset type have been impacted. Thus, if a deal is performing poorly, it is very important to look at the reasons why.

---

[2] Gus Harris, "Commonly Asked CDO Questions: Moody's Responds," Moody's Investor Service, *Structured Finance, Special Report* (July 13, 2001).

Diversification

So far, we have examined what to focus on when looking at an individual deal—making the case that rather than focusing on the manager's track record, focus on the performance of outstanding CDO deals, and how the manager has balanced his interests with those of the noteholders. We now shift gears, and examine the argument that not only should CDO buyers look at individual deals, but they should look at their CDO holding in a portfolio framework.

The key to managing a CDO portfolio is diversification. One of the few indisputable facts is that the types of securities purchased (the style) is key—far more important than skills of a particular manager. Roger Ibbotson, one of the key researchers in the performance area, writes:

> ...relying on past performance is not as simple as it appears. The investment styles of mutual funds typically explain more than 90 percent of the variation in returns. Just knowing that a fund is a large or small capitalization fund, a growth or value fund, an international stock fund, or a combination of these categories largely explains its performance. The skill of the manager is demonstrated relative to the fund's investment style...[3]

While it is indisputable that style matters, there is a question as to whether good or poor performance in one period is indicative of the performance going forward. That is, are some managers just far superior to others? While there have been studies of mutual funds that have examined this issue, in short, the debate seems to be whether style (asset class) accounts for 90% or 99% of return variation. There is no disputing the fact that it is the key factor. Bottom line—diversify across asset classes.

---

[3] Roger Ibbotson, "Style Conscious," *Bloomberg Personal* (March/April 2001).

Many investors buying a large number of positions still tend to look at each purchase individually. Yes, it is important to look at each deal, but some parameters may be unacceptable if a particular deal was the only one purchased, and less important when the security will become part of a portfolio. Diversity is one such parameter.

In fact, it is important to look at holdings on a consolidated basis. Adding deals with low diversification may, in some circumstances, help a CDO portfolio. For example, a REIT-only deal may have a low-diversity score, but if it was part of a larger CDO portfolio, and REIT holdings elsewhere are limited, then purchasing it may actually increase diversification. By contrast, if one purchased three high-yield deals within a short period of time, each with very high-diversity scores, the additional diversification provided by buying all three deals may actually be limited, as they may own substantially the same securities. The rating agencies generally tend to require less subordination on a deal with a higher diversity score. However, when an investor purchases a large number of CDOs, they are creating their own diversification.

In point of fact, favoring deals with low diversity scores actually conflicts with the Rule 3—trying to collect CDOs backed by different types of collateral. High-yield and investment-grade corporate deals tend to have much higher diversity scores than do structured finance or CDOs backed by other CDO deals. Thus, if one was trying to accumulate deals with low-diversity scores, you would be accumulating predominately ABS deals and not achieving that desired diversification.

Thus, the practical advice is

1. an investor should not shun low diversity score deals since the investor also creates his own diversification; and
2. an investor should look at holdings in his CDO portfolio on a consolidated basis.

DATE DUE

DEMCO 38-297